W9-AGL-613

CELEBRATION OF LIFE

CELEBRATION OF LIFE Studies in Modern Fiction

WILLIAM R. MUELLER

SHEED & WARD • NEW YORK

Library of Congress Cataloging in Publication Data

Mueller, William Randolph, 1916–
    Celebration of life.

    CONTENTS: Man and vocation: James Joyce: Genesis
of an artist. Jean-Paul Sartre: A portrait of the existentialist
as a young man. Ralph Ellison: A portrait of the Negro as
a young man.—Man and nature: Joseph Conrad: Nostromo
and the orders of creation: an ontological argument. Albert
Camus: Microbe against man. Thomas Mann: "For everything there is a season".—Man and other men: D. H. Lawrence: The paradisal quest. George Orwell: The demonic
comedy. Virginia Woolf: The soul's sad delight. [etc.]
    1. Fiction—20th century—Addresses, essays,

lectures. I. Title.
PN3503.M76   809.3'3   70–39868
ISBN 0-8362-1078-6

Copyright © 1972 by Sheed and Ward, Inc.
Library of Congress Catalog Card Number: 70-39868

Manufactured in the United States of America

This book is for Frances,
whose selflessness and generosity
are constant as the sun's rising.

Contents

Preface

Had it not been for my suffering an at least modestly propor-
tioned dark night of the soul a few years back, this book might
never have been written. I'm not sure what brought on that
night, but I suspect that prolonged exposure to a relatively
joyless body of literature may have helped. I do know that
during the early and middle 1960s various of my literary excursions, particularly those into the absurd theater of Beckett,
Ionesco, and Genet, began to make of near and happy certainties something closer to haunting doubts. The time had come,
I then realized, to reexamine both my beliefs and my self. Convinced that modern fiction offers the most perceptive and comprehensive view of the life of our time, I felt it possible that the
novels of this century, some read for the nth time, some for
the first, might help give at least partial answers to questions
that I had asked before and had answered before, but which I
knew I must ask again. The questions, remarkably unoriginal,
are among those Socrates would consider central to an examined life. The first and most general is that of who I am and
who I should be, a question embracing the search for identity
and vocation. The others are complementary to it and also
possess an intrinsic interest of their own. What is my relationship to the vast natural order of creation, to the creation's four
elements and its animal, vegetable, and mineral kingdoms?
And what is, or should be, my relationship to other human
beings, both as individuals and as composite groups of larger
social orders? Finally, what comprehension do I have of the
God of whom Scripture speaks, and what do I sense to be my

relationship to him? The reading later gave way to writing, and the four questions to the four sections of this book: Man and Vocation, Man and Nature, Man and Other Men, Man and God.

Such, briefly, is the genesis of this book. The place to which the reading and writing led me I attempt to describe in the Afterword.

Miss Barbara Levitz and Mrs. Sylvia Wagonheim, good friends and former students, I wish to thank for assistance in matters bibliographical. The refreshing and welcome candor of another friend, the Reverend Ralph Harper, influenced the final drafting of the Afterword to this book. And I remain, as ever, warmly indebted to Dr. Nathan A. Scott, Jr., whose contributions to the whole area of literary and theological study are legion.

The chapter on Hermann Broch first appeared in *Theology Today* XXVII (April 1970), and the chapter on Joseph Conrad in *Thought* XLV (Winter 1970). I am grateful to the editors of these journals.

I am grateful also to those publishing houses (noted at the beginning of each chapter) from whose books I have quoted extensively.

Introduction

In this section entitled "Man and Vocation" I have chosen to discuss three novels whose lonely protagonists are, above all, intent upon discovering their proper role in life. Each one asks "What should I do?," a question most of us ask—and with great frequency. I find myself forever planning the hour, day, year, or decade, hoping not so much to pass the time as to seize it. Like Thoreau I do not want to approach death, later or sooner, and discover that I have not lived.

A first step toward answering the question is to ask a prior one: To what basic authority or first principle should I turn for direction, for apprehension of my proper place in the world? Though many answers are possible, most of them fall into one of three categories. I may fashion my life in accordance with a divine will, with my society's needs, or with the demands of my own intrinsic being. My motivating source may be primarily religious, ethical, or existential. Most probably I will be influenced by all three: the sources need not be, and seldom are, mutually exclusive.

For a period of many centuries prior to our own, Western man judged biblical teaching a major touchstone for determining appropriate attitudes and righteous behavior. Biblical writers make quite explicit their conviction that God wills for every man a particular way of life and calls him to it. God's will for Noah was to build an ark; for Abram to leave his homeland, go forth, and father a chosen people; for Moses to lead the chosen from bondage in Egypt toward the freedom of a Canaan rich in milk and honey. From Ephesians we learn that God may call men to be apostles, prophets, evangelists,

3

pastors, teachers; from Luther that God also may call men to dignified labor in the fields and women to worthy household chores. A man's calling, ordained by God's will for him, is for sufficient semantic reason known also as his vocation. The biblical doctrine of vocation affirms that we are born with certain preconceived, predetermined talents which comprise our divine inheritance, and that our devotion to their use is both the measure of our obedience and the prerequisite of our freedom. Freedom's perfection is found in Holy Week when, in one person, man's will was wrestled into harmony with God's.

Men are sometimes called not only *to* a specific mission but also *by* the name appropriate to that mission. Jahweh changed the name of Abram ("exalted father") to Abraham ("father of a multitude") shortly before the birth of Isaac, the son through whom the chosen race was to continue. Isaac's son Jacob was given the name Israel ("he who strives with God") after his nocturnal wrestling with the angel. Peter (from the Greek *Petros*) was the rock (from the Greek *petra*) upon whom Christ chose to build his Church. Parents continue to name children after persons they hope their offspring may emulate. George Washington Carver, Ralph Waldo Ellison, Aristotle Socrates Onassis are, in greater or lesser degree, famous examples. And there are a few Homers and Virgils and many Ruths, Stephens, Davids (and some Nathans), Pauls (and some Sauls). One of my elementary school classmates was named Moses Moses, a fact endowing our daily roll call with at least a modicum of wonder.

The Bible affirms no doctrine more persistently than that of vocation. The man of biblical faith seeks his proper action, immediately and over the long run, by inquiring through prayer, meditation, and ecclesiastical guidance God's will for him. Thoughtful men of medieval, renaissance, and reformation times took the doctrine of divinely inspired vocation with high seriousness. But there has been a tapering off in more recent times until, with the growing acceptance of God's death, the doctrine has lost for many its life-giving source. "What should I do?" is a question still asked, but its answer, in the literature of our time at least, is generally sought outside a biblical context. Thus T. S. Eliot's five plays, variations on the theme that man should first seek God's will and then follow it, are the exception rather than the rule of contemporary letters.

A man may also choose to base his actions, and feel that others should base theirs, on whatever would seem best to serve society's needs and welfare. The most famous classical text stressing this concept of vocation is Plato's *Republic*. Its goal is to define justice, its conclusion that justice is the product of every man's minding his own business, defined in turn as what he is equipped to do best. The citizen of the Republic does not, like Jew or Christian, discover his calling through prayer, meditation, or ecclesiastical guidance. His place in the community is determined by his aptitude, measured by a rigorous training and education program administered by the state's wisest leaders. The end product will be a hierarchical society composed of artisans, warriors, and guardians. For a member of any one of the three classes to indulge in the business of either of the other two is to commit injustice and court disaster. A citizen's vocation, therefore, is fixed by his superior's judgment, based on a testing program, of how that man can best promote the health of the body politic.

In their concepts of vocation, both the Bible and the *Republic* are concerned with the welfare of both the individual and the larger community. Yet there is a difference of emphasis. The Bible—particularly the New Testament, whose God numbers the hairs of a man's head—is more person-oriented than the *Republic:* individual members of the Body of Christ, of the Church Militant and Triumphant, are viewed with more tender compassion than Plato's imaginary citizens˙ The Bible calls each man above all to personal salvation; the *Republic,* to his proper place in the larger order. Though the biblically redeemed are members of a larger society, and though Plato's just society could not exist without just men, the Bible and the *Republic* do entertain different priorities.

There are, of course, modern writers who stress the good (or bad) of the social or political body and whose protagonists feel called to amend social and political injustice. One thinks, for example, of the literature of the Spanish Civil War, including Malraux's *Man's Hope* and Hemingway's *For Whom the Bell Tolls*. Also in the political tradition, but with a reverse twist, is anti-utopian fiction like Zamiatin's *We*, Huxley's *Brave New World*, and Orwell's *1984*.

A third concept of vocation, younger in tradition than the other two, has been prominent in the literature of the last half century or so. Its protagonists are called to their life's action by neither God nor society's needs. Largely areligious and apolitical, they find their directing principle within themselves. In their autonomy, their apartness from God and other men, they are profoundly lonely. It is ironic that one major impetus to the contemporary literature of loneliness is the work of a Christian, the mid-nineteenth-century Danish theologian Sören Kierkegaard. The God-possessed Kierkegaard believed that the "crowd" is untruth, quite incapable of fathoming God's will, and that only the "individual," confronting God directly and quite apart from other men, can apprehend religious truths. Such an individual, the rarest of persons, Kierkegaard called the knight of faith. The most exemplary knight of faith is Abraham, who alone heard Jahweh's call to sacrifice his only son Isaac, and who then obediently moved toward an action which the crowd, ignorant of God's command, would have judged sheer murder. Abraham, his agony increased by uncertainty even as to whether it was the one God he had heard, had to act on faith, in utter loneliness, and in fear and trembling. Two decades after the publication of *Fear and Trembling* (1843) another Christian, Dostoevsky, wrote another classic of the solitary man, *Notes from the Underground*. And two decades later a third lonely man, Nietzsche, proclaimed in *Joyful Wisdom* (and elsewhere) the death of the God to whom his predecessors Kierkegaard and Dostoevsky could turn in their loneliness.

These three massive nineteenth-century figures are the roots of a way of thinking that has dominated our own century and is called existentialism. The word has assumed so wide a variety of meanings that precise definition is impossible. Yet among the attributes shared by many existentialists are a sense of deep loneliness; a conviction that man must take with supreme seriousness the freedom which is his birthright; and a belief that a man's inner-directed, autonomously chosen actions will continue to make him, decision by decision, the man that he is. The contemporary atheistic existentialist (there are religious existentialists as well) is, in short, called by himself. The twentieth-century apostle of this philosophy is Jean-Paul Sartre, whose atheistic existentialism bears remarkable similarities to Kierkegaard's Christian existentialism. Sartre is in highest degree a Kierkegaardian knight of faith—without a God!

The protagonists of the three novels discussed in this section begin with different premises, endure disparate lives, and end with the common decision to write novels tracing their search for identity. Of all twentieth-century fiction, James Joyce's *A Portrait of the Artist as a Young Man* is to me the very model of the novel of vocation. Stephen Dedalus rejects the calls of family, Church, and State to answer the imperative resting only in his own deepest being and impelling him toward the role of artist. The more philosophically oriented Antoine Roquentin of Sartre's *Nausea* never considers the possibility of divine impulse and rejects out of hand the bourgeois call to follow what the Sartrean scorns as the lifeless, thoughtless ways of society. Through the writing of a novel Roquentin would hope to call rather than to be called and he would call his readers to shame for sedulously aping the crowd rather than attending their own free and autonomous spirits. The protagonist of Ralph Ellison's *Invisible Man*, after years of doing what he is told, resolves that he must find in himself his proper impulse to action, though he will proceed in a more explicitly social context than either Stephen or Roquentin. Of the three protagonists Stephen alone even considers God's call, only to turn away from it. All three, when they do in differing degrees take into account the health of the social order, see themselves as beckoning, not following, others. The novels, each in its own way, argue that the unexamined life is not worth living and that the examined life, whatever its loneliness and agony, leads to a self-determination which is also a self-creation.

Genesis of an Artist

He would create proudly out of the freedom and power of his soul. . . .*

I will try to express myself in some mode of life or art as freely as I can and as wholly as I can. . . .

I

—Heavenly God! cried Stephen's soul, in an outburst of profane joy.

He turned away from her suddenly and set off across the strand. His cheeks were aflame; his body was aglow; his limbs were trembling. On and on and on and on he strode, far out over the sands, singing wildly to the sea, crying to greet the advent of the life that had cried to him.

The advent of Stephen Dedalus's new life is signaled not so much by what he sees as by how he sees it. He sees a girl standing alone in a stream and gazing out to sea—her legs slender, her bared thighs full and ivory-hued, her bosom soft and slight, her hair long and fair, her face touched with wondrous beauty. There was a time, several years earlier, when the same vision would have elicited from him a lustful desire for possession, and a time just a little later when, his desires mortified, he would have lowered his eyes at the sight of a woman. But he now regards the girl, as indeed she regards him, "without shame or wantonness," impelled neither to take nor to ignore her. For the first time in his adolescent life his spirit and flesh

---

* Quotations are from the definitive text, corrected from the Dublin holograph by Chester G. Anderson and edited by Richard Ellmann (New York: Viking, 1964). Reprinted with the permission of The Viking Press,

9

are in harmony: his *soul* cries out in *profane* joy. It is a heady discovery, this bursting knowledge that he can look upon the world with neither the passion to possess nor the urge to eschew. Having cast aside the vestments of both seducer and ascetic, Stephen is now joyfully arrested by life's wonder and beauty. His apostrophe to the Heavenly God bespeaks his gratitude that he can now see with the eyes of one who celebrates the world, of a man now free to become an artist.

Stephen has experienced the miracle of revelation through the commonplace. To see a girl in a stream is hardly in itself an extraordinary event. Yet for Stephen the event is a great and revealing moment, though its cause would seem a frail vessel for its overwhelming effect. From it springs his conviction that he is, or is on his way toward becoming, an artist. Indeed, to look at the whole unfolding of Stephen's life in *A Portrait of the Artist as a Young Man* is to know that for James Joyce a man comes to know himself and his world by means of epiphanies, of revelations through the commonplace. A man sees through the surface qualities of ordinary phenomena, reaching to their radiance, their quintessence or "whatness." The person most open to this miraculous mode of apperception is the artist, called to translate the raw material of earthly phenomena and of his own imagination into words which, in turn, bring sight and sense to men of lesser vision and sensitivity. Stephen's sight of the girl is the climactic experience of his young life, the informing source of "the advent of the life that had cried to him." What in his early years prepared him for this revealing moment and to what end does the moment lead?

II

The novel's five chapters move from Stephen's memories of early childhood to his decision to leave family, Church, and homeland, and to seek in exile a new life free from the inhibiting nets of his past. The notebook jottings which bring the novel to its end were written in March and April of 1902, when Stephen was twenty years old. *A Portrait* records Stephen's search for himself and his gradual maturing toward the artist he is to become.

We are first introduced, through Stephen's memories, to his childhood world and his manner of responding to it with vivid sense impressions and frightening reveries. From his storytelling father, Simon, he identifies himself with "a nicens little boy named baby tuckoo," who was once upon a time met by a moocow. He notes, from wetting his bed, that "first it is warm then it gets cold," and that the bed's protective oil sheet has a queer smell; through sense association he remarks that his mother has a nicer smell than his father. We learn too that, a few years later, his first term at the Jesuit Clongowes School brings him sickness and sorrow. The bully Wells pushes him into a watery ditch, later remembered for its ugly slime and the big rat once seen there. In his feverish sickness consequent upon his wet exposure, his reveries move from a blissful, nostalgically induced dream of returning home to a vision of rats to an imaginative, sentimentalized fantasy of his own death, complete with a mass whose beauty transports his corpse to tears. His family, particularly his mother, was deep in his childhood affection, and he already has a sense of *amor matris,* in both its subjective and objective case, which he is later to ponder in *Ulysses.* One of his few pleasures at Clongowes is each day to diminish by one that series of numbers pasted inside his desk and reckoning the days left before Christmas vacation.

Nor are his memories limited to purely personal misfortunes and heart's desires. Engraved grimly and frighteningly in his mind is the Christmas dinner at home following upon his first sad term at Clongowes. He has the full experience then of what he had even earlier known to be true: that politics (and religion as well, he might have added) is the thing that people argue about. And he learns that, in matters of politics and religion, Mrs. Dante Riordan, with her inviolable faith in the Irish Church, takes one side and his father and Mr. Casey, Irish Nationalists whose god is the recently dispossessed and now dead Charles Stewart Parnell, the other. The high-passioned dinner scene is one of the most memorable in literature; it is also late nineteenth-century Ireland in miniature, embracing the inseparables—politics and religion—and ending in frustrated, anguished rage. The embittered conversational exchange ends with Dante's abrupt departure, screaming oaths on Parnell's head; with Mr. Casey sobbing convulsively for his "dead king"; and with Stephen "raising his terrorstricken face . . . [and seeing] that his father's eyes were full of tears." Stephen, as he grows, is to opt for neither Parnell and his Ireland nor the Church nor family ties and rifts around the dinner table. But memories of and continuing exposures to such discords are to be among the nurturing forces of a life which is to reject State, Church, and family in order to move on toward the calling of an artist.

We learn of Stephen's early sense impressions, his personal fears and disappointments, his exposure to the high winds of political and religious passions. We learn also of his acute sensitivity to words and sounds, a quality indispensable to the artist-to-be. As he once thinks of "his belted grey suit," he realizes simultaneously that "belt was also to give a fellow a belt." And when his schoolmate Simon Moonan is derisively called his prefect McGlade's "suck," Stephen's mind goes word- and sound-tracing:

Suck was a queer word. The fellow called Simon Moonan that name because Simon Moonan used to tie the prefect's false sleeves behind his back and the prefect used to let on to be angry. But the sound was ugly. Once he had washed his hands in the lavatory of the Wicklow Hotel and his father pulled the stopper up by the chain after and the dirty water went down through the hole in the basin. And when it had all gone down slowly the hole in the basin had made a sound like that: suck. Only louder.

The word *wine,* on the other hand, was to Stephen a beautiful word, leading him to "think of dark purple because the grapes

were dark purple that grew in Greece outside houses like
white temples." Yet Stephen also remembers from his first
communion that the smell of wine on the rector's breath, far
from conjuring up lush Grecian images, simply induced a
slight nausea. Stephen is fascinated by proper names—of places
and persons—as well. Learning from Dante the name of the
highest mountain on the moon is to him a fact of sufficient interest to record, and in his geography book he writes not only
his own name but every identifying place name from that of
his Class to that of the Universe. He records his infirmary
mate's observation that the name Dedalus is like Latin. He observes that his schoolmate Tusker Boyle is sometimes called
Lady Boyle because of his fastidious regard for his fingernails.
And he puts the pandybat-swinging Father Dolan in his place
by noting (to himself) that Dolan's name is like that of a
washerwoman.

To the artist—at least to the artist whose growth is traced
in *A Portrait*—sensitivity to personal fortunes and men's passions, to words and sounds and sights and smells, is not enough.
He must also learn to be free, both free from and free for.
The bullying and unjust Father Dolan triggers Stephen's first
major step toward freedom and thus toward the necessary pre-
condition of his artistry. His glasses having been broken, Stephen, excused from his written Latin exercise and thus sitting
seemingly idly in class, is first berated in front of his classmates
and instructor by the roving prefect of studies, Dolan, and
then whipped across the palm of his hand by the disciplinarian's pandybat. The event leads Stephen to his first crucial
question and decision. What is the proper response to so unjust and cruel an act? Should injustice be ignored or brought
to the attention of the school's highest court, its rector, Father
Conmee? In trembling and dignity and with the encouragement of his fellows, Stephen goes to the rector, tells his tale,
and is assured that Father Dolan will not make the same mistake again. It is a glorious triumph for Stephen, whose schoolmates cheer him for his courage and bear him aloft in the
cradle of their locked hands. "He was happy and free," we are

told, and Clongowes is at that moment for him transformed from a place of slimy water and a large rat to a scene most peaceful and pastoral.

This episode marks Stephen's first challenge of onerous tyranny in the dreary world in which he finds himself. Freed from the injustice of Father Dolan, he can savor the earliest fruits of a revolt which will extend to a casting off of far more than the oppressiveness of a prefect of studies. Stephen has taken the first step in his long odyssey leading to exile, to an eschewal of all influences tending to inhibit the movement toward the vocation of the artist.

III

Stephen's memories of Clongowes—he was not to return after that bleak year—are sad ones. Even his one triumph turns somewhat bitter, as he is later told by his father that he and Father Dolan have enjoyed a hearty laugh over the pandybat episode. Stephen, humiliated and alienated by the bullies— young and old—of his childhood, becomes more and more a spectator of life rather than an active participant in its events. His greatest solace in an increasingly lonely existence is found in words. In the summer following Clongowes, during long walks with his father and his Uncle Charles, he *listens,* learning more of politics and family and enchanted by the words, familiar and unfamiliar, which convey the thoughts and prejudices of his elders and which serve, so he believes, to reveal to him the nature of the mysterious, yet real, world of persons and things:

Words which he did not understand he said over and over to himself till he had learned them by heart: and through them he had glimpses of the real world about him. The hour when he too would take part in the life of that world seemed drawing near and in secret he began to make ready for the great part which he felt awaited him the nature of which he only dimly apprehended.

Yet he feels that his movement toward apprehending this real world is a slow one, and that there is for him a disparity be-

tween the daily round of events, the sum and substance of life
to others, and those inner images born of his imagination.
Sensing his difference from other children in this respect, he
can only watch them excitedly giving themselves to the activities of the moment, while he remains "a tranquil watcher of
the scene before him."

But if Stephen cannot enter with abandon into the world
of events, he can reflect in words those actions in life which
seem always to elude him. Once, as he and the lovely Emma
return from a party, he yearns to yield to her attractively provoking gestures and to kiss her. He cannot. But he can return
home and realize in verse what he could not accomplish in
fact. He writes of the night, the breeze, the moon, and a tender parting which bore the fruition of a kiss, relished in words
if not by lips. And when, not long after, his father, whose
impoverishment had broken Stephen's ties to Clongowes, ar-
ranges that his son be admitted to Belvedere College, the
young Stephen has behind him the romantic verses of a very
young poet.

In his first two years at Belvedere, Stephen gives full evidence of those cuttings of ties which are to lead to the drastic
severing known as exile. Taking on the youthful robes of
heresy, he shows that a challenging of orthodoxy may be a
richly positive gesture—not only a breaking with a past, but a
commitment to a future. He not only derides his fellow students' favorite poet, Tennyson ("Lawn Tennyson, gentleman
poet" in *Ulysses*); he also champions Byron and will not be
forced, despite a caning, to opine Tennyson's superiority. His
heretical impulses embrace theological matters as well. Once
having written in a class essay that the soul is "without a possibility of ever approaching nearer" its Creator, Stephen does
retreat before his master's attack and amend the offending
phrase to "without a possibility of ever reaching," but his
movement toward a rejection of the Church and its doctrines
is under way, to be abruptly though briefly reversed at a later
period, and then to be unleashed. There will be many urgent
petitions to Stephen that he be a good Catholic or an Irish

patriot or a "gentleman," but he will pay them increasingly less heed.

During his Belvedere years Stephen's rebellion is primarily against his family and their wishes that he be a boy like other boys. For a brief moment, when he takes part in his school's Whitsuntide play, he forgets his introspective moodiness, his deep awareness of his difference from his peers, and seems a boy like other boys. The mood is short-lived. The play over, he emerges from the theater, sees his parents waiting for him, and, feigning an errand, rushes away, emptied of pride and hope and desire, feeling an anguished frustration and a sense of the vanity and futility of all things. It was a feeling that Joyce knew well and that another "Stephen," the young protagonist of the *Dubliners*' "Araby," experienced as he left the dismal and disillusioning bazaar, as empty-handed and empty-souled as Stephen now is.

A little later but still within the Belvedere days, a trip to Cork with his father, some of whose steadily diminishing property is to be auctioned off, serves only to increase Stephen's sense of estrangement. Simon, returning to the city of his youth (a youth which he never outgrew), proves little more than a source of embarrassment to his far more introverted son. Simon's excessive talkativeness, his empty boasting, his adolescent flirtatiousness, his fatuous and Polonius-like preachments to his son, do nothing but underline for Stephen the vast gap between his own temperament and his father's—and convince him that his father is more of a child than he. But the trip does far more than increase Stephen's disenchantment with his father. One of its incidents serves to show him that the motions of his own mind and those of the real world are in closer conjunction than he once thought. While visiting the anatomy theater of Simon's alma mater, Queen's College, Stephen sees the word *Foetus* cut several times into the wood of a desk top. The word does more to reincarnate Queen's past for Stephen than all his father's reminiscences. He can picture the student who pressed the knife, his fellows standing by in laughing admiration. And he now realizes that his thoughts, his cruder ones at least, are reflected in an outer world once seemingly so distant from him.

It shocked him to find in the outer world a trace of what he had deemed till then a brutish and individual malady of his own mind. His recent monstrous reveries came thronging into his memory. They too had sprung up before him, suddenly and furiously, out of mere words. He had soon given in to them and allowed them to sweep across and abase his intellect, wondering always where they came from, from what den of monstrous images, and always weak and humble towards others, restless and sickened of himself when they had swept over him.

Some months after his unhappy trip, Stephen makes one last effort to stem the increasing restlessness and loneliness that is overtaking him. He longs to renew or solidify his ties with his parents and to hold on to the tender motions of affection that had marked his feelings toward Eileen and then Emma. With the prize money won through his literary efforts he showers on his family a round of delicacies and entertainments. And as his more brutish sexual impulses grow in insistence, he gains momentary relief in memories of the lovely Mercedes in *The Count of Monte Cristo* and of the few restfully idyllic scenes of his childhood. But such thoughts of the tenderly romantic do little to quiet the feverish lust stirring his blood. Stephen's heart beats more in harmony with what the engraved *Foetus* had suggested than with all that beckons him to his family, to Mercedes, to visions of a white house and moonlit rose garden. Dublin's "dark slimy streets" win the night. As Stephen once rebelled against the capricious injustice of Father Dolan, he now rebels against his family and the Mercedeses, Eileens, and Emmas of literature and life. He had kissed Emma only in verse, not giving his physical being to her provoking, yet innocent, openness. But the Dublin whore is not to be put off by an indecisive Stephen, as his inner "den of monstrous images" is at last to find its matching counterpart in the real world. His family and all they repre-

sent cast aside, he is now free for a new experience. As the
woman pressed herself upon him, Stephen

closed his eyes, surrendering himself to her, body and mind, conscious of nothing in the world but the dark pressure of her softly
parting lips. They pressed upon his brain as upon his lips as though
they were the vehicle of a vague speech; and between them he felt
an unknown and timid pressure, darker than the swoon of sin, softer
than sound or odour.

I V

Whatever the meanderings of Stephen's conduct, his mind remains consistently thoughtful and introspective. His actions
he weighs with deliberation and passes on them the Church's
own judgment. He sees his soul in a state of sin, thus acknowledging God, since sin is the contravention of the will of God.
He thinks in terms of grace, knowing he has placed himself
outside the stream of sanctifying grace, that providentially
constant intrusion of God's spirit, and yet hoping that an occasional act of charity may bring him some small measure of
actual grace. With King Claudius he knows that his sinful disposition renders prayer impossible. Yet the image of Mary,
conceived without sin, presses upon his imagination. He is
entranced by her spikenard, myrrh, and frankincense, by her
garments and emblems, by her compassionate eyes gazing
down upon him from the chapel altar. And he reflects that
his lips which speak her name are lewd channels for so holy a
sound. Enamored of lust as he is, he calls it by the name of sin.

Shortly after his own first "swoon of sin," the sixteen-year-
old Stephen is called with his fellow students to a school retreat. The sermons preached there by Father Arnall have an
overwhelming effect on him. The hope voiced in the priest's
first sermon—that the retreat may prove a turning point for
any soul alienated from God's grace—is strikingly fulfilled, at
least briefly, in Stephen's life. The sermons are eschatological,
speaking of last things—of death, judgment, hell, and heaven.

Stephen learns that, if the Clongowes ditch nursed one rat, the grave which swallows death is besieged by a host of them, scuttling about, plump-bellied with the glut of dead flesh. He learns too the horrible rigor of the judgment meted out to one who prefers a sated appetite to a disciplined love. He is reminded of the proud motto of Lucifer—"Non serviam: I will not serve"—one that he, after a short period of conversion, is to adopt as his own. He learns of hell, of its exterior darkness, its awful stench, its tormenting fire, its intensity, its company of the damned and of devils. And he learns, most frighteningly of all, of its spiritual torments, spun through an eternity and described by Father Arnall in a measured detail and concreteness which sting Stephen's vivid poetic imagination with devastating pain.

Stephen again is emptied, this time of all lustful desire, his whole being in torment. He adds to Father Arnall's vision of hell—one which, it seems, could have no addition—a vision of his own. He is surrounded by goatish creatures, their malignity unexceeded. They wander about in eerie complaint, moving "in slow circles, circling closer and closer to enclose, to enclose, soft language issuing from their lips, their long swishing tails besmeared with stale shite, thrusting upwards their terrific faces." The whore too had turned to Stephen with "frank uplifted eyes." From face of whore to faces of goats—and Stephen rises from his vision terrorized in conscience and vomiting in agony.

The imagery abruptly changes. Spiritually and physically purged, Stephen goes to the window, sees a faintly luminous heaven, and breathes a sweet air. He is now ready to confess, not that Tennyson outshines Byron, but that he is contrite for his sins and ready to receive God's sanctifying grace. It is his third major decision. He had sought and found justice against the tyrannic authority of Father Dolan; he had put aside his family and dreams of tender romance to take refuge in the arms of a harlot. And now, confessing his sins and hearing the priest's words of absolution, Stephen's prayers (in purple passage!) "ascended to heaven from his purified heart like perfume streaming upwards from a heart of white rose." He had felt "happy and free" when he left his petitioning interview with Father Conmee at Clongowes; he had felt a pressure "darker than the swoon of sin, softer than sound or odour" in the prostitute's arms. Now he feels "fair and holy once more, holy and happy." And in the communion which follows, Stephen accepts tremblingly not the body of a whore, but that of his newly found Lord.

V

Irony, in one of its more intriguing modes, stems in part from the distance between author and protagonist, from the ability of the former to view the latter with a degree of objectivity. As author and protagonist move toward identification, this kind of irony approaches zero. First-person narrative and autobiography can be ironic as long as the writer is able to look at himself, at least in part, as another self. One of the most tender and satisfying modes of irony takes the form of reminiscence, the looking back to a childhood or adolescence either real or imaginary. The art of this form lies in the author's ability to present simultaneously (1) the young protagonist's feelings about and responses to events as they occurred in the past and (2) his own present, mature, adult reflections upon those earlier feelings and responses. A superb such model is Joyce's short story "Araby," whose reader experiences both the young boy as he was and the older Joyce's somewhat aloof, yet fully sympathetic, present assessment of him. The story's perfect tonal control lies in the balanced, simultaneous presentations of a dramatic past and a present reflection upon it.

That Stephen Dedalus is in most of his contours the young James Joyce is of greater relevance to biographer than to literary critic. But of considerable interest to the critic is Joyce's view or appraisal of his protagonist or younger self. To interpret this appraisal, to determine the varying degrees of approximation between author and character—the degrees of identification, sympathy, ridicule—is a task difficult and fascinating. *A Portrait* was completed in 1914, when Joyce was thirty-two years old, twelve years after the concluding action of the novel. The book was, in one form or another, in composition over a period of ten years, from the very short prose work written in 1904 and entitled "A Portrait of the Artist," through the lengthy *Stephen Hero,* and culminating in *A Portrait of the Artist as a Young Man* itself, published in 1916. *A Portrait* records an embryonic artist's growth toward artistry, in terms both of literary style and of intellectual and emotional maturity.

The development of Stephen's style is charted ironically from the declarative simplicity of his youngest days—"His father told him that story: his father looked at him through a glass: he had a hairy face"; to the awkward complexity of the Clongowes period—"All he had to do was when the dinner was over and he came out in his turn to go on walking but not out to the corridor but up the staircase on the right that led to the castle"; to the sixteen-year-old purple prose—". . . his prayers ascended to heaven from his purified heart like perfume streaming upwards from a heart of white rose"; to the twenty-year-old crisp and straightforward economy—"Long talk with Cranly on the subject of my revolt. He had his grand manner on. I supple and suave. Attacked me on the score of love for one's mother." Such stylistic development foreshadows the vastly more complex "Oxen of the Sun" episode in *Ulysses,* where Joyce parodies English prose styles from Anglo-Saxon to contemporary times.

Joyce is at his most ironic in his depiction of Stephen's prose style and emotional disposition toward the end of chapter 3, which narrates the latter's confession and communion, and at the beginning of chapter 4, when Stephen subjects himself to the most intensive mortification of the flesh. We are, previously, sympathetically amused by the simple declaratives of earliest childhood and the ungainly prose complexities

of early school days. But we are perhaps inclined to find a
little ridiculous the utterance of palpitating phrases whose
preciosity tends to embarrass us: the claim to "a heart of
white rose" is excessive. The ironic imprint is engraved not
only on Stephen's phraseology but on the psychic temperament which it reflects. The earlier Stephen at the brothel, committed as he then felt to the pleasures of the flesh, hardly
viewed them as the sum of all life to come. But with the
communion comes the conviction that he has reached the center of a life which will no longer be subject to changing wind
and tide. "Another life!" thinks Stephen as the priest-borne
eucharistic bread approaches him. "A life of grace and virtue
and happiness! It was true. It was not a dream from which he
would wake. The past was past." The past *was* past, but it
always is, as Stephen is later to learn. The dream, punctuated
by exclamatory effusions, is one from which he will awake, as
he has already awakened from dreams of perfumed flesh. Stephen here knows himself even less well than usual, the heightened irony perhaps implying that, for Joyce, nothing seemed
more restrictive to his own artistic freedom than subservience
to the Church.

At the beginning of chapter 4, the flesh, at whose altar
Stephen has for a time served, is consigned to outer darkness.
His daily regimen, a careful and systematic mortification of the
senses, is extreme. "Resolute piety" is Joyce's term, the qualifying adjective a perfect underlining of the mechanical rigidity
of Stephen's new phase. To the souls in purgatory, whose
earthly lives had fallen far short of his own, he offers his
supererogatory works and intercessory prayers, disturbed only
that he receives no strict accounting of his gifts. Joyce's imagery is devastating: at times, he writes, Stephen seems "to
feel his soul in devotion pressing like fingers the keyboard of
a great cash register and to see the amount of his purchase
start forth immediately in heaven, not as a number but as a
frail column of incense or as a slender flower." Stephen imposes on his senses the strictest discipline: he will look at nothing pleasing, certainly not into the eyes of a woman; his nose

seeks out what is to it most revolting—"a certain stale fishy stink like that of longstanding urine"; his taste bows humbly to fasting; and he discovers the avenues to every itch, pain, and sting that may assail his flesh. We smile, recalling the Bergsonian principle that the sight of rigidity evokes laughter. And when we learn that Stephen, despite all his sober meticulousness, remains open to moments of petulance and slenderly motivated anger, we remember another Bergsonian precept: that the futile effort of the human spirit to control human passions is another source of the comic. Stephen's "resolute piety" we cannot take with full seriousness.

The sign and seal of his rejection of the world, Stephen now believes, will be his ordination to holy orders. But when confronted by his spiritual director and encouraged to a priestly vocation, he draws back, discovering that, once again, the past is past. Hugh Kenner has remarked on the imagery through which the meeting of Stephen and his director comes to us. The priest's back is to the light, his face in total shadow; like a hangman he dangles and loops the cord of one of the window blinds. Freedom, Stephen senses, is not to be found in darkness and nooses, not in the grave, chilled, passionless life which he sees as that of the priesthood. The appeal of the name "The Reverend Stephen Dedalus, S.J.," and of the ordered life which it implies, is finally no match for the attraction, to Stephen, of the snares and disorder of the fallen world. As he leaves the priest and walks toward his own untidy and malodorous home, he smiles "to think that it was this disorder, the misrule and confusion of his father's house and the stagnation of vegetable life, which was to win the day in his soul."

A short time later, having matriculated at University College in Dublin, Stephen, walking seaward, is beckoned, not by the name "The Reverend Stephen Dedalus, S.J.," but by the bantering shouts of his young friends: "Stephanos Dedalos! Bous Stephanoumenos! Bous Stephaneforos!" And he thinks not of the stoned martyr whose name he bears, but of the sunward-flying escaper from his own labyrinth, of the free hawklike man, the great Daedalus who now becomes the guiding symbol of his life—"a symbol of the artist forging anew in his workshop out of the sluggish matter of the earth a new soaring impalpable imperishable being." The past again is past, but the present present bears a difference from former ones. Stephen, in recognizing "the call of life to his soul" in its distinct contrast to "the inhuman voice that had called him to the pale service of the altar," is now ready for the major epiphany which will direct him, no longer subject to the sharp veerings of the past, through his four remaining decades of life as Stephen Dedalus-Joyce.

As Stephen had previously moved from brothel to the Lord's altar, he now moves from altar to the sea's strand, there finding a new and life-sustaining promise. He is ripe for an artist's vision of the girl in the stream, whom he beholds with neither desire nor loathing, but, as he is later to phrase it, after Aquinas, in her wholeness, her harmony, her radiance. He now knows that he is henceforth "to recreate life out of life," to take "the sluggish matter of the earth" and to re-create in words "a new . . . impalpable imperishable being." Thus Stephen defines the calling of the artist that he will *become*. He *is* a young man, not yet the mature artist, as his stylistic reflection on his new world attests: "Glimmering and trembling, trembling and unfolding, a breaking light, an opening flower, it spread in endless succession to itself, breaking in full crimson and unfolding and fading to palest rose, leaf by leaf and wave of light by wave of light, flooding all the heavens with its soft flushes, every flush deeper than other." The ironic distance between the younger Stephen and the older Joyce remains, in spite of the young man's progress toward self-knowledge.

VI

The last chapter of *A Portrait* is, properly, the last will and testament of the artist as a young man. Stephen puts his mind, as it responds to Ireland, Church, family, and art, in order, and he chooses exile. To what condition of being and thought have his twenty years brought him?

Stephen is to tell Leopold Bloom, some two years later in the early hours of June 17, 1904, that he (Stephen) is not important because he belongs to Ireland, but that Ireland is important because it belongs to him. It is an attitude prefigured in *A Portrait,* where Stephen's indifference to the body politic is seen in global dimensions. By the rugged MacCann he is denounced as an antisocial being interested only in himself. And when Stephen refuses, somewhat later, to sign a testimonial pledging himself to the pursuit of universal peace and brotherhood, MacCann has the wit to observe: "Minor poets, I suppose, are above such trivial questions as the question of universal peace." Only Temple, another student, sees Stephen as the lone man in the university who "has an individual mind." Stephen will surrender his allegiance neither to a universal society nor to Ireland. "When the soul of a man is born in this country," he tells his fellows, "there are nets flung at it to hold it back from flight. You talk to me of nationality, language, religion. I shall try to fly by those nets."

He must disavow not only Ireland, but the Catholic Church as well. Not only to the call of the priesthood, but to that of the Church itself Stephen replies in Lucifer's words, "I will not serve." Severance from Church also means for him severance from his mother. His decision to leave his sacred studies and enter the university has already occasioned the "first noiseless sundering of their lives," a cleavage which deepens when he later refuses his mother's request that he "make . . . [his] easter duty" communion. The waning relationship is a link in the chain that leads Buck Mulligan's aunt in *Ulysses* to think that Stephen killed his mother by refusing to pray for her at her deathbed. In *A Portrait* Cranly, wishing to stay Stephen's growing estrangement from his mother and the Church, asks him if he had not been happier in his days of faith. Stephen's reply—"I was someone else then"—is a most appropriate remark from a person whose psychic journey has been so extended as his. The journey is by no means confined, however, to a series of rejections; as Stephen rejects, he also accepts:

I will not serve that in which I no longer believe, whether it call itself my home, my fatherland or my church: and I will try to express myself in some mode of life or art as freely as I can and as wholly as I can, using for my defence the only arms I allow myself to use—silence, exile and cunning.

The silence, exile, and cunning are not to be used as ends in themselves, but rather as protective weapons to ward off all forces that inhibit artistry. In the last chapter of his book we learn from Stephen what are, to him, the conditions and nature of art.

Stephen's aesthetic discussion with the fire-lighting dean of studies—his quoting Aquinas to the effect that the beautiful is that which pleases the eye, and the good that toward which the appetite tends—is but a brief preliminary to his longer exchange with Lynch, which he begins with a consideration of art's proper effect. True art evokes a static emotion, arresting a person and holding him fast in a condition of awe. It infuses its spectator with neither desire nor loathing and is thus neither pornographic nor didactic. To create a work of art, the apprehension of which pleases the eye and induces a static emotion, a man must first be able to perceive an object in its three basic qualities of wholeness, harmony, and radiance. An object is seen in its wholeness when seen in its separateness from everything that is not itself. It is, next, seen in its harmony, in "the rhythm of its structure," when its constituent elements are perceived in their perfected interrelationships. The object's radiance, its self-revelation, is grasped when the informing imagination strikes through to the object's "whatness," its quintessential being; the sensing of radiance is the moment of rapture, of epiphany.

This supreme quality [of radiance] is felt by the artist when the esthetic image is first conceived in his imagination. The mind in that mysterious instant Shelley likened beautifully to a fading coal. The instant wherein that supreme quality of beauty, the clear radiance of the esthetic image, is apprehended luminously by the mind which has been arrested by its wholeness and fascinated by its harmony is the luminous silent stasis of esthetic pleasure, a spiritual state very like to that cardiac condition which the Italian physiologist Luigi Galvani, using a phrase almost as beautiful as Shelley's, called the enchantment of the heart.

Stephen's lessons in aesthetics came partly through his reading of Aristotle, Aquinas, Shelley, and others; they came also through his observation of the girl in the stream. He had never, before his vision of the wading girl, actually experienced that wondrous static emotion which arrests. The prostitute he saw only as a physically desirable object, and his days of resolute mortification of the senses turned him only to a loathing of what he had formerly desired. His rapture at the moment of apprehending the wading girl springs from his sudden knowledge, not only that he can be ecstatically arrested, but that to see in this way, "without shame or wantonness," is to see with the eyes of an artist. Stephen experiences Luigi Galvani's "enchantment of the heart." He then knows that he is called to become an artist, that the heart's enchantment is to be shared, and that the literary artist's means of sharing are words. Most men, in unmediated confrontation with the real world of persons, places, and things, remain blind to the inherent wholeness, harmony, and radiance of those objects. The literary artist is one who must first perceive those qualities and then so translate them into words that his readers, formerly seeing through a glass darkly, may in turn be possessed of the beautiful.

Stephen, in fact, rejects one kind of priesthood to take up another. He loses his more strictly religious faith, but his mind, steeped in its Jesuit heritage, never relinquishes its mode of interpreting and categorizing the world's actions and passions in theological terms and images. He sees literature as "the highest and most spiritual art," and himself as "a priest of eternal imagination, transmuting the daily bread of ex-

perience into the radiant body of everliving life." The daily
bread is life itself; the radiant body is the artist's interpreting
and blessing and celebrating of life through words. Stephen
likens the artist's act of creation to the Virgin Mary's: "In the
virgin womb of the imagination the word was made flesh."
And he compares the artist himself to God: "The artist, like
the God of the creation, remains within or behind or beyond
or above his handiwork, invisible, refined out of existence, indifferent, paring his fingernails." The image can be misleading. God may be to Stephen indifferent, but Stephen views
neither his own artistry nor its desired effect with indifference.
His indifference is expressed only in his affirmation that art
should not, through the pornographic or the didactic, beckon
its perceiver to physical action. But Stephen would, through
his art, call his readers to change, to become, in freedom to
cast off the nets which have bound them, and to move to the
point where they may say, with him, "I was someone else
then."

A primary reason for Stephen's leaving Ireland is that he
may find elsewhere the nurturing soil that will free him to
free Ireland from what he several times calls its batlike soul.
The birds which he sees on a late March evening shortly before his departure call him to his exile, but as a hawk, not a bat.
How, he asks himself a little later, can he capture the con-
sciences and imaginations of his countrymen that they may
henceforth "breed a race less ignoble than their own"? How
can he transform "the thoughts and desires of the race to
which he belonged flitting like bats, across the dark country
lanes, under trees by the edges of streams and near the pool-
mottled bogs"? He must, he determines, gain his own freedom
before he can bequeath freedom to others; he must, like the
hawklike Daedalus and like the dwellers in Plato's shadowy
cave, turn sunward. He is, like Plato's enlightened men, his
brothers' keeper, called to move some of them at least, not to
physical action, but to the radiance which is wisdom and self-
knowledge.

Stephen's final terse journal entries see him off to his voyage. Everything—his family and friends (male and female), his Church and State—he is to leave behind. As his mother, tenderly and sadly, helps ready him for the voyage he cries out to his future: "Welcome, O life! I go to encounter for the millionth time the reality of experience and to forge in the smithy of my soul the uncreated conscience of my race. . . . Old father, old artificer, stand me now and ever in good stead." With this final invoking petition to his mythological father Daedalus, Stephen, someone other than he once was, is on his way.

A Portrait of the Existentialist
as a Young Man

*All I wanted was to be free.**

I want to leave, go to some place where I will be really in my own niche, where I will fit in. . . . But my place is nowhere; I am unwanted, de trop.

They have washed themselves of the sin of existing.

I

Jean-Paul Sartre's *Nausea* records the genesis of an existentialist and could appropriately be subtitled "A Portrait of the Existentialist as a Young Man." As James Joyce's *A Portrait of the Artist as a Young Man* is an artist's account of the maturing of an artist, Sartre's *Nausea* is an existentialist's account of the maturing of an existentialist. Both are first novels, written when their authors were in their early thirties, old enough to proclaim to the world their manifestoes, purchased through severe growing pains and serving to make clear some of the meanings of art and existentialism. The protagonist of each novel equates his personal freedom with the discovery of his vocation.

Joyce's novel is more overtly autobiographical, taking Stephen Dedalus-Joyce through his first twenty years, from his

* Quotations are from the New Directions edition, translated by Lloyd Alexander (New York: New Directions, 1964). Copyright © 1964 by New Directions Publishing Corporation. Reprinted by permission of the publisher. The novel was first published in 1938.

30

earliest memories—of his father Simon's tale about the moocow and baby tuckoo, of the changing temperature of the urine-wet bed, of his mother's nice smell—up to the journal notations of March–April 1902, announcing his exile from family, Church, and homeland, his flight to the continent and into the practice of art. Stephen's progression toward his craft is a well-defined, rhythmical series of rises and falls, each a necessary step toward finding his calling. Though he was not to remain long in his early ecstatic abandonment to fleshly delights, or in the ensuing period of rigorous mortification of the senses, such stages were necessary preliminaries to the crowning epiphany of his young life—his observing the lovely, slender-legged, ivory-thighed, soft-bosomed, fair-haired girl, wading in a stream and gazing out to sea, and his realizing that he regards her not with desire or loathing but with wondrous delight. Arrested by her radiance and eager to communicate this stunning sense of the world's beauty, Stephen is soon ready to try the wings of his artistry. *A Portrait,* moreover, is the fulfillment of its own promise, the novel that Dedalus-Joyce sets out to write in the freedom of exile.

Antoine Roquentin, thirty-year-old protagonist of *Nausea,* comes to us through a more abridged time scheme. With the exception of some brief introductory material, we are confined to his notebook entries of one month, from Monday, January 29, through Wednesday, February 28, 1932. Early in that year he comes suddenly under the heavy oppressiveness of what he calls "Nausea." His notebook or diary is the record of his initial awareness of the disease, of his efforts to define and account for it, of its growth, and of his finally countering its more paralyzing effects through his own existential wisdom.

Roquentin's metamorphosis, his movement from being overcome by Nausea to overcoming (or giving promise of overcoming) it, is not so clearly stratified as Stephen's growth toward artistry. At the end of each of *A Portrait*'s first three chapters, Stephen reaches a solution to the problem of that particular chapter, freeing himself from one kind of bondage only to enter another in the next chapter, until, with the epiphanal vision of the wading girl, he is released to his freedom beyond bondage, the artist's freedom to pursue his calling. The rhythm of Roquentin's psychic journey is less well defined because he does not, throughout the novel, move from one condition to another clearly distinguishable from it, thus leaving behind one to enter another. Instead, extending to almost the very end of *Nausea* and presented with little apparent order, a diverse series of episodes illustrates his many inducements to the disease. He occasionally gains some relief at the end of a particularly traumatic episode, but only to be plunged again into much the same dilemma that had seemed on its way to solution. It is not until the very last diary entry, following upon the most severe attack of his treacherous malady, that he gives promise of escaping its ravages. As Stephen's major epiphany comes through his vision of a wading girl, Roquentin's comes through his hearing of a song, one which, through various previous hearings, had temporarily assuaged his Nausea, and which, at the last, points his own path to a more enduring freedom. He too will become an artist; he sets out, finally, to write a novel, though his journey to that end has been a different one from Stephen's. *Nausea*, like *A Portrait*, is a fulfillment of its own promise; it *is* the novel that Roquentin-Sartre sets out to write at its own end. In the end was the beginning; in the beginning, the end. Both novels are their own records of how they came to be written.

Nausea's claim to a reader's time, however, is hardly based on whatever relationship it may bear to *A Portrait*. It is an important novel because it sensitively and artistically conveys the feelings of an existential man confronting his world. In his systematic, expository writings ranging from the vast, difficult *Being and Nothingness* to the short, lucid, popular "Existentialism Is a Humanism," Sartre writes only *about* existentialism. But to experience the texture of a particular way of life, a reader turns to belles-lettres, not to exposition. Among Sartre's novels and plays, *Nausea* is the best guide to the existential heart and psyche, probably the best of all books for the reader who wishes to explore the existentialist from the inside, to gain an immediate sense of the anguish of the existentialist facing existence. To follow Roquentin is to trace the genesis and maturing of such a man.

I I

Late in the novel we learn from Anny, Roquentin's sometime sweetheart, that he had, as a younger man, been stolid and normal, healthy and contented. But Roquentin has now reached thirty, the year of truth for existentialists and absurdists, the year of trial for both Kafka's Joseph K. and Camus's Meursault, and the year, according to *The Myth of Sisyphus,* of unnerving self-disclosures. It is in January of 1932 that Roquentin becomes aware of a strange and radical change. His three placid previous years, spent in the town of Bouville at work on a biography of the Marquis de Rollebon, now dead for over a century, give way to a new and bewildering disquietude.

The transformation is abrupt. On what begins as a thoroughly ordinary day, Roquentin, casually observing some children at the game of ducks and drakes, picks up a stone to skim it over the water. But for some mysterious reason he feels impelled to drop the stone. He wonders anxiously whether his eerie and unsettling reaction is provoked by something in the stone or the sea or perhaps in himself. There develops a recurrent pattern, a sequence of unpleasant changes in his relationship to various objects. His hands relate to a pipe, a fork, a doorknob, in a new way, and the hand of the Self-Taught Man in his own seems "a fat white worm." Even more disconcertingly, he, for whom picking up stray pieces of paper has long been an obsession, discovers that he is now unable to pick up a dirty, detached notebook page lying by a puddle. Of one thing he becomes certain: he is no longer free; some devastating form of paralysis has overtaken him. He traces his disease to the stone, whose tactile unpalatableness had wrenched him from his desire to skim it. The touch of the stone, pipe, fork, knob, hand, the untouchability of the dirty piece of paper—it all adds up to "a sort of nausea in the hands."

Accompanying this malaise, which intensifies in the early days of February, is Roquentin's sense of his difference from other persons and his consequent aloneness. He observes the card-playing cronies who frequent the Café Mably. Their hands can deal cards and gather chips—and they could doubtless skim stones and pick up stray papers if they so willed. They talk agreeably and in agreement with one another. Trivial and banal as they may be, they enjoy certainties, meet no recalcitrance in the world of objects, and find their companionship mutually solacing. They manage "to pass the time," to live at ease in Bouville, to remain strangers to the growing introspection which oppresses Roquentin. Nor is it simply the cardplayers who seem immune. Roquentin comes to recognize that virtually all of the Bouville citizenry—patrician and plebeian, past and present—have been and are untouched by the sickening paralysis that grips him. The more he observes and reflects, the more he knows his solitude.

Consider, for example, his visit to the Bouville Museum on Saturday afternoon, February 17. Adorning the walls are portraits of those who, from 1875 to 1910, had guided with firm and successful hands the town's affairs. The achievements of that generation were many. They had built, at a cost of fourteen million francs, Sainte-Cécile-de-la-Mer, the church whose construction was inspired by the mayor's wife's vision of Sainte Cécile, who charitably argued that the Bouville elite should no longer attend mass in the company of shopkeepers at the older churches. The men of that distinguished era had also developed and enlarged the town's shipping facilities, founded schools for technical and professional studies, and married women who established various philanthropic projects and raised their children in the best traditions of France.

The portraits breathe assurance; they are of men whose looks show clearly that Nausea (in the hands or elsewhere) had never assailed them. Intent upon the progress of Bouville, convinced of the contributions of their lives and works to the unchallenged goodness and rightness of that progress, they had never chanced an introspection that might raise haunting doubts and induce the sickness felt by Roquentin. More than this, Roquentin feels, the over one hundred and fifty pairs of eyes staring out of the portraits are questioning his very right to exist. For what has he, by their standards, ever done to justify his existence? What is an unfinished biographical manuscript compared to the accomplishments of the Bouville elite?

To no portrait is Roquentin more attentive than that of the merchant Jean Pacôme, a man who had, consciously or unconsciously, shielded himself well against self-questioning.

For sixty years, without a halt, he had used his right to live. The slightest doubt had never crossed those magnificent grey eyes. Pacôme had never made a mistake. He had always done his duty, all his duty, his duty as son, husband, father, leader. He had never weakened in his demands for his due: as a child, the right to be well brought up, in a united family, the right to inherit a spotless name, a prosperous business; as a husband, the right to be cared for, surrounded with tender affection; as a father, the right to be venerated; as a leader, the right to be obeyed without a murmur. For a right is nothing more than the other aspect of duty.

To be convinced of the presence of duties is a great comfort. For behind every duty lies its prerequisite, some code or construct or system, some way of life whose rules, carefully spelled out, assure the faithful that virtue is rewarded and that the dutiful will gain a treasure house of rights. A man likes to know where he stands, and Pacôme's knowledge was precise: he had done his duty; he had enjoyed his rights; he had done well by the system; the system had done well by him. It is no wonder that he "had never looked any further into himself"—or into the system either. Why challenge or question a way of life so reassuring and unthreatening?

Pacôme was not alone in his arrogant assurance. There was his contemporary Jean Parrottin, whose conviction of *his* rights guided all his thoughts and actions. Roquentin speculates that Parrottin, on his deathbed and following upon his wife's most assiduous, vigilant, and tender care, had turned to her with the gracious farewell: "I do not thank you, Thérèse; you have only done your duty." Nor was arrogance confined to a past generation. Worthy of notice is Roquentin's contemporary, Monsieur Coffier, president of the Chamber of Commerce, who has done his duty so well that, on his Sunday morning walks after mass, he enjoys the right of ignoring the passersby of less established repute. On his portrait, perhaps, future generations may gaze.

The Bouville elite escape Nausea through trust in a system of values or way of life which they have comfortably inherited, a system, moreover, whose criteria for success they fulfill admirably. More than this, the elite's very presence, dead or alive, proves a shelter against Nausea for the town's more ordinary citizenry. More than once Roquentin mentions Gustav Impétraz, erstwhile school inspector and author, now dead thirty years, whose gigantic bronze statue dominates the Cour des Hypothèques. How solacing it is to the Bouville women who need only look at the man to realize that "he thought as they do, exactly as they do, on all subjects." The impressive (if seen not too closely!) bronze Impétraz is one of the town's guardians, assuring those who see him of the soundness of their ways and values, and thus enabling them to return to their daily round of unthinking activities and rest secure under his protective wisdom.

Not unlike the women strolling through the Cour des Hypothèques are a husband and wife who enter the museum during Roquentin's visit. They view the portraits with respectful awe, opining that Bouville is what it is because of the Pacômes and Parrottins. And so it is. But the couple's grateful response to this fact is different from that of Roquentin, whose parting sentiments to the portrayed town fathers are brief, eloquent, unambiguous: "Farewell, beautiful lilies, elegant in your painted little sanctuaries, good-bye, lovely lilies, our pride and reason for existing, good-bye, you bastards!"

III

Roquentin's Nausea is a consequence of his aversion to the physical world of objects and his disgust with the persons who have successfully eluded the disease which engulfs him. Why is he revolted by the world of objects and persons and scornful of those who seemingly rest on easy terms with the same world? It is as we observe Roquentin's response to what he calls "existence" that we begin to learn the reason for and to experience the feeling of existential man's Nausea.

In the early evening of February 21, some weeks after the first incursion of the disease, Roquentin, sitting in the town park and gazing at the black, knotty roots of a chestnut tree, suddenly comes to a visionary grasp of what existence is and why he is so repelled by its presence:

If anyone had asked me what existence was, I would have answered, in good faith, that it was nothing, simply an empty form which was added to external things without changing anything in their nature. And then all of a sudden, there it was, clear as day: existence had suddenly unveiled itself. It had lost the harmless look of an abstract category: it was the very paste of things, this root was kneaded into existence. Or rather the root, the park gates, the bench, the sparse grass, all that had vanished: the diversity of things, their individuality, were only an appearance, a veneer. This veneer had melted, leaving soft, monstrous masses, all in disorder—naked, in a frightful, obscene nakedness.

We see that each part of the created order, certainly at its inception, is to Roquentin a gelatinous thereness, a vast, sprawling disorder in which there is no separate identity of objects (no "wholeness," in the Thomistic, Joycean sense), but only an oozing merging of all things. In such a universe, birth or creation is in itself a waste, for simply to come into existence is to be *de trop,* to be in the way, to overflow absurdly into a world already crowded with other existents. Sheer existence, in its lack of outline or boundary, in its meaningless viscosity, is an imperfection, an incompleteness. A circle, whose careful order and definition mark its difference from the absurd, massive conglomeration of the chestnut root, defies existence and is an example of what existents may *become*. But Roquentin's world has many roots—and no circles.

The Pacômes, Parrottins, and Impétrazes evoke Roquentin's scorn not because they had warded off Nausea, but because they had done so at the expense of truth. They had, with what degree of consciousness and deliberation it is impossible to tell, shielded themselves from the, to Roquentin, frightening evidence that existence, their own as well as that of a chestnut root, is simply a contingency, an accidental addition to a world already too full, an occurrence which might just as well not have happened. They had been the victims of of what Sartre elsewhere calls bad faith—a self-deception at once recognized and not recognized by its perpetrator, an ambiguous relationship of a person to himself, not unlike what George Orwell defines as "doublethink" in *1984*. The Pacômes, unable to face the fact of their own incompletion or superfluity, had self-deceptively yielded to a pleasant untruth —that a certain sanctity and an a priori goodness inheres within the system of life that they nurture. And for having done their duty by the system, for having sustained and promoted the unquestioned traditions, they had been well rewarded. Pacôme had not seen himself as "in the way" or as a gelatinous addition to an already gelatinous mass. He had been, in his own eyes and in those of the mass of people believing in duties and rights, a well-defined man in a well-defined universe. But men like Pacôme deceive themselves, refusing to recognize the contingent, accidental quality of existence and, instead, attributing to it a necessity—a meaning and purpose. To know, as Roquentin affirms that he does, that existence *is* contingent "turns your heart upside down and everything begins to float . . . here is Nausea . . . is what those bastards . . . try to hide from themselves with their idea of their rights. But what a poor lie. . . ." Roquentin would ward off Nausea without accepting the lie.

IV

Roquentin's disdainful reflections on others extend to himself with the growing realization that he too has devices for buoying his spirits, for trying to protect himself, perhaps through self-deception, from Nausea. After several years of busy research, he recognizes that his work on Rollebon is his only justification for existence, or—more to the point—that his research has served the useful, but desensitizing, function of preventing his feeling existence. To keep busy, or to kill time, is to put off the reflection that invites Nausea. No longer deceived about the role of his research, Roquentin puts all his therapeutic hopes in a reunion with Anny, his former sweetheart, whom he now meets in Paris after an absence of six years. But she proves perhaps even more difficult, acidulous, and elusive than she had formerly been. Now, with neither Rollebon nor Anny serving to shield him from the brutal fact of existence, Roquentin must look elsewhere to escape the dreaded disease. He must look directly at existence itself. If he cannot escape it, he must, through frontal attack, transform it.

He had been moving gradually toward this persuasion, perhaps without full awareness, well before his ill-founded hopes in Rollebon or Anny dissolved. Fairly early in his odyssey, on February 11, he refers to "something which needs . . . [him] in order to come to life." This "something" is unformed existence. The entire universe of matter, events, and persons remains formless and lifeless until experienced in a very particular way. A human being, Roquentin becomes convinced, must lay hold upon the sheer events of existence, experience them in some kind of focus and order, and then bequeath upon them a continuing and well-defined life by revealing the experience through words. Until that moment, neither the perceivable nor the perceiver is freed from the nothingness of an amorphous, undifferentiated existence. Most men remain fairly much as they were born; they are existents simply existing among and in the way of other existents; they rest passively and relatively unchanged in a sea of existence. On rare occasions, however, a man moves from such complacent endurance of the events of life to the active experiencing of and creating of what Roquentin calls "adventures." Between "event" and "adventure" is *all* the difference.

The meanings of "event" and "adventure" seem to change during the course of the novel. But finally, for Roquentin, the experiencing of an adventure is to recognize that a metamorphosis has occurred, that the events of existence have in some way assumed or, more accurately, been given shape and order. It is like a creation out of chaos, a waving of some magic wand which transforms the gelatinous mass into sharp focus. To experience an adventure is also to acknowledge the presence of a dynamic, transcending force. It is not simply that the sticky mass is modified into a series of static shapes. There is also movement, a beginning advancing surely toward an end. The unfolding progression is a testimony of purpose, for in an adventure necessity has replaced the contingency of mere events. Roquentin describes the inception of an adventure: "Something is beginning in order to end: adventure does not let itself be drawn out; it only makes sense when dead. . . . Each instant appears only as part of a sequence." It is like the grain of wheat which, fallen onto the ground, must die before it can bear fruit. It is as if each individual event were a still, fuzzy picture, insignificant in itself, and assuming definition and meaning only when experienced in its disparate and temporal relationship to other events. An adventure reveals itself in the form of a motion picture, showing the relationship of one event to another *in time,* which is the annihilation of one moment that another may be born:

This feeling of adventure definitely does not come from events: I have proved it. It's rather the way in which the moments are linked together. I think this is what happens: you suddenly feel that time is passing, that each instant leads to another, this one to another one, and so on; that each instant is annihilated, and that it isn't worth while to hold it back, etc., etc. And then you attribute this property to events which appear to you *in* the instants; what belongs to the form you carry over to the content. You talk a lot about this amazing flow of time but you hardly see it. You see a woman, you think that one day she'll be old, only you don't see her grow old. But there are moments when you think you *see* her grow old and feel yourself growing old with her: this is the feeling of adventure.

With this ability to distinguish between event and adventure, Roquentin is on his way toward becoming the existentialist defined in Sartre's essay "Existentialism Is a Humanism," published eight years after *Nausea*. The term *existentialist* is in its Sartrean meaning confusing, for it refers to a person who is able to escape or transform existence and to construct what Sartre calls an "essence." An event is a property of existence, is a static imperfection which cannot transcend itself. An adventure is a prerequisite to essence, is a purposeful, perpetually transcending movement through time. In learning to distinguish between event and adventure, Roquentin is also groping toward the crucial distinction between existence and essence and toward the conviction that man alone in the entire created order is capable of, and condemned to, the painful, glorious freedom of making those choices which will transform his existence into his essence. To ignore the opportunity of such freedom is to settle for the life—or lifelessness —of an object.

An object—in "Existentialism Is a Humanism" Sartre cites a paper cutter as an example—*is*, but cannot *become;* it is at its creation everything that it can ever be; it has neither the freedom nor the will to change. A paper cutter could not come into existence without a previous concept in the mind of its maker of what a paper cutter *is* and must *remain*. Such a concept is also the object's permanent essence, since it is incapable of change. Thus it can be said that an object's concept or essence precedes its existence and that, with its creation, its existence and essence are congruent. A man, on the other hand, should always be in the process of *becoming*, never satisfied with what he *is*. This condition through which man should continue to move himself, adventure by adventure, is defined as his essence. Not until death, when he will be the sum of all his choices, will he be frozen—for good or bad—in his essence, as the three main characters of Sartre's *No Exit* so well exemplify.

Roquentin is moving toward comprehension of the Sartrean "truth" that man's distinctiveness in the created order lies in the fact that his existence precedes his essence. Unlike an object, no human being comes into existence with his function or purpose already determined. In Sartre's and, we may assume, Roquentin's atheism, there is no God to superimpose a goal or calling on man. It is the very contingency of human existence that makes for its flexibility, its openness to man's choice; this contingency is "the perfect free gift." Man is consequently born absolutely free, whether or not he chooses to take advantage of this accessible freedom. The contingency —or "nothingness," as Sartre sometimes calls it—of man's existence is thus devoid of any predetermined end toward which he should strive. Man's choices, incarnate in his self-determined actions, are the powers which transform the nothingness of his existence into the something of his essence.

Roquentin's diary notations trace his growing apperception of man's basic difference from the world of objects. One striking example of such discernment occurs as Roquentin, riding on a streetcar after his dramatic luncheon engagement with the Self-Taught Man, notes that the seat upon which he rests his hand would not *be* had there been no prior *idea* of the essence of a seat: "They made it purposely for people to sit on, they took leather, springs and cloth, they went to work with the idea of making a seat and when they finished, *that* was what they had made." But if a seat lacks the capacity to become something which it is not, lacks the freedom to transcend itself, man does not. The Pacômes of the world offend Roquentin because of their contentment with themselves and with their way of life. Accepting without question the rightness of the way things are, they are willing to rest in their bourgeois community's "progressive" ways, seeing them as absolute values and thus perceiving in them no incompleteness. Such men, willing to settle for what is, abrogate their possibility of human freedom and, in their staticity, approach closely the status of inanimate objects. They cannot experience adventure, since they lack the insight or courage to accept the death of one moment that another may be born.

V

Roquentin's Nausea comes from his experiencing existence as "all soft, sticky, soiling everything, all thick, a jelly," and from his belief that most men rest content with existence, not choosing to exercise their human freedom. The more he becomes aware of the causes of his Nausea, and of the vanity or cowardice of trying to stem it through his research on Rollebon or his reunion with Anny, the more he becomes its victim. Once he puts his research aside, he is flooded with the Nausea engendered by the oppressiveness of existence: "The thing which was waiting was on the alert, it has pounced on me, it flows through me, I am filled with it." And when the next attempted anodyne, the meeting with Anny, fails him too, he seems stripped of all defenses and plunged into the deepest abyss of his thirty years. Returning from his visit with Anny, he writes that, all hope of adventure seemingly past, he will surrender himself to the boredom which has recently threatened him, will confine himself to eating and sleeping, and will exist "slowly, softly, like . . . trees, like a puddle of water, like the red bench in the streetcar." His deepening despair is, moreover, accompanied by an increasingly acute awareness of the great gulf that separates him from other men. The world which is to him an amorphous mass is to them reassuring in what they feel to be its rigid dependability. They can count on what will follow from the twist of a water tap, the flick of a light switch. They know the closing hour of the public park and the local streetcar schedule. They inhabit a world of petty assurances, going about their daily business with an easy sense of achievement and satisfaction. Only Roquentin knows that,

all this time, great, vague nature has slipped into their city, it has infiltrated everywhere, in their house, in their office, in themselves. It doesn't move, it stays quietly and they are full of it inside, they breathe it, and they don't see it, they imagine it to be outside, twenty miles from the city. I *see* it, I *see* this nature . . . I know that its obedience is idleness, I know it has no laws: what they take for constancy is only habit and it can change tomorrow.

In a ghastly, apocalyptic passage Roquentin envisages certain changes whose utter unpredictability, massive evasion of every known law of cause and effect, and appalling consequences would evoke unimaginable horror. His recital of them, moreover, brings the novel's readers to their own experience of Nausea. We are told of a man who is walking along the pavement, sees across the street what appears to be a red rag being blown toward him, but discovers, at its closer approach, that it is "a piece of writhing flesh rolling in the gutter, spasmodically shooting out spurts of blood"; of another man who feels a strange sensation in his mouth, goes before a mirror, and finds that his tongue is an enormous centipede; and of others who, suddenly detecting within themselves a brooding, frightful sixth sense, commit suicide by the hundreds. Such untoward events, to all those persons habitually confident of a rational order, would be devastating. Roquentin, on the other hand, would only burst into laughter, asking the frantic citizens what had become of their science and their dignity. Nor, should such events take place, would Roquentin's misery increase, for nothing could be more frightening or painful to him than the existence which he already feels in full. Indeed, the outer events which he imagines are but the correlatives of his inner feelings.

His research plans scrapped, his relationship with Anny at an end, Roquentin seems, on February 28, his last day in Bouville, on the point of complete surrender to his disease. Little by little, those activities and hopes that previously had to a degree diverted him from Nausea have worn thin. But as he despairingly awaits his time of departure, he experiences an adventure that proves the key to and pattern of his own transcendence and essence.

This experience of adventure comes through the hearing of a song, "Some of These Days," one to which he had listened on the Café Mably phonograph at various times before this day of his departure. To a remarkable degree, Roquentin's philosophical position grows out of his attentiveness to this popular composition. As early as February 2, suffering keenly from Nausea, he had asked that the record be played, and had perceived in the order of the musical notes a quality that would later enable him to recognize the presence of an adventure. Of the notes he had written:

They know no rest, an inflexible order gives birth to them and destroys them without even giving them time to recuperate and exist for themselves. They race, they press forward, they strike me a sharp blow in passing and are obliterated. I would like to hold them back, but I know if I succeeded in stopping one it would remain between my fingers only as a raffish languishing sound. I must accept their death; I must even *will* it. I know few impressions stronger or more harsh.

We find here the basis for Roquentin's later definition of adventure. The song, comprising a number of individual moments or notes, gains its gratifying beauty through the relationship among them, each one dying that the next may be born. Thus the song is always becoming, always transcending itself. A single note, cut off from the rest, would be imperfect, deprived of a completion or perfection to be attained only through its taking its place *among* the other notes. To arrest the song, as one might be tempted to do at the sounding of one beautiful note, would be to produce a living death, a paralysis into existence, and not the kind of death which, painful as it may be, makes way for a new life.

On at least three occasions during Roquentin's agonizing month, the song came to him when he needed it most. On February 2 the music assuaged the worst attack of Nausea he had yet endured. Again, on February 19, at another time of crisis—Roquentin on that day decided to forgo his research —the song drew him back from the edge of despair. Finally on this last day in Bouville—after the unhappy reunion with Anny and the harrowing library scene involving the Self-Taught Man—Roquentin sits in the Café Mably and asks that the record be played for him one more time.

With this playing Roquentin goes beyond a recognition that the song has those qualities which define an adventure, and that the arrangement of the notes and the singing of the words bring to him the joy of an adventure. He also recognizes that, prior to *his* adventure in hearing the song and prior to *the* adventure which the song is, there were the creators of the adventure, the song's Jewish composer and Negro singer. The sequence has been from the creators to the creation to the effect of the creation; from the adventure-makers, to the audible, substantial adventure which is the song, to the song's instilling in Roquentin his own, vicariously derived sense of adventure. And Roquentin realizes not only that the song is a gift to him, but that its very creating and performance had served to redeem its composer and singer from existence:

She sings. So two of them are saved: the Jew and the Negress. Saved. Maybe they thought they were lost irrevocably, drowned in existence. Yet no one could think of me as I think of them, with such gentleness. No one, not even Anny. They are a little like dead people for me, a little like the heroes of a novel; they have washed themselves of the sin of existing. Not completely, of course, but as much as any man can. This idea suddenly knocks me over, because I was not even hoping for that any more. I feel something brush against me lightly and I dare not move because I am afraid it will go away. Something I didn't know any more: a sort of joy.

The final hearing of "Some of These Days" is Roquentin's epiphany much as the seeing of the lovely girl wading in the stream was Stephen Dedalus's. Stephen knew, from his aesthetic response to the vision of the girl, that he was growing into an artist. Roquentin not only perceives in the movement of the song a paradigm of life itself, a constant transcending toward the achievement of an essence; he also comes to realize that he must go beyond the stage of vicarious participation in the adventure of another and turn to the creation of his own adventure. If the composer and singer had "washed themselves of the sin of existing" and served as a source of revealing truth for Roquentin, he in turn will seek to accomplish the same end for himself and others.

Roquentin had earlier affirmed that a man must choose between living his life and telling about it. The distinction seems a strange one until it is realized that he is equating "living" with being plunged into existence, impotently caught up in the daily round of events. "Nothing happens while you live," he had written. "The scenery changes, people come in and go out, that's all. There are no beginnings. Days are tacked on to days without rhyme or reason, an interminable, monotonous addition. . . . That's living. But everything changes when you tell about life. . . ." "Telling" follows upon a stepping back from the blur of events and ordering them in much the same way the musical composer ordered his notes. Composing, telling, ordering—each comes to the same thing, each is a counter to Nausea, and each points the way toward fulfillment of the novel's central imperative: man, to realize his human freedom, must transform the nothingness or formlessness of existence. Roquentin can most clearly and persistently give meaning to the world by telling about it; he will do so not in the sense of *discovering* an a priori meaning (there is none), but in *creating* a meaning through the ordering of events and experiences. He can best do this, not by writing a biography of one long dead, but by writing a novel. Such a novel, he hopes, may do for others what "Some of These Days" had done for him—make them "ashamed of their existence," arouse the Pacômes from their thoughtless satisfaction with their deathlike lives. Perhaps the day may even come when persons reading Roquentin's novel will think of him with the same affection that he feels for the composer and singer.

That day *has* come, for the novel which Roquentin sets out to write on February 28 is in fact completed. The diary *is* the novel and is its own account of how it came to be written. More than this, *Nausea* does succeed in persuading the reader, perhaps with some shame, to take another look at his life.

V I

Nausea does not talk *about* existentialism, any more than the plays of Samuel Beckett and Eugène Ionesco talk about absurdity. The art of Sartre's novel lies in its absorption of the reader into the fabric of existential man's response to life. The reader learns not only the philosophical nature of existentialism, but the actual feeling of living within its experience. Sartre's literary method in *Nausea* is largely surrealistic, with Roquentin conveying his inner feelings most intensively through a series of nightmarish visions. One of the earliest and most striking, chronicled on February 2, involves his looking into a mirror and seeing himself as a jellyfish, his "insipid flesh blossoming and palpitating with abandon." The image is extended: all human facial characteristics disappear—the pulp twists, swells, uncovers, opens, "on pink, bleeding flesh." And there are other such passages, including the already mentioned climactic phantasms of blood-spurting flesh, tongue turned centipede, and mass suicides. They provide, impressively and nauseatingly, the visible, tangible correlatives of the inner motions of Roquentin's psyche. They also enable the reader to feel both what and as Roquentin feels. Thus is Nausea defined *and* felt.

Yet for Sartre, art is always handmaiden to a philosophically based exhortation to action, never primarily an aesthetically oriented end in itself. Sartre proclaims no Joycean indifference. An earnest and sometimes humorous evangelist, he uses his artistry to awaken his reader to both the terrible anxieties and the gratifying triumphs attendant upon taking freedom seriously. The Pacômes are invulnerable to both the agony and the exaltation. They will not make the descent into Nausea, preferring (in Sartre's view) the empty contentment of self-deception to the lonely suffering of a more knowledgeable Roquentin. But out of the agonizing descent and the horrific vision of nothingness arises the one human imperative: make those choices, carry through those actions, that will transform the world of matter and of human beings into an order whose beholding is a joy. Each man is free to usurp the function traditionally ascribed to the gods: the task of creating order out of chaos. Roquentin chooses a most explicitly creative mode: the diary-novel which traces the growth of an existential man who learns to use his freedom well.

A Portrait of the Negro
as a Young Man

*I myself, after existing some twenty years, did not become alive until I discovered my invisibility.**

"Freedom," I said. "Maybe freedom lies in hating."
"Naw, son, it's in loving."

Life is to be lived, not controlled; and humanity is won by continuing to play in face of certain defeat.

There's a possibility that even an invisible man has a socially responsible role to play.

I

The unnamed protagonist of Ralph Ellison's *Invisible Man*, as he speaks to us from his well-illuminated underground suite after the novel's main action, is modest in ambition. He asks only the freedom to "exist in the real world," by which he means the privilege of respectful recognition, the loss of invisibility. Compared to Stephen Dedalus's resolve to forge the uncreated conscience of his race, or Antoine Roquentin's to bring his future readers to shame of their existence, the hope for visibility seems an exercise in humility. And so it is, in a way. Yet if the hope itself is a modest one, the use to which the visibility would be put—the attempt to lead men from hating to loving—is hardly unambitious.

Like James Joyce's *A Portrait of the Artist as a Young Man* and Jean-Paul Sartre's *Nausea*, Ellison's narrative is of a young man in search of himself and his place in the world. The protagonist is a Negro who, toward the end of his junior year in a southern state college for Negroes, goes, not totally voluntarily, to New York City, where most of the novel's action takes place. As Joyce shows through Stephen the maturing of an artist, and Sartre through Roquentin the maturing of an existentialist, Ellison shows through his invisible man the maturing of a Negro in the mid-twentieth-century United States. Maturation inevitably involves the gaining of freedom both from something and for something. Stephen has to escape the restraining nets of family, Church, and nation, then fly toward an artistry serving to free others; Roquentin to escape the nothingness of existence and find his freedom as an existentialist novelist. The invisible man's net or nothingness is his invisibility, the torturous discovery of which leads to his possibility of freedom, once he feels ready to leave his underground retreat.

Aside from the Prologue and Epilogue, there are three major sections in *Invisible Man*, which Ellison designates, after Kenneth Burke, as a movement from "purpose to passion to perception" *: (1) the college years, initiated by a scholarship certificate and terminating, at the end of chapter 6, with seven letters of "recommendation"; (2) the early New York period, beginning with the letters and ending, at chapter 14, with a slip of paper bearing the protagonist's new name as a member of the Brotherhood; (3) the later New York period of activity in the Brotherhood, from the new naming to the descent into a coal cellar and the burning of various accumulated papers. This odyssey, like those of Stephen and Roquentin, is sparked by epiphanies, by the protagonist's gaining of insights along the way, largely through his seeing those per-

* *Shadow and Act* (New York: Random House, 1964), pp. 176–7.

sons and organizations which he had trusted betray him at every critical juncture of his life.

Throughout virtually the whole of *Invisible Man*, the protagonist, unlike Stephen in large degree and Roquentin in smaller measure, makes few independent choices. For the most part he does what he is told to do—or at least tries to do what he is told to do—by Mr. Norton, Dr. Bledsoe, Brother Jack, among others; and his actions, most of them, serve to deepen his wretchedness. The imagery of the novels, not surprisingly, supports their respective rhythms. Stephen, like his Daedalean namesake, is engaged in an upward spiral, an arrow-like flight into freedom; Roquentin seems contained by a circular motion (an image implied, not expressed) from which he breaks free only at the last. The invisible man is caught in a downward pressure, a plummeting from the highest of hopes with which he entered college into the disillusioning abyss of the underground cellar, though there is, finally, promise of reversal of direction. To him the world moves not like an arrow in rising spiral, but like a boomerang. Himself victim of a series of betrayals—the major ones by Dr. Bledsoe and the college, by Brother Jack and the Brotherhood—his possibilities in life constantly narrowing as one hope after another vaporizes, he seems appropriately to have fixed on the frustrating boomerang motion. By the novel's end, his every tie cut, he has at the moment no place to go. He cannot go back to anything he has known, for all that has failed him, depriving him in his reduction to invisibility of a place in the world. And if he cannot go back, he is not yet ready to go forward either, since he at this time knows only what the world does, not offer him, not what it may offer him. Thus he hibernates and reflects, gradually coming to the conviction that, given himself in the context of mid-century America, there was an inevitability about the events which befell him: as the last sentence of the novel proper (not counting the Epilogue) puts it, "The end was in the beginning." But the Epilogue also intimates that there is another and obverse apothegm: the beginning is in the end. As in Greek and Roman mythology, there is the inference that, prior to reaching a cherished goal, a descent must be made (into Hades or a coal cellar), in the process and duration of which the hero is revitalized and reeducated, thereby apprised of the new direction he must take to gain Ithaca or Rome or a sane and united United States. "All sickness," we are told, "is not unto death, neither is invisibility."

II

A Portrait's predominant interest is aesthetic as Joyce traces his own coming to age as an artist. The artist, moreover, is portrayed in Olympian splendor, aloof from the diurnal events of common humanity. Stephen makes the most of this role, once eliciting from his friend MacCann the exasperated comment: "Minor poets, I suppose, are above such trivial questions as the question of universal peace." And Stephen himself compares the artist to the God of creation, who "remains within or behind or beyond or above his handiwork, invisible, refined out of existence, indifferent, paring his fingernails." Though Stephen sees his work also as an impetus toward a new Irish conscience, he for the most part assumes an artistic purity. Sartre, fervent evangelist of existentialism, views literature above all as a means toward a philosophic goal: through Roquentin's example, Sartre's readers may learn to become men of good faith, transcending themselves with each new decision and moving toward their proper essence.

Ralph Ellison has neither the developed aesthetic of Joyce nor the dazzling philosophy of Sartre. He does have his own clear conception about the relationship between literature and life, clearly expressed in his collection of essays and interviews entitled *Shadow and Act*. When he speaks of *Invisible Man*'s "attempt to return to the mood of personal moral responsibility for democracy which typified the best of our

nineteenth-century fiction," he is enunciating his own first principle of literary composition. He is not equating novelist with pamphleteer or social philosopher, believing as he does in the possibility of "a fiction which, leaving sociology to the scientists, can arrive at a truth about the human condition, here and now, with all the bright magic of a fairy tale." The novelist of most appeal to Ellison is the artist whose conscience is awakened to problems of deepest human dimension and whose inclination is to protest conditions offensive to the human spirit. Thus he approvingly asserts that André Malraux, in writing *Man's Fate,* "was the artist-revolutionary rather than a politician . . . and [that] the book lives not because of a political position embraced at the time, but because of its larger concern with the tragic struggle of humanity." And he goes on: "Most of the social realists of the period were concerned less with tragedy than with injustice. I wasn't, and am not, primarily concerned with injustice, but with art. . . . I recognize no dichotomy between art and protest."

Invisible Man is both protest and art. It protests the abuse of human power to manipulate human beings, showing vividly that power's abuse may lead to every conceivable indignity, as well as to the crushing of the human spirit unless it is of remarkable resiliency. It is also art, its large body of material beautifully organized, with each succeeding episode illuminating the protagonist's present condition, at the same time erasing one more of his hopes and leading him with fine inevitability closer to recognition of his invisibility. There is also a rich variety of style, from the lyrical, pastoral descriptions of campus scenes (though, retrospectively, the narrator recalls "only the yellow contents of the cistern spread over the lawn's dead grass") to the brutality of the Harlem riot; from the realism of events in the Liberty Paints factory to the nightmarish surrealism of the hospital episode immediately following. There are, moreover, scenes of intense dramatic power: the opening battle royal, Jim Trueblood's well-practiced narrative of his incestuous excursion, Mr. Norton's visit to the Golden Day, Ras the Exhorter's brave-spirited championings of his people. The novel's artistry is sustained over the long run and punctuated with brilliantly drawn individual episodes. And of great importance in any serious work of protest is the presence of humor: the protagonist's fortunes with two ardent female admirers, whose interest in the "Woman Question" was less theoretical than his own, are among those lighter touches which help make for the book's balanced perspective.

The novel is first-person narrative, the invisible protagonist appropriately nameless. We know neither the name with which he began his life and lived for twenty years, nor the name given him by Brother Jack at baptism into the Brotherhood. The nymph Sybil, with measured syllabic economy, calls him Boo'ful. In Harlem he is mistaken for a versatile man of all trades, professions, and accomplishments—largely illegal or spurious—and is miscalled by his name, Rinehart, which, Ellison once remarked, is "my name for the personification of chaos." The first-person novel is not, as we learn from its author in *Shadow and Act*, autobiographical, at least not in the sense that events in the narrator's life bear a one-to-one relationship to those in the writer's. Yet in a larger and psychological sense there is certainly close affinity between author and narrator. Ellison, once noting how difficult it is for a Negro to express what he feels rather than what he is supposed or encouraged to feel, asserts his own eagerness to convey as precisely as possible the Negro's life in its total American setting. It was out of this concern, he writes, that

fiction became the agency of my efforts to answer the questions: Who am I, and how did I come to be? What shall I make of the life around me, what celebrate, what reject, how confront the snarl of good and evil which is inevitable? What does American society *mean* when regarded out of my *own* eyes, when informed by my *own* sense of the past and viewed by my *own* complex sense of the present?*

* *Shadow and Act*, p. xxii.

Both author and narrator of *Invisible Man* ask the same questions about identity and vocation and try to reflect the American situation as it is (or was), not as a man is supposed or encouraged to feel that it is. And I doubt that any work—literary, scholarly, sociological—surpasses *Invisible Man* in its ability to convey, compellingly and comprehensively, in both emotional and conceptual dimensions, what it was like for an intelligent, sensitive Negro to grow into manhood in mid-century America. Though conditions have changed in the two decades since the novel's publication, *Invisible Man* remains far more than either a monument to its own brief period of action or a work of historical import in the chronicle of race relations in the United States. It is, most significantly and gratifyingly, a work of art incarnating the dignities and indignities celebrated and endured by the human spirit at all times.

Before turning in more detail to the novel's unfolding, one vexing problem: what to call a nameless one when he must be referred to again and again? how to avoid the graceless monotony induced by a repetitious "the protagonist," "the central character," "the invisible man"? Memory recalls that I was asked, long ago, "What is your name?" And I replied, with literal fidelity to catechismal text, "N. or M." The hero I christen, in the cause of simplicity, "M."

I I I

At the time of his high school graduation and of our first meeting with him, M. possesses a gift—the art of speaking well; a hope—that of becoming a second Booker T. Washington; and a memory—his grandfather's deathbed words. His eloquence wins for him a college scholarship and assumes a large role in his later New York days. His hope dissipates with the recognition of his invisibility. His memory, forever

haunting him, is of his grandfather's dying mandate to his son, M.'s father:

Son, after I'm gone I want you to keep up the good fight. I never told you, but our life is a war and I have been a traitor all my born days, a spy in the enemy's country ever since I give up my gun back in the Reconstruction. Live with your head in the lion's mouth. I want you to overcome 'em with yeses, undermine 'em with grins, agree 'em to death and destruction, let 'em swoller you till they vomit or bust wide open.

The grandfather, meek throughout his life, was thought simply mad, and M.'s parents, far from seeking to commemorate the dying man's last words—"Learn it to the younguns"— warned the children to forget. M. never did.

It is the gift of eloquence which initiates his slow journey toward self-discovery. Invited to repeat his impressive graduation speech to a gathering of the community's leading white citizenry, he witnesses a striking, nauseating example of power's cruel abuse. The meeting, ostensibly to pay tribute to a good young speaker, is orgiastic—with a nude, belly-grinding blonde; brutal—with a command performance of a savage, blindfolded battle royal performed by M. and nine other Negroes; sadistic—with a wild scramble for coins wired for violent electrical charges. M.'s oration finally given, he is rewarded with a handsome calfskin briefcase, to which he clings throughout the novel's action, and a college scholarship, to be supplanted three years later by seven letters of reference. That M. learns so little from this early episode, overlooking the obscene depravity of his benefactors and continuing to aspire to their kind of world, underlines one of the novel's major ironies: the reader gains much more quickly than the protagonist an awareness of the way things are. M., as is later said of him, "registers with his senses but short-circuits his brain . . . takes it in but . . . doesn't digest it." In this early sequence M.'s thoughts seem embraced, to the exclusion of all else, by the scholarship and all that it promises. That night he has a dream, the first of many in which his grandfather plays a major role. The old man orders him to read the scholarship paper. The document spells out not the gift of college tuition but, instead, the true intent of its donors: "To Whom It May Concern . . . Keep This Nigger-Boy Running." The dream is prophetic, and of more than M.'s college years.

The novel's first major section (through chapter 6) culminates in a frantic day of activity toward the end of M.'s junior year in college. At the day's beginning M. is the administration's darling, entrusted with the care of the institution's most distinguished trustee and benefactor, Mr. Norton; on the next morning M. is on his way to New York, expelled by the president, Dr. Bledsoe. In this brief period the reader learns three important ground rules of the world of *Invisible Man:* (1) the white man delights in and gives encourage ment to any evidence of Negro weakness or failure; (2) the white man will not knowingly tolerate Negro success; (3) the dying counsel of M.'s grandfather, if carried out by a diabolically clever man under propitious circumstances, can be frighteningly successful and lead to a terrible power.

The events of this short span can be simply expressed. M., given temporary charge of Mr. Norton during one of his campus visits, is chauffeuring him over a back road near the college. Intrigued by the sight of a log cabin and learning that it belongs to the Negro Jim Trueblood, whose daughter is pregnant by him, the trustee, in morbid fascination, orders the car stopped and insists upon talking with the black man. Shocked by Trueblood's meticulous narration of his incestuous encounter, Mr. Norton falls ill, requests a stimulant, and is driven by M. to its nearest source, the notorious Golden Day, filled at the time with the Negro inmates of the nearby veterans' mental institution on one of their periodic frolics. In the ensuing melee, Mr. Norton gets roughed up, loses consciousness, and is tended by a former doctor, a Negro now confined at the institution. M. eventually delivers Mr. Norton back to the campus and is soon sent packing by an enraged Dr. Bledsoe.

Out of these frenetic events issue some facts of life whose implications are not at the time fully grasped by M. For example, Trueblood has discovered that, since his forbidden intimacies have become known to the white community, he has never had it so good. He has been invited by them to tell his story again and again, to both the openmouthed uneducated and the pencil-poised social science researchers "from the big school way cross the State." He has, to his perplexity, been showered with gifts and declared a celebrity. His value to the white folks is, of course, his confirming their favorite, obdurately held image of the Negro, that of a no-man who exhibits his uncivilized nature through failing to conform to conventional standards of human respectability. Mr. Norton, who affirmed that his fate lay in the lives of the graduates of Dr. Bledsoe's college, is moved to give Trueblood a $100 bill before departing for his stimulant.

The novel's second ground rule is complementary to the first. If the white man will reward the Negro who falls farthest short of white self-aspirations, he will root out the Negro who achieves them. Many of the inmates encountered by Mr. Norton were formerly doctors, lawyers, and teachers, and the man who expertly tended him had been a surgeon. But that the saving of human lives is a profession reserved for white men only, the doctor learned after his scalpel had saved a (white?) life: he was summarily whipped by ten masked men. When M. boards the bus for New York, the doctor, with an attendant, is also departing. He had, the day before, ministered to a white man, and without yessing and grinning him to death. The college had found no effort sufficient to wrest Jim Trueblood from local soil, but Dr. Bledsoe encountered no white opposition to the removal of a once skilled black surgeon who, in his meeting with M. and Mr. Norton, told more of white and Negro attitudes and motivations than whites and Negroes were willing to hear. The doctor was one "Nigger-Boy" they really kept running.

To the fortunes of Trueblood and the doctor, M. reacts with little fervor. But Dr. Bledsoe's uncompromisingly unjust response to the Norton–Trueblood–Golden Day incident shakes and confuses him immeasurably and through it he learns something of the novel's third ground rule: that the successful pursuit of his grandfather's counsel can nurture a treacherous power. For three years he had judged Dr. Bledsoe the humblest, wisest, most honest of men, working in harmonious concert with his institution's white benefactors to the end that young Negroes might take their modest place in a white man's world. He now learns that his president is the shrewdest of manipulators.

Dr. Bledsoe is incensed that M. has taken Mr. Norton to see what he wanted to see rather than what he should have seen, and that M. had not, if necessary to divert his guest's attention from the log cabin country and Trueblood, lied to him. He owes his own success, he tells M., to accommodating his words and actions to any mode which increases his control, and he would be willing to have every Negro in the county hanging from a tree if such were required for the maintenance of his power. M. cannot reconcile this ruthless image with that of the man who had always bowed obsequiously to his white guests, deferentially declined to eat with them, and stood hat in hand to await their bidding. In his fusion of the figure he had for nearly three years deemed the epitome of humility with the enraged man now counseling lying, deceit, and destruction, M. "felt suddenly that . . . [his] grandfather was hovering over . . . [him], grinning triumphantly out of the dark." For Dr. Bledsoe is a traitor, a spy in enemy country, living with his head in the lion's mouth and yessing and grinning others to death. Yet Dr. Bledsoe does seem to be going M.'s grandfather at least one better: he is a traitor to white and black man alike, though this distinction is not at this time drawn by M.

M. had come to college with a scholarship document. He leaves with seven letters of reference from Dr. Bledsoe to trustees of his college living in New York, letters presumably recommending their holder for a summer job, but actually apprising the addressees of M.'s expulsion and urging them to keep him on the run. With this "exchange" of one paper document for others we enter the second major section of the novel, extending to the time M. receives still another paper, that one containing the new name bestowed upon him at his induction into the Brotherhood.

I V

M. enters this second phase with, as he puts it, his "old confidence and optimism," qualities soon to show marks of erosion. For with his learning of Dr. Bledsoe's ultimate treachery in the matter of the letters, he is launched on the journey toward knowledge of his invisibility, of his being little more than an object manipulated to the advantage of other men. The launching is a shock, an early one among many, yet, like those to follow, necessary to his successful quest for identity.

Another soon comes, in the early afternoon of a painfully long day at the Liberty Paints factory, to which a well-meaning young man had directed M. to a short-lived employment. It takes M. but a few hours to learn how congenial to some people are the emotions of fear, distrust, and hate. The boiler explosion which climaxes the day—a blast taking place in "a deep basement," presage of M.'s later underground station—does violence to both his body and mind and leads him to a reassessment of his condition and expectations. The ensuing hospital scene is fittingly composed around the imagery of seeing. The first object of his attention as he gains semiconsciousness is that of a doctor looking at him "out of a bright third eye that glowed from the center of his forehead," a Cyclopean image constituting one of the novel's many references to eyes, glasses, glass eyes, one-eyedness, bat-blindness.

But the doctor is as blind as the maimed Polyphemus. For as M. observes in the Prologue, his own invisibility is consequent not upon an inadequacy of the physical eyes of others, but upon "their *inner* eyes." And when, in the hospital scene, he complains of inner pain and is viewed through still another eye, an X-ray machine, even that is blind to his true desperation. The scene is a compound of fantasy and reality, making impossible a precise knowledge of the treatment rendered. The doctors talk, casually and banteringly, of lobotomy and castration, operations not in fact performed, but symbolic of mutilations white men daily visit upon black. It is only when one of the doctors asks M. what his name is and who he is that the real root of his malady is touched. It is appropriate that he can answer neither of these questions. Important, however, is the fact that he now begins to recognize their profound relevance.

Chance and eloquence combine to move M. yet another step toward self-knowledge. After his release from the hospital it is chance that brings him upon the scene of a Negro couple's eviction at its most critical moment, and eloquence that enables him to rally the sympathetic, enraged onlookers to protective action and a sense of solidarity. It is chance too that Brother Jack, white leader of a leftist Brotherhood and a critical force in M.'s future, should be at the same place at the same time. That phase of M.'s life which began with seven letters and a bus ride to New York ends with his joining the Brotherhood, an initiation marked by a slip of paper given him by Brother Jack and bearing his new name.

V

As a rule, to name is to identify; to name anew, to reidentify. With a new name, M. reflects, he "had best leave the old behind." And he can indeed go through the physical, outward motions of so doing. He can and does put aside old clothes and buy new ones, and move from the home of Mary Rambo, who had befriended him, to the impersonality of a furnished apartment. But the inner man is more resistant to change than the outer, and those material remnants of the old life which M. carries into the new symbolize such resistance. He clings to the calfskin briefcase with which he had begun his long journey; and he carries also from Mary Rambo's, as embarrassing circumstances decree, the dismembered cast-iron figure of the stereotyped slave boy—black-skinned, red-lipped, wide-mouthed and grinning, wide-eyed and staring—the disposal of which he finds vexingly difficult: it is difficult to shake the familiar Sambo image of everything that some persons would wish a black boy to be. And even with the prospect of an existing new world of achievement and freedom there remains the obsessive memory that seems never to lose its hold on M. "Perhaps the part of me," he reflects, "that observed listlessly but saw all, missing nothing, was still the malicious, arguing part; the dissenting voice, my grandfather part; the cynical, disbelieving part—the traitor self that always threatened internal discord. Whatever it was, I knew that I'd have to keep it pressed down." He thinks back also to Bledsoe and Norton, who, he now believes, have by their very kicking of him "into the dark" enabled him to see the possibility of achievements previously undreamed of. And not knowing that Jack and the Brotherhood are to cast him into an even deeper pitch, he sets out again with great hopes, only to see them turn to ashes.

M.'s experiences with the Brotherhood are disillusioningly educative. Off to an auspicious beginning, he soon finds himself, with bewildering rapidity of change, now in their favor, now out of it. As he is moved like a disk on a checkerboard from Harlem to the Woman Question and then back to Harlem and is rebuked upon every exercise of his own initiative, he learns that he is being used as surely by Brother Jack as he had been by Dr. Bledsoe. He finds it difficult to comprehend and absorb the Brotherhood's basic, frequently

expressed conviction, voiced by Brother Jack as early as their
first meeting, that the individual counts for nothing, and
"the necessity of the historical situation" for everything. This
principle's corollaries are various: historical necessity is whatever the Brotherhood determines it to be; to live outside the
organization's discipline is to live (and die, as in the case of
Brother Tod Clifton) outside history itself; the individual
must in every case be sacrificed to whatever the organization
considers the good of the whole, a whole which in turn seems
almost indistinguishable from the Brotherhood's small core
of leaders. Such a principle accounts for the Brotherhood's
unsentimental readiness to disavow the delinquent Clifton
and to reprimand M. for organizing his elaborate funeral
tribute. Brother Jack's insistence that his group's function is
not to *ask* but to *tell* characterizes the position held by all
the self-appointed dictators M. has encountered, whether in
college administrations, paint factories, or political organizations. And when Brother Hambro informs him that the Brotherhood, intent upon new and expedient political alliances, is
ready to play down its role in Harlem and sacrifice the community "for the good of the whole," M. doubtless remembers
the passionate utterances of Ras the Exhorter, the Harlem
black nationalist, calling for an exclusively black coalition and
warning that M.'s allegiance to the predominantly white
Brotherhood was a betrayal of his own people. M. comes,
finally, to a major revelation:

And now I looked around a corner of my mind and saw Jack and
Norton and Emerson merge into one single white figure. They were
very much the same, each attempting to force his picture of reality
upon me and neither giving a hoot in hell for how things looked to
me. I was simply a material, a natural resource to be used. I had
switched from the arrogant absurdity of Norton and Emerson to
that of Jack and the Brotherhood, and it all came out the same—
except I now recognized my invisibility.

With this recognition M. decides to lay his own plans in
Harlem, simultaneously and with grins and yeses persuading

the Brotherhood that he remains their man. But his deceit
is elemental compared to their master plan which leads to
the riot corroborating Ras's earlier insistence that white men
"don't have to be allies with no black people. They get what
they wahnt, they turn against you." As the riot gathers force,
M. bitterly realizes how he and the black men have been
duped, how the Brotherhood's deliberately relinquishing Harlem leadership to the militant Ras has in fact led to the
suicidal self-destruction of his own people, and how his apparent acquiescence to the Brotherhood has boomeranged with
frightful consequences.

Between that early orgiastic, brutal, sadistic smoker and
M.'s flight from the riot, he has come a long way—through the
shock of Dr. Bledsoe's hypocrisy to the white man and
treachery to the black, through the paint factory interlude,
and through the collapse of his idealistic faith in the Brotherhood. Out of the sequence of broken hopes has come the
self-knowledge sought so long: he has reached the point of
"knowing now who I was and where I was and knowing too
that I had no longer to run for or from the Jacks . . . and the
Bledsoes and Nortons, but only from their confusion, impatience, and refusal to recognize the beautiful absurdity of
their American identity and mine." In flight he finds temporary refuge in a coal shelter, defined in *Shadow and Act* as
"a source of light, power and, through association with the
character's motivation, self-perception." His downward plunge
"is a process of *rising* to an understanding of his human
condition." The next morning, hoping to chart his way out of
darkness, M. opens the omnipresent briefcase and removes
the accumulated papers that will serve as his only torch. He
kindles first his high school diploma; then a disquieting,
anonymous letter received long ago and now recognized as
the work of Brother Jack; and lastly the slip of paper bearing
his Brotherhood name. Each piece has served as a link in the
chain which has painfully brought him to where he now is,
and each is a reminder of a former identity relievedly no

longer his. That document of which he had dreamed, reading "To Whom It May Concern. . . . Keep This Nigger-Boy Running," is not there to ignite, but M. is now fully aware of its meaning and practice.

He will run no more. As his exhausted mind, now in its underground habitat, seeks to fix the present and sort the past from the future, it tells him in a state between waking and sleeping that he must choose his own course, not have it imposed upon him by a Norton, a Bledsoe, a Jack, a Ras, or anyone else. He dreams also of his castration at the hands of white men who would maintain their control over him, and he comes simultaneously to the knowledge that all destroyers are eventually victims of their own destructive acts. Free from the multitude of illusions which had titillatingly nourished him during the various stations of his journey, he feels empty and pained but, importantly, now free to reflect in peace and lay plans for a new life.

V I

The novel's main action, from battle royal to coal cellar, is framed by the Prologue and Epilogue and is a flashback from the former, through which we learn that an invisible man is hibernating in a light-flooded basement apartment, that he has become alive only with the discovery of his invisibility, and that "a hibernation is a covert preparation for a more overt action." His decision to remain temporarily underground is the first major self-determined action of his life. Previously in docile service to others, never more in their favor than when telling them what they wished to hear and doing what they wished done, he had been their construct, a specter given flesh, bones, words, and actions by them. Thus his underground life is appropriate to the kind of no-man he has in frustration, humiliation, and suffering found himself to be. Yet he is not content with "simply the freedom not to run." Scouting his next move he ponders again his dying grandfather's legacy. Could his grandfather, he asks, have meant that the Negro should try to overcome the oppressors of his race, yet remain true to the democratic principles so frequently, though hypocritically, professed by them? Could his grandfather actually have seen his own "traitorousness" as something which might ultimately enable all men to live by those principles? M. is not certain.

He has, however, come to certain truths of his own: that conformity to rigid, demeaning conventions and traditions is not the way to health and vitality; that insistence upon such conformity is the weapon of the death-bearing tyrant too power-crazed and fearful to let lives be lived rather than controlled; that "humanity is won by continuing to play in face of certain defeat"; that, despite all the nightmare past, he still loves, and that those who love cannot sustain a permanent underground station. The Prologue's reefer dream in which the slave woman defines freedom as loving, not hating, and its resurrection imagery, affirming that "a bear retires to his hole for the winter and lives until spring; then he comes strolling out like the Easter chick breaking from its shell"—both inform M. of his proper subsequent action. At the end, he is ready to shed his old skin and move aboveground, still uncertain of his precise future role but determined to assume an independence of compassionate action through which invisibility may be made visible.

Given the merciless facts of the novel, remembering its heartless flow of seemingly endless indignities and humiliations, a reader may well question the credibility of M.'s decision to live again and ask if his innocence will never end. The world endured by him has been almost exclusively a fierce struggle for personal reward, with evidences of love and understanding quite minimal. He does, however, enter upon his second major decision in choosing to make his underground condition a hibernation rather than a death. And he does so out of the persuasion that, whatever the odds may be against the fashioning of a sane world, a man *should* be a socially responsible being. He is now ready to exercise and direct this responsibility as he has never done before. His decision to live again is made credible, above all, by Ellison's genius, his disposition to celebrate life. No series of events seems capable of transforming into lasting bitterness his strong-spirited resilience. *Invisible Man* is marked by a thorough humanity which laughs tenderly at man's folly as well as condemns his vice and which maintains a balanced hope and sanity as a bulwark against despair. Ellison portrays a young Negro at mid-century, but *Invisible Man* is a book encompassing the whole of American society. And it is more— a novel about the human heart, leading each reader to answer affirmatively its narrator's closing question: "Who knows but that, on the lower frequencies, I speak for you?"

Introduction

From Sir James George Frazer's *Golden Bough* we learn of Siamese monks who would no more have broken the branch of a tree than the arm of a man; of Austrians who would beg a tree's pardon before felling it; of Indonesians who accorded identical courtesies to pregnant women and blossoming cloves, in whose presence they made no noise, displayed no light at night, and doffed their headgear to ward off abortion. To harm nature was to court punishment: in ancient Germany a bark-peeler's navel was cut off and nailed to the offended tree, around which he was driven until his entrails encircled the trunk in replacement for the bark. There was a time when men were tenderly compassionate of natural phenomena.

Ancient peoples also believed that the human order and the natural order enjoyed the closest of relationships, a conviction best exemplified in their fertility rites. Enduring a four-day sexual abstinence before the planting of crops, Central American tribesmen believed that their consequent, passionate enthusiasm on the eve of the sowing carried sympathetic vibrations to the earth. Javanese, leaving less to chance, practiced intercourse in the very fields. And the aforementioned courteous Indonesians, when the clove crop was scanty, fertilized the trees with their own sperm, shouting all the while, "More cloves!" There were, moreover, fertility gods as well as fertile men, gods who would symbolically die with the harvest, ritually to rise again with nature's conceiving season. Gods, men, trees, crops, streams, stars—the whole of creation—beat with one pulse.

71

The mainstream of our civilization, however, has been arrogantly anthropocentric. We have paid a measure of awed tribute to the heavenly host; we have been more or less concerned with our brothers; we long have been obsessed with our individual destinies; but we have throughout the centuries shown meager interest in the welfare of the natural world. To this neglectful disposition we have come understandably: the Greek and biblical thought comprising our major heritage affords little stimulus to our viewing the natural order as dignified and sanctified. In the Old Testament the nature gods, or baalim, worshiped by Canaanites and Phoenicians were but antagonists (and not very potent ones) of the one Father of Abraham, Isaac, and Jacob, and the nature gods of the Greek mystery religions bore little kinship to the triune God. Plato's interests were numerous—metaphysics, ethics, logic, politics—but hardly included the study and reverence of nature. Aristotle, for all his concern with science and physical phenomena, saw the natural world as an object to be studied, not as a subject to be revered.

It is true, of course, that Jahweh would have no other gods (including baalim) before him, and that for a monotheistic God there is accommodation for no other gods before or behind. It is also true that Jahweh was very much pleased with his creation of all that is, and that, from the biblical perspective, man's reverential gratitude *for* nature should be expressed *to* God. In the Bible there are gracious, if sporadic, references to the nonhuman order: the whale was highly serviceable; the natural imagery of the Psalms and the Song of Solomon is of rare loveliness; the fall of sparrows is divinely watched over; the lilies of the field are not forgotten. But in the biblical narrative the created world is hierarchically stratified: man shares his high stage with nothing else, nor is he asked to. He is instructed to subdue the earth and to dominate every other living thing that moves through or over sea, air, or earth.

There is the palatable argument that God conceived man

as a good steward, a kind of vice-regent born to care tenderly and unselfishly for the rest of the Creation, and that man, self-corrupted through sinfulness, has become a tyrant over nature rather than the steward God would have him be. Such a contention in no way lacks theological reasonableness. Yet if the Bible affords no iota of encouragement to man's subtle and unsubtle modes of desecrating sea, air, and earth and the animal, vegetable, and mineral orders thereof, it is also lacking in strong encouragement to view them with reverence. The Bible is man- (and God-) centered to the degree that little thought is given to the vast universe of nonpersons.

Neither the world of Frazer's *Golden Bough,* nor of the pagan tribes and nature gods of the Old Testament, nor of the Greek mystery religions is the normative world of a Western culture rooted in Greek philosophical and Judeo-Christian theological traditions. Man has, predominantly, seen himself as against rather than with nature. When Francis Bacon approvingly affirmed that knowledge is power, he spoke for virtually the whole of modern Western civilization. His *New Atlantis* indicates that "knowledge" is to be largely of the physical world, is the science of understanding nature to the point where it may be harnessed to man's desires. For most men nature is seen as something to be subdued: minerals exist solely for human wealth and comfort; the soil, even at the cost of its own chemical health and balance, is for the production of man's food; birds of the air, beasts of the field, and fish of the sea furnish man an opportunity for sport, fun, and games.

Not until the late eighteenth century do we find in our culture a serious, sustained viewing of nature as sacramental, as a subject to be loved rather than as an object to be extravagantly manipulated. With the English preromantic and romantic poets we come upon men stunned by nature's loveliness and convinced of her exemplary power to teach those who would observe her the meaning of a harmonious life. Through nature, Wordsworth writes in "Tintern Abbey," "We see into the life of things." He recognizes "In nature and the language of the sense, / The anchor of my purest thoughts, the nurse, / The guide, the guardian of my heart, and soul / Of all my moral being." No early Greek, Jew, or Christian went so far. And although the seventeenth-century poets Henry Vaughan and Thomas Traherne voiced sentiments similar to those of the later Wordsworth, the major writers of their time—Donne, Milton, Bunyan—hardly sustained so ecstatic and grateful a response to nature. But several decades after Wordsworth's main work, we find quite kindred spirits in the American transcendentalists Emerson and Thoreau.

In the Christian era no other century has accorded to nature such love, admiration, and respect as the nineteenth. Supremely grateful for God's gifts of streams and ponds, mountains, fields, and forests, birds and beasts, writers like Wordsworth, Emerson, and Thoreau saw in the world of nature a paradigm of how human life might best be lived. They revered the physical universe for its own intrinsic being, seeking not to harness or overpower it, but to live in its rhythms and learn from its grace. A cursory glance at more recent times, particularly the last decade with its conservationist fervor, might lead us to believe that we are carrying on the same tradition. But there is a difference. With the pollution of all that is, we have come to the sharp realization that to destroy nature is, finally, to destroy ourselves. Man must breathe air, drink water, and eat food to live. His present disposition to protect the physical world seems to spring more from a passion for self-survival than from a love for nature herself. Pestilent vapors billowed into the air, human and other waste poured into the waters, destructive chemicals loosed on the earth, and wholesale deforestation are not only outrageous affronts to nature; they invite and promise a universal plague that will annihilate man himself. Ecology has become the most urgently popular of sciences. But if it calls man to a stewardship of nature, it is a stewardship nurtured more by self-interest than by a sense of the sanctity of all that

God made. Whatever the informing source and compelling motivation of conservation's call, however, man is now probably giving more serious attention to the natural order than at any other time in his history.

The novels discussed in this section represent three quite diverse twentieth-century views of man's relationship to a natural or cosmic order. No one of the authors is a Wordsworthian romanticist, a transcendentalist, or an ecological activist. Joseph Conrad, in *Nostromo,* writes of man's violation of one of nature's kingdoms. The principal motivating force of the novel's dramatic action is man's passion for silver resting deep in the San Tomé mine. Some of the lesser characters greedily wish the silver for gratification of personal whims— comfort, splendor, power; other more major ones for more idealistic reasons—a community's welfare, another person's happiness. Nostromo himself finds the mining enterprise an opportunity to show off his many talents. The many characters, diverse as they are, share one attitude: the earth's rich mineral store exists *only* for man's benefit and has no bill of rights of its own. To what degree Conrad is proffering a philosophical or an ontological thesis is uncertain. Quite clearly, however, in *Nostromo* man's exploitation of the earth invites a counteraction which spares virtually none of the human ravagers from death or a wretched death-in-life.

Whereas Conrad sees man's rapacity as initiating the agon which brings him misery, Albert Camus in *The Plague* sees man as, for the most part, innocent victim of cosmic forces which assail him: nature is the predator, man the prey. *The Plague* is a dramatic fable, a symbolic narrative embracing Camus's related philosophies of absurdity and rebellion. The absurd is the disparity between man's hopes and the world's realities. Man treasures life in a universe which demands death. No matter what he does or how he does it, he will inevitably be struck down by nature's most pervasive element: the death-bearing germ or microbe or plague. The rebel whom Camus counsels every man to be will recognize *and* resist the absurd basis of all life, fighting a noble though losing battle against nature's destructive edict. Dr. Bernard Rieux, the novel's central protagonist and Camus's prototypical rebel, recognizes absurdity without understanding its cause and does all he can to alleviate the misery and delay the death which the plague harbors.

As Camus's protagonists fight to soften or stay the plague's fury, the protagonists of Thomas Mann's *Buddenbrooks*, particularly Thomas Buddenbrook, strive to slow a cosmic law decreeing that those individuals and collective groups—families, business firms, social classes—that rise to fortune's peak will inevitably fall from it. Mann's novel seems at first glance strange bedfellow to the other two. Its characters neither despoil the earth nor bear a deep philosophic grudge against some cosmic malignancy; its action is initiated by neither ravaging men nor deadly microbes. Like Hermann Broch's *The Sleepwalkers*, to be discussed later in this book, *Buddenbrooks* expresses a philosophy of history. Man's life is determined not primarily by his own will, selfish or unselfish, or by some specifically identifiable part of nature, whether mineral or germ. Life's course is ordained by what may best be called historical determinism, by recurring and predictable historical cycles, by an undulating rise and fall which is the prevailing law of cosmic motion. The Buddenbrooks are not presented as simply helpless pawns who supinely accept this law. Thomas especially, in recognizing and fighting the invisible forces bringing his family's and firm's majestic dynasty to an end, is a worthy antagonist. But the novel's thesis is that not even the most worthy can reverse the law of historical inevitability.

The three novels, with their quite different premises and perspectives, share the conviction that man's destiny is to struggle, suffer, and die in an uneven battle with forces, within or without, beyond human control.

Nostromo and the Orders of Creation: An Ontological Argument

*He groaned over the injustice, the persecution, the outrage of that mine.**

"There is something in a treasure that fastens upon a man's mind."

She saw the San Tomé mountain hanging over the Campo, over the whole land, feared, hated, wealthy, more soulless than any tyrant, more pitiless and auto-cratic than the worst government, ready to crush in-numerable lives in the expansion of its greatness.

I

Most pervasive of the various epic struggles informing Joseph Conrad's *Nostromo* is that between man and nature. The novel's conflicts are acted out on many levels. We follow, for example, the inner turmoil of such introspective characters as Martin Decoud and Dr. Monygham, as well as the vast, politically oriented battle between armed men who would lay

* *Nostromo* by Joseph Conrad (New York: The Modern Library, 1951). Copyright 1951 by Random House, Inc. Reprinted by permission of the publisher. The novel was first published in 1904.

77

claim to a relatively primitive South American territory and its subterranean treasure. But to me at least, *Nostromo's* real fascination lies neither in its unfolding of the anxieties of individual men nor in its larger-scaled revolutionary conflict, but in the continuing confrontation between the human and the natural orders of creation—between man, who, for whatever reason, would unrestrainedly rape the earth, and those natural forces that would destroy him for his intrusion.

A major, perhaps insoluble, problem is how we are to interpret Conrad's drawing of the enduring attack and counterattack between man and nature. Is he implying an ontological conviction that men are intemperate ravagers of the natural order of creation—specifically, in *Nostromo,* of the San Tomé silver mine—and that the natural order in turn possesses some inherent reflexive mechanism which will give embattled response to its despoilers? If his argument is of such metaphysical character, is he attributing to nature some degree of deliberation and intention which is consciously responsive, or is he characterizing nature as a scourge, not self-motivating but used by some other force as an instrument to punish man for his intemperance? Or is he, on the other hand, indulging in a purely literary device, personifying nature simply to heighten the novel's dramatic quality and not to imply any substantial philosophical position? An examination of some of Conrad's other works may help clarify the problem, even if it gives no certain solution.

Particularly in that period between the publication of his first major work, *The Nigger of the "Narcissus"* (1897), and the appearance of *Nostromo* seven years later—a span including *Youth, Typhoon, Lord Jim,* and *Heart of Darkness* —Conrad strikes again and again the theme of enmity between man and nature. Few novelists of any place or time match his awe of the world's cosmic forces, and perhaps no other writer succeeds so well as he in expressing this wonderment through description of nature's dreadful power. Nature's immense vitality is conveyed in such a way that storms and seas and jungles seem at times not merely blind, errant forces, but purposeful, consciously motivated antagonists, committed to the destruction of a mankind which goes beyond appropriate limits, which overruns and violates the nonhuman orders of the created universe. In *The Nigger of the "Narcissus,"* the gale is seen as "an avenging terror," with the qualifying adjective suggesting deliberation. The battle for James Wait's body is described as "a personal matter between us [the crew members] and the sea," and his corpse must be surrendered to the sea before nature will send her solacing, haven-directing winds. As old Singleton remarks, "The sea will have her own." The early pages of *Lord Jim* even more explicitly attribute to nature a conscious effort to destroy those who sail the seas. Reflecting on the "many shades in the danger of adventures and gales," the narrator affirms that at their worst they possess

a sinister violence of *intention*—that indefinable something which forces it upon the mind and the heart of a man, that this complication of accidents or these elemental furies are coming at him with a *purpose* of malice, with a strength beyond control, with an unbridled cruelty that *means* to tear out of him his hope and his fear, the pain of his fatigue and his longing for rest: which *means* to smash, to destroy, to annihilate all he has seen, known, loved, enjoyed, or hated; all that is priceless and necessary—the sunshine, the memories, the future—which *means* to sweep the whole precious world utterly away from his sight by the simple and appalling act of taking his life. [Italics mine.]

Perhaps nowhere more than in *Heart of Darkness* do we find that prevailing "violence of intention" which Conrad attributes to natural forces. As Marlow moves farther and farther along the snakelike river into the heart of the dark Congo, he becomes increasingly conscious of his, or any other "civilized" man's, unwelcome. It seems, he writes at one point, "as if Nature herself had tried to ward off intruders"; he speaks twice of the wilderness as waiting for the passing away of man's "fantastic invasion"; and he sees the thick vegetation as ready "to sweep every little man of us out of his little existence." It is the metamorphosis of Kurtz, however, which seems most clearly to denote nature's vengeance. That self-assumed idealist, would-be savior, and eager standard-bearer of the International Society for the Suppression of Savage Customs entered the Congo to bear, as he saw the matter, light to darkness, civilization to savages. But his mission, however he originally may have intended it, is in fact an unwelcome invasion which elicits full retribution in the form of a sobering, terrifying reversal: the wilderness, viewing Kurtz as a trespasser who must be transformed to be acceptable, took him, "loved him, embraced him, got into his veins, consumed his flesh, and sealed his soul to its own. . . ." Kurtz learns not only the awful power of the wilderness of forest and river outside the human soul; he is persuaded also of a wilderness within the soul, convinced that savagery is the natural state of human beingness and that altruism and good will are but surface pretensions. His attempted proselytism of the savages is an offense against the wilderness which claims them for its own, not geographically so much as psychically. His unrestrained pursuit of ivory, moreover, suggests the unrestrained pursuit of silver in *Nostromo*. The wilderness, Marlow tells us, takes upon Kurtz "a terrible vengeance for the fantastic invasion," leading him with sure inevitability to his last words: "The horror! The horror!" Yet horrifying as his final vision is, it is also a victory of sorts in its perception of the dark, stalking forces always ready to do battle with man's intrusiveness, even when it is motivated by the intruder's most noble hopes and aspirations, which, sadly, are but illusions. William Golding's *Lord of the Flies* is a fitting companion-piece to the Kurtzian-Marlovian-Conradian descent into the cosmic heart.

In his writings of that seven-year period from *The Nigger of the "Narcissus"* to *Nostromo,* Conrad plays many variations on the theme of man against nature. In the sea stories—*The Nigger, Youth, Typhoon*—the human protagonists do enjoy their moments of triumph over the sea's wrath: most of the *Narcissus* crewmen reach shore; the Marlow of *Youth* comes upon that magic vision of a splendid East; Captain MacWhirr outlasts his typhoon and brings the Chinamen and their money to port; and in most cases the waves and winds bring courageous men together in that human solidarity so prized by Conrad. But the survival and solidarity come at the price of a terrible suffering born of struggle against elemental forces, as if the sea, jealous of her rights, would seek to destroy those who intrude upon her. The Conrad who, as a very young man, took so eagerly and lovingly to the sea found that the passing years brought second thoughts. There came a point in his marine career, remarked on retrospectively in his autobiographical *The Mirror of the Sea* (1906), when his early, romantic enthusiasm turned to darker colors. In the moving section entitled "Initiation," he notes his growing conviction, born of his voyages, that "the sea has never been friendly to man," that "the ocean has no compassion, no faith, no law, no memory," and "has remained the irreconcilable enemy of ships and men ever since ships and men had the unheard-of audacity to go afloat together in the face of his frown." And he goes on to describe his feelings just a few years after he has taken to the sea:

Already I looked with other eyes upon the sea. I knew it capable of betraying the generous ardour of youth as implacably as, indifferent to evil and good, it would have betrayed the basest greed or the noblest heroism. My conception of its magnanimous greatness was gone. And I looked upon the true sea—the sea that plays with men till their hearts are broken, and wears stout ships to death. Nothing can touch the brooding bitterness of its soul. Open to all and faithful to none, it exercises its fascination for the undoing of the best. To love it is not well. It knows no bond of plighted troth, no fidelity to misfortune, to long companionship, to long devotion. The promise it holds out perpetually is very great; but the only secret of its possession is strength, strength—the jealous, sleepless strength of a man guarding a coveted treasure within his gates.

The last phrase of this disillusioned comment on the brooding, jealous sea is an appropriate epigraph to *Nostromo,* whose San Tomé silver mine cannot successfully guard her

coveted treasure, but can and does wrest from her assailants
a price exceeding the value of the metal. As the sailors of the
ocean try "to wrest from him the fortune of their house, the
dominion of their world," the workers of the mine—which,
like the sea, is a "dangerous abettor of world-wide ambitions"
—enter ambitious quest for fortune and dominion. And the
characters of *Nostromo*, like Kurtz, claim more of the world's
bounty than is rightfully theirs. They too are cursed with a
lack of restraint—for silver, not for ivory and savage rites—
and with a rapacity luring them to cross that cosmic line separating their proper territory from nature's domain, in this
case her mineral kingdom. They lack the wisdom which intuits boundaries and foresees the consequences of trespass.

It seems to me that the central theme of *Nostromo* involves not so much the actions and reactions among men as
the motions and countermotions of the human and natural
orders of creation and that Conrad is proffering an ontological comment on the universe's structural economy.
Whether, in *Nostromo,* the expressed attribution of conscious
purpose to the San Tomé mine is to be taken figuratively or
literally I am less certain. The modern age, unlike more
primitive ones, views animism with more than skepticism. Yet
a reading of Conrad with a willing suspension of our habitual
rationalism makes for a particularly exciting venture, one
which, I believe, Conrad encourages. And I am quite willing
to indulge myself in what may seem a rash or quaint pro-
cedure.

II

Nostromo is the most epic and complex of Conrad's novels. Its
characters are many, their interrelationships sometimes difficult to follow. Its events, spanning many years, come to us in
no consistent chronological sequence. Its action is played in
great part on the insurgent streets of Sulaco, seaport city of
the South American territory of Costaguana. We are quickly

introduced to the first day—a May 2, as we are later able to calculate—of a three-day riot, a period also encompassing the novel's main action. Through various flashbacks we learn the earliest history of the San Tomé mine, of past revolutionary activity in Costaguana, of the courtship and marriage of Charles and Emilia Gould, of the building of a railway eighteen months before the opening action. We are also taken beyond those riotous days in May to the military victory of the loyalists, the building of a lighthouse, and the death of the incomparable Nostromo. Perhaps William Faulkner alone is Conrad's peer in the stunning use of unchronological sequence, that deployment of time which engenders suspense and issues in a complex structure of considerable aesthetic satisfaction. The primary motivating source of the massive struggle illuminating the pages of *Nostromo* resides in the competing claims for that great attractor of "Material Interests," the San Tomé mine, "from which," Conrad avers in a prefatory note, "there is no escape in this world." Impelled by a variety of reasons, ignoble and noble, the inhabitants of Costaguana are led to plunder the mine, their insatiable passions leading, in turn, to San Tomé's unremitting resistance to its human invaders.

The history of San Tomé, the novel's great antagonist and its counter to human ambitions, is chronicled early. First mined by slaves, its treasure won at the expense of their overworked lives, it was abandoned when it "had ceased to make a profitable return no matter how many corpses were thrown into its maw." The pillaging was later successfully resumed for a time by an English company, only to be abruptly ended when the English chiefs, actuated, as the *Diario Official* put it, "by sordid motives of gain rather than by love for a country where they came impoverished to seek their fortunes," were murdered by the revolted and revolting native miners. Still later, the strange exigencies of politics brought the concession of San Tomé to Charles Gould's father, who, after years of protesting "the injustice, the persecution, the outrage of that mine," was, in accordance with his own prophecy and his son's post-mortem judgment, killed by San Tomé. Charles, despite his father's long-time warning to eschew the mine, became bent upon redeeming her history, upon transforming a moral disaster into a moral success. But the ensuing history of San Tomé would seem to suggest that the mine is less impressed than Charles by his idealistic intention to draw from her riches a stabilizing, ordering, and saving panacea for the Costaguanan province. The natural order, it appears, is offended by man's trespass, whatever its motive.

Nostromo's characters, most of them, are most clearly bound through common interest in San Tomé, and most sharply distinguished through their widely differing motives behind that interest. At one extreme are the utterly self-indulgent Commandant Sotillo and Pedro Montero, who, one by sea and one by land, assault the beleaguered and defenseless city of Sulaco on May 3 and May 4. The cowardly, frenzied Sotillo, in his mad search for silver, is true to his life's single guiding principle, the quest for riches whereby to indulge his lavish tastes. Pedro Montero, brother to the less than illustrious rebel general, matches even Sotillo in ignobility, looking forward only to the treasure that would become his through rebel victory. Sotillo, in defeat, is thrust through with a sword. Montero, his hopes dashed, makes, we may assume, a quick retreat into the hills. At the opposite pole, yet equally interested in the mine's productive working, are Don José Avellanos, his daughter Antonia, and Captain Mitchell, all of whom seek not personal aggrandizement but their country's health. "Don José Avellanos loved his country"—so Conrad sums up the perfect patriot, whose unpublished *Fifty Years of Misrule* eloquently proclaims the tragic injustices that have corrupted Costaguana. The beautiful Antonia also loves her country, placing its welfare above her happiness with Martin Decoud. Don José dies, his death hastened by tireless resistance to brutal forces which, in search of riches, assail his land; and Antonia must endure the death of her affianced

Martin, whose interests finally touched too closely upon San Tomé. With Captain Mitchell, superintendent of the Oceanic Steam Navigation Company which oversaw the shipments of silver beyond Sulaco's coast, San Tomé deals more leniently, perhaps that he may serve for long after the May crisis to relate its history. Patriotic like the Avellanoses, representing the "allied and anxious goodwill of all the material interests of civilization," proudly responsible for bringing Nostromo's rare talents to the Gould Concession, Captain Mitchell narrates his tale pompously but well.

And what can be said of the novel's five main characters —Martin Decoud, Dr. Monygham, Charles and Emilia Gould, Nostromo—of their motives and their misfortunes in relation to the great silver mine? Whatever their ruling passions—two are moved by love for a woman, one by love of "progress," one by love for a man, one by love of reputation—and however far most of them remain from the more insidious lures of material interests, all of them fall, through indirect or direct involvement with San Tomé, to death or a living misery. None escapes the vengeance of a mine which would have remained quiescent had her treasure not been stolen.

Martin Decoud, initially cynical about any form of national or human aspiration, and possessed of an ironic disposition which keeps at bay the claims of patriotism or interpersonal fidelity (except for his sister), is aroused from indifference by the charms of Antonia Avellanos, "the only being capable of inspiring a sincere passion in the heart of a trifler." When Antonia, out of love for her country, rejects his petition to flee Costaguana with him for a safer and more civilized land, the once trifler invests his wisdom and energy in a patriotic cause which means little to him, much to his beloved. His service on Sulaco's small-arms committee, his editorship of the loyalist newspaper *Provenir,* his proposing a political separation which works to the good of Sulaco—all stem from his love for Antonia.

It is supremely ironic that Decoud, greatest ironist of all, is lured to his death by the great white symbol of material interests for which he has neither desire nor direct concern, and that he is, finally, borne to his watery grave by four bars of silver, which some deemed requisite to the life abundant. Left alone on the Great Isabel to which he has accompanied Nostromo and the lighterful of silver, finding no other being on whom his irony can feed, discovering in his lonely introspection his lack of faith in both himself and others, unable to face the solitude of that quiet island, he feels stripped of every reason for living. "In our activity alone," the narrator tells us, "do we find the sustaining illusion of an independent existence as against the whole scheme of things of which we form a helpless part. Decoud lost all belief in the reality of his action past and to come. . . . Both his intelligence and his passion were swallowed up easily in this great unbroken solitude of waiting without faith." And so, sitting on the gunwale of his dinghy just off the island shore, gun to breast and four silver ingots in his pockets, Decoud pulls the trigger, falls forward into the sea, and surrenders himself to the welcome oblivion. A single sentence sums up his fate: "A victim of the disillusioned weariness which is the retribution meted out to intellectual audacity, the brilliant Don Martin Decoud, weighted by the bars of San Tomé silver, disappeared without a trace, swallowed up in the immense indifference of things."

Dr. Monygham, misshapen in body and wounded in spirit and pride by a traumatic past, is more militantly cynical than Decoud, viewing other men with suspicion and hostility, not merely indifference. He shares with his younger acquaintance that freedom from illusion which enables them both to see far more perceptively than the other inhabitants of Sulaco into the heart of matters. He too is moved by love for a woman, in his case Emilia Gould. As Antonia alone inspires Decoud, for a time at least, to put aside his indifference, Emilia alone keeps the doctor's cynicism from engulfing him. But whereas Decoulĕd's love requires for its fruition possession of Antonia, Dr. Monygham's is of the rare kind that sustains itself without hope of acquisition. He seeks no favor except Emilia's smile and occasional presence, and is led to oppose the rebellious forces not in behalf of patriotism or material interests, but in defense of the peace of mind and body of Emilia. When the Gould Concession is in worst danger of toppling and Sotillo and Montero are closest to success, Dr. Monygham risks his life for the saving of a treasure—not San Tomé, however, but Emilia:

The doctor was loyal to the mine. It presented itself to his fifty-year-old eyes in the shape of a little woman in a soft dress with a long train, with a head attractively overweighted by a great mass of fair hair, and the delicate preciousness of her inner worth, partaking of a gem and a flower, revealed in every attitude of her person. As the dangers thickened round the San Tomé mine, this illusion [Dr. Monygham's only illusion!] acquired force, permanency, and authority. It claimed him at last! This claim, exalted by a spiritual detachment from the usual sanctions of hope and reward, made Dr. Monygham's thinking, acting individuality extremely dangerous to himself and to others, all his scruples vanishing in the proud feeling that his devotion was the only thing that stood between an admirable woman and a frightful disaster.

To this "claim" the doctor devotes his full energy. His clever duplicity leads Sotillo to search the sea for a sunken treasure that is not there, thus diverting the madman from the sack of Sulaco. His persuasive power leads Nostromo to the daring railroad journey which figures in the loyalist victory. Though Dr. Monygham risks his life, he does not, like Decoud, lose it. He lives on, rewarded, it is true, by Emilia's gratitude, but deeply grieved by her growing, agonizing awareness that her husband cares more for San Tomé than for her. Neither Decoud nor Dr. Monygham is attracted by material interests, but each is led by indirection to their defense, with the result that one suffers death, the other keen sorrow, for his intercession.

If Martin Decoud and Dr. Monygham are most free of illusions, Charles Gould is, certainly at the beginning of his career, least so. It is in *Heart of Darkness* that we are introduced to his prototype. About to begin his chilling tale to those gathered on the *Nellie*'s deck, Marlow distinguishes between the ways of the ancient Romans who sailed up the Thames bent on conquest and those of his contemporary English colonists who share the same thirst. In ancient times such adventure was compounded of brute force, of violent robbery and large-scale murder, of the strong wantonly subduing the weak. But the human mind, grown more subtle through the centuries, has now crowned the concept of conquest with a halo, justifying its practice through a kind of intellectualization or, at least, rationalization: "What redeems . . . [conquest]," Marlow tells his companions, "is the idea only. An idea at the back of it; not a sentimental pretence but an idea; and an unselfish belief in the idea—something you can set up, and bow down before, and offer a sacrifice to. . . ." Just such an idea obsessed Kurtz, who made his serpentine way into the Congo committed to winning a host of savages to the benign ways of civilization, and giving voice to his hopes in a most eloquent and high-minded essay of seventeen pages. But as his well-intentioned ideal was overtaken by a towering passion for ivory and an embracing of the uncivilized horror which he had set out to combat, he displayed a capacity for violence, savagery, and murder equal to that of any Roman.

Charles Gould, in many ways a lesser man than Kurtz, starts out by holding in common with him devotion to an idea. The "King of Sulaco," as he comes to be called, refuses to heed history and his father's wise counsel. For him it is not enough that San Tomé has never laid down her arms against those who, through many years of intermittent conquest, would steal her treasure. On the contrary, the disasters that have attended her working serve only as a stimulus to Gould, who feels he can turn the tide and, in a moral sense, redeem what has been lost. He is, like the early Kurtz, a man with an ideal before whose altar he is ready to bow down and offer the sacrifice of mind, heart, and hands. As

Kurtz would redeem savages from savagery, Gould, who also sees himself as something of a missionary, would redeem Costaguanans from the instability, poverty, and ill governance which rides herd over them. Gould does have faith in material interests and does set out to make of San Tomé a vastly profitable enterprise, but his objective is unquestionably to use the treasure for the Republic's welfare.

In Marlovian terms, then, Gould justifies his conquest through belief that it will redeem Costaguana. Not surprisingly, Decoud questions his motives, deeming him a victim of self-deception who, he tells Mrs. Gould, "cannot act or exist without idealizing every simple feeling, desire, or achievement. He could not believe his own motives if he did not make them first a part of some fairy-tale. The earth is not quite good enough for him, I fear." Somewhat later, Decoud writes to his sister in much the same vein, asserting that Gould is among those typical Englishmen who can do nothing "unless it comes to them clothed in the fair robes of an idea." And if Decoud would define Gould, the embodiment of the English character, as a sentimental idealist, he also has a word for the "progressive" Europeans who have long claimed Latin American treasure for their own: they are a fusion of "Don Quixote and Sancho Panza, chivalry and materialism, high-sounding sentiments and a supine morality, violent efforts for an idea and a sullen acquiescence in every form of corruption."

It takes a man of Gould's inherent idealism a long time to realize that, when chivalry and materialism contend, the victory is, finally, to the latter. To work San Tomé, he gradually discovers, is to force compromise. Though he is committed to placing the earth's riches in the service of a people's welfare, there are others who see the treasure as valuable only when at their personal disposal. For a Don Quixote (and Gould, of course, is an indefatigable tilter at his own kind of windmill) to come to such knowledge is a painful awakening. The constant necessity of compromise opens

Gould's mind to the power of the Sancho Panzas and the darker lures of material interests. But if he becomes slowly aware that his father had been wiser than he thought and that moral disaster is a constant for those who would touch San Tomé, he believes that there is for him no turning back. Once across the Atlantic in pursuit of a moral success, he is trapped, confined increasingly and simply to making the disaster minimal. And to attain even this reduced goal, the once visionary King of Sulaco is forced to the extreme of joining forces with the once most notorious bandit of the Costaguanan Republic, Hernandez, who, interestingly, also has a strain of idealism in his proud character.

San Tomé is as merciless to Charles Gould as to others. The mine finally gets hold of him, we are told, "with a grip as deadly as ever it had laid upon his father." The man who once begged the hand of Emilia and journeyed off to improve man's lot at the expense of nature's treasure is, by the novel's end, a fractured shadow of his former self. On his ideal he has confidently gambled everything, and he is at last left with little, not even a son to whom he may bequeath the dark wisdom, richer by a generation, which his own father had tried to impress upon him.

San Tomé is instrumental to Decoud's death, to the long-afflicted Dr. Monygham's increased measure of sorrow, and to the bankruptcy of the principles and aspirations on which Gould has based his life's work. To Emilia the mine is an antagonist of a different kind: San Tomé is the loved but unloving mistress of Charles, bearing him the silver monsters which are to destroy him and to dissolve in all but name the Gould marriage. It takes the usually intuitive and perceptive Emilia a long time to pierce through her partially blind devotion to her husband and know that she has been betrayed.

At the time of their betrothal on a country road in Italy, Emilia was as confident as Charles that their grand future lay in the conquest of San Tomé and that they would succeed where all others had failed. Her disillusioning is gradual. She learns early that not all men are moved by the high ideals which beckon her husband. She comes quickly, for example, to the judgment that the wealthy Holroyd, endower of churches and financial backer of the Gould Concession, is more devoted to his own material interests than to religion or social welfare and views his God "as a sort of influential partner, who gets his share of profits in the endowment of churches." But not until much later does she realize that her own white knight, for whom material interests are not ends in themselves, is nevertheless being undone by their pervasive influence. Her expressions of doubt about the direction and outcome of the silver enterprise, however, elicit from her husband only the balladic refrain that there is no going back.

There is more than a touch of sainthood in Emilia, with her capacity to be gracious ministrant and hostess to all Sulaco without neglecting her wifely duties, and to evoke Dr. Monygham's devotion without the slightest questioning of the honor of either. But if she never forgets her own first and proper object of fidelity, Charles quickly forgets his, as Decoud, observing to his sister that Gould lives more for San Tomé than for his wife, recognizes more quickly than does Emilia. But even when Emilia does come to see herself as victim of one of the more subtle forms of conjugal infidelity and to see San Tomé, her husband's mistress, as a dreadful force "hanging over the Campo, over the whole land, feared, hated, wealthy, more soulless than any tyrant, more pitiless and autocratic than the worst government, ready to crush innumerable lives in the expansion of its greatness"—even then, she judges Charles a perfect man, not guilty of his blindness to the truth. Only with the fatal shooting of Nostromo does Emilia despair of both her husband and his enterprise, finally knowing that nothing is worth the price San Tomé extracts for the rifling of her womb. Seeking to console the weeping Giselle Viola, mourning the loss of her beloved Nostromo, Emilia declares that he would in time have forsaken her through his obsessive passion for the hidden treasure. When the young girl protests that she had been loved by Nostromo as no girl had ever been loved before, Emilia, with a severity foreign to the whole tenor of her previous life, replies in the *past* tense, "I have been loved too." And Giselle's insistence that Emilia will be loved to the end of her life is received in silence by the habitually gracious and self-forgetful hostess of all Sulaco, who now knows that the marital rupture effected by San Tomé is beyond healing.

It is not extravagant to suggest that neither Holroyd and all the capital he pours into Costaguana nor Charles Gould and all his technical and administrative skill are more important to the silver enterprise than Nostromo. "A fellow in a thousand," "my capataz de cargadores," "a man absolutely above reproach," "a perfectly incorruptible fellow," as Captain Mitchell calls him, Nostromo seems a man beyond the reach of failure or ignobility. He is also a man of great simplicity, his every daring and well-accomplished deed springing from a single motivating force, an inexhaustible passion for personal prestige. Decoud, whose judgment of others is extraordinarily dependable, observes that Nostromo's very incorruptibility is the product of a vanity which will not suffer him to be otherwise, and that to him death would be preferred to loss of esteem. And Emilia is correct in suggesting that he loves prestige for its own sake, with the important implication that he takes no unprincipled advantage of his esteemed position. Nostromo is, during his years of service to the Oceanic Steam Navigation Company and the Gould Concession, talented, incorruptible, vain, innocent.

And so he remains until what he regards as his betrayal. When, on the dark night of May 3, he undertakes with Decoud to preserve the lighterful of silver from revolutionary forces, he has no self-interest in the treasure and seeks no monetary gain. Instead, true to his love of fame, he views the adventure as "the most famous and desperate affair" of his life, as an act that will "be talked about when the little children are grown up and the grown men are old." But when, having left Decoud and the silver behind on the Great Isabel, Nostromo returns to the mainland, knowing himself to be a hunted man no longer able to swagger openly in the streets, bitterness begins to set in. As Decoud needs others on whom to vent his criticism and exercise his irony, Nostromo needs others before whom to perform those incomparable deeds which earned him the description "a fellow in a thousand." Returned from the island and forced to keep cover, he is thus deprived of his life's most nourishing provision. It strikes him, moreover, that he has been asked to risk his life for a shipment of silver which, in comparison to the limitless riches of San Tomé, is but a pittance. Concealed in the darkness of Sulaco, the great Nostromo, feeling he has been betrayed, suffers his first keen disillusionment:

The renowned capataz, his elbows on his knees and a fist dug into each cheek, laughed with self-derision, as he had spat with disgust, straight out before him into the night. The confused and intimate impressions of universal dissolution which beset a subjective nature at any strong check to its ruling passion had a bitterness approaching that of death itself. And no wonder—with no intellectual existence or moral strain to carry on his individuality, unscathed, over the abyss left by the collapse of his vanity; for even that had been simply sensuous and picturesque, and could not exist apart from outward show.

Yet even with this recognition, Nostromo has still not quite learned his lesson, and it is Dr. Monygham whose cleverness entices him to surrender once again to his thirst for esteem. Just one day after Nostromo's conviction of his betrayal, the doctor, with Emilia's welfare most in mind, persuades the capataz to make the spectacular railroad journey for the purpose of summoning the loyalist General Barrios back to the besieged Sulaco. "And to you," Monygham tells Nostromo, "I offer the best means of saving yourself . . . and of retrieving your great reputation." The "means" of salvation is to reach Barrios; the word which springs Nostromo from his sullen apathy is "reputation." The mission success-fully accomplished, Nostromo returns to discover Decoud's disappearance.

He returns to discover also how costly, finally, his reputa-tion-seeking has been. For he now believes not only that he has been betrayed, but that he has twice betrayed others—once, in his haste to guide the treasure-burdened lighter to safety, by refusing to summon a priest to Teresa Viola's deathbed for the administering of last rites; once by leaving Decoud alone on the island to a fate the precise nature of which he is ignorant, but which he senses to have been a desperate one. The high cost of his vanity exposed, Nostromo disdain-fully throws aside both the vanity itself and the incorrupti-bility which it nourished. The "lost" silver, which by everyone else is thought to rest hidden somewhere under the sea's large expanse, he determines to make his own, becoming through its secret sale, ingot by ingot, a rich man. The silver is all that a once proud man has left.

Thus San Tomé, in terrible malediction, bestows her curse on that "perfectly incorruptible fellow." For Nostromo, his bondage to San Tomé complete, knows no peace after that day of decision. Not even the lovely Giselle Viola, who wishes to flee with him the Great Isabel and live henceforth in married bliss far from a frightful past—not even she can wedge herself between Nostromo and the fruit of the mine. They will depart, Nostromo assures her, but not before they grow rich. Yet to a man whose insatiability always sees rich-ness as one step beyond his present wealth, "rich" is a rela-tive term and "richness" an ever-receding condition. As the frightened Giselle astutely remarks to her lover and loved one: "Your love is to me like your treasure to you. It is there, but I can never get enough of it." And before Nostromo can get enough of his prize, he is dead, killed in his pursuit of a treasure instrumental in triggering the first shot fired on the Great Isabel. The man who holds the gun is, ironically, Nostromo's father-surrogate, Giorgio Viola, who all his life has fought in self-forgetfulness and with striking singleness of purpose for universal love and brotherhood, and to whom all the world's material treasure is dross. Thus even Giorgio, by tragic obliquity, comes under the power of San Tomé, on whom he has never laid a hand. No one, from the most sinister to the most pure, seems free from the wrath of a natural order constantly vigilant and jealously guarding her rights.

The dead Nostromo is to have one last triumph. Linda Viola, elder sister of Giselle and the woman for whom Nostromo was originally intended, can admit no defeat for the once great mover of men. Her final piercing cry—"Never! Gian' Battista!"—is a ringing benediction. Her passionate denial of the incomparable man's death, we are told, is

another of Nostromo's successes, the greatest, the most enviable, the most sinister of all. In that true cry of love and grief that seemed to ring aloud from Punta Mala to Azuera and away to the bright line of the horizon, overhung by a big white cloud shining like a mass of solid silver, the genius of the magnificent capataz de cargadores dominated the dark gulf containing his conquests of treasure and love.

Such a benediction, however, is but a minor triumph within a near-total disaster.

III

The San Tomé is close kin to the sea which Conrad, in *The Mirror of the Sea,* describes as responding alike to "the basest greed or the noblest heroism," exercising "its fascination for the undoing of the best," and possessing "the jealous, sleepless strength of a man guarding a coveted treasure within his gates." In *Nostromo* it is a large net that encompasses persons so diverse as Sotillo and Montero, Don José and Antonia Avellanos, Decoud and Dr. Monygham, Charles and Emilia Gould, and Nostromo. San Tomé is instrumental in fastening upon Sotillo a madness leading to death and upon Montero dreams of glory which quickly disintegrate, in weighting Decoud to the bottom of the sea, adding grief to an already depressed Dr. Monygham, making a shambles of Gould's fervent idealism, robbing Emilia of a husband, and corrupting the incorruptible Nostromo before beckoning him to the path of a bullet. Whatever the individual's ruling passion—sheer greed, patriotism, love for another person, desire for a country's economic, political, and social welfare, self-esteem—each protagonist meets death or a living misery. If it is possible to speak of a poetic justice in *Nostromo,* it is not a justice allotted each man in terms of his apparent deserts, but a judgment upon the whole of mankind seen in its communal aspect. The judgment of the human order might call for Sotillo's death and Montero's ignoble retreat, but hardly for the grievous fates of the novel's major characters.

The common denominator linking *Nostromo*'s widely diverse characters is their interest, for whatever reason, in the successful working of San Tomé. In one aspect of its structure, the novel conceives, not so much a division among characters into protagonists and antagonists, as a division between the human characters envisaged as a kind of communal protagonist and San Tomé as antagonist. Human beings, of course, motivate the novel's action. Some work in concert with, some in discord against, others, but all act with common effrontery toward the mine. Whether selfishness or unselfishness marks their benign or malign interpersonal relationships, the protagonists are in the mutual accord of judging that San Tomé exists only to serve mankind; in this judgment lies their only human solidarity.

Conrad, I believe, would tell us that there is a wide difference between man's proper stewardship of the other orders of creation and his habitual disposition to regard them as objects to be used solely and unrestrainedly for human comfort. There is in his view of the natural universe something sacramental, a belief that each order of the world possesses its own kind of integrity, dignity, and beauty. When such integrity is violated by man's heedless rapacity, the offended order will strike back, and strike not only at the individual men who, in the court of human judgment, seem most selfish in their assaults on the world's treasures, but at the whole of mankind. In his Preface to *The Nigger of the "Narcissus,"* Conrad affirms that the artist is one who "speaks to our capacity for delight and wonder, to the sense of mystery surrounding our lives . . . to the latent feeling of fellowship with all creation. . . ." Much has been remarked upon the central importance of human solidarity, of the fidelity of man to man, in Conrad's philosophy. But his concept of solidarity reaches beyond the strictly human order, extending to the whole of creation. Man is called to a sacred sense of fellowship with all that is. When he arrogantly usurps the inherent rights of the natural world, he invites its vengeance upon his head. Important to an understanding of *Nostromo* is an understanding of its basic ontological position, of Conrad's feelings about the proper relationships among the world's various orders of being. *Nostromo* would impress upon us, perhaps above all else, the incalculable virtue of self-restraint in a universe calling for man's wise, humble, compassionate sovereignty, not his manic tyranny. When this virtue is lacking, a destruction initiated by man and wrought by nature falls upon the human order.

Microbe Against Man

*Everybody knows that pestilences have a way of recurring in the world.**

"And until my dying day I shall refuse to love a scheme of things in which children are put to torture."

"What's natural is the microbe."

I

My proposal about Conrad's sense of the relationship between man and nature is speculative. Albert Camus's view of the relationship can be expressed with more certainty. Both men believe in the possibility of human solidarity. Conrad would seem also to hold out a slight hope for cosmic solidarity, if only man would moderate his passionately acquisitive instinct; it is man's lack of restraint which incurs nature's counter, vengeful, destructive powers. For Camus, cosmic solidarity is beyond hope: man is innocent victim of a natural order whose inherent disposition is uncompromisingly hostile or indifferent to his being.

For Camus the relationship between man and the natural world can be defined in one word: *absurd*. It is in *The Myth of Sisyphus* (1943), the first of his philosophical treatises, that he writes most extensively of the absurd juxtaposition of

* *The Plague* by Albert Camus, translated by Stuart Gilbert (New York: Alfred A. Knopf, 1948). Copyright 1948 by Stuart Gilbert. Reprinted by permission of the publisher. The novel was first published in 1947.

the human order and the natural order. Put in its simplest terms, the absurd is the "divorce between the mind that desires and the world that disappoints." * Evidences of the divorce are many, their recognition beginning to shatter the placidity of a person at the mythical age of thirty, when he suddenly realizes the invalidity of assumptions which have borne him through his earlier, unreflective years. He has previously longed for every tomorrow, perhaps under the thoughtless illusion that life protracts itself forever, but at thirty he comes to know that time, progenitor of mortality and harbinger of death, is his greatest enemy. He has previously felt at home in the world, sensing it a kind of paradise in close and benign kinship with himself, but he learns that it is, in fact, either hostile or indifferent to his presence. And he has savored his human beingness, judging it unique and distinct from all else that is, but he then detects in himself a mechanical perfunctoriness of gesture and movement which persuades him of an underlying inhumanity. He comes to realize, in short, that the world of time and space can and does deny him those aspirations that have seemed to him most precious: a never-ending procession of tomorrows; an accommodating, sympathetic home; a style of life and movement which implies his humanity.

It is for man sufficient burden that the world of time decrees his death, the world of space his homelessness, and the world of robotism his inhumanity. But absurdity does not end here. Equally contributory to man's frustration is what Camus calls "the unreasonable silence of the world": not only does the world balk the specific human hopes already enumerated; it gives no reason for its unyielding obduracy. Early in *The Myth* Camus defines the "mind's deepest desire" as "an insistence upon familiarity, an appetite for clarity." It is one thing to endure suffering while understanding its cause, quite another to suffer through, apparently, the arbitrary, capri-

* *The Myth of Sisyphus and Other Essays,* translated by Justin O'Brien (New York: Alfred A. Knopf, 1955).

cious, and whimsical. In Conrad there is at least the intimation that man bears responsibility for his misery, which can thus to a degree be understood, but such is not so in Camus. Petitioning the world for the lucidity which is balm to the human heart and mind, for the kind of clarity for which Jacob wrestled the angel, Camus finds that, from the twentieth-century world at least, the angel has withdrawn, leaving the universe sphinxlike and beyond reasoning. Thus there is an additional absurdity, product of "the confrontation of this irrational and the wild longing for clarity whose call echoes in the human heart." And this absurdity, Camus goes on to affirm, binds together the world and man, "one to the other as only hatred can weld two creatures together."

Through his recognition of the abysmal disparity between what he desires and what the world legislates, man is led to reflect on what Camus, in *The Myth,* calls "the one truly serious philosophical problem," that of suicide, of whether life is, under its absurd conditions, worth living. Certainly it is a question which has been asked by thoughtful men of all periods, but it gains heightened intensity at a time when God's death, or at least his apparent withdrawal from concern with human affairs, is an increasingly prevailing persuasion. And the acceptance of God's death leads perhaps to the greatest absurdity of all, for the deepest hopes of the Western world have over many centuries rested in biblical promises, particularly the promise of immortality for the faithful.

The Myth not only defines the absurd but describes the three basic responses to it. First, a man may be so oppressed by the apparent heartlessness of the world and its disappointment of human hopes that he escapes it through suicide. A second and somewhat more subtle way of eluding the absurd is the alternative called by Camus "philosophical suicide" and attributed by him to such religious existentialists as Leo Chestov, Sören Kierkegaard, and Karl Jaspers. These men, each in his own way, do not fashion a physical escape from life's miseries through physical suicide; instead they indulge in a more metaphysical excursion, a leap of faith, not denying the world's wretchedness any more than do the physical suicidists, but postulating a transcendental world into whose peace the faithful will ultimately be raised, leaving behind all mortal, transient disappointment. Camus cites, as what he believes a typical though caricatural example of such philosophical suicide, the illogical logic of Jaspers, who, out of his failure to find the transcendental sovereignty of good in this world, formulates a questionable escape: "Does not the failure reveal," Jaspers observes, "beyond any possible explanation and interpretation, not the absence but the existence of transcendence?" And Camus, later noting Kierkegaard's agreement with Ignatius Loyola that God rejoices most in man's willingness to sacrifice his intellect, concludes that, for the religious existentialist, God "is maintained only through the negation of human reason." Both physical and philosophical suicide are, for Camus, forms of evading the absurd condition which is life itself, each a retreat from the world, a withdrawal from life.

Camus urges rejection of both forms of suicide and acceptance of a third response to the absurdity of life, the response of revolt. To commit physical suicide is to surrender to the absurd, not revolt against it; to commit philosophical suicide, under the assumption that the absurd is for the faithful man a temporary condition to be replaced ultimately by the glory of eternity, is to withdraw attention from the absurd and thus not revolt against it either. Camus would have us acknowledge, but not accept, the absurd. It is this nonacceptance or revolt, he writes, that "gives life its value." This argument is the link between *The Myth* and Camus's other major philosophical treatise, *The Rebel*, published eight years later, in 1951.

The Rebel, ignoring the option of physical suicide, focuses on two basic responses to life: philosophical suicide characterized by the leap of faith, and metaphysical rebellion. "It would be possible to demonstrate," Camus asserts, "that

only two possible worlds can exist for the human mind: the
sacred (or, to speak in Christian terms, the world of grace)
and the world of rebellion." * Such rebellion "is the movement
by which man protests against his condition and against the
whole of creation." Moreover, it is in this rebellion that man
finds his solidarity with other men, a solidarity clearly growing
out of their mutual resistance to a world which, finally,
demands from every man the same price: death. If Conrad
intimates that man initiates the natural world's hostility, certainly Camus argues that the natural world initiates man's.
The movement in Camus is from recognition of absurdity
("that divorce between the mind that desires and the world
that disappoints") to rebellion against it, to the human solidarity born of rebellion, to man's majestic but losing battle
against the world, ending in his death. The novel which
best charts this movement is *The Plague,* published in 1947
and related to *The Rebel* in much the same way that Camus's
first novel, *The Stranger,* is related to *The Myth of Sisyphus.*

II

"But my real interest in life was the death penalty." So remarks Jean Tarrou to Dr. Bernard Rieux some seven and a
half months after the outbreak of plague in Oran, Algeria.
The pestilence had struck in a mid-April of the 1940s, the
germ first asserting itself in the death of rats and quickly claiming its human victims as well. By summer the toll of the city's
population of 200,000 soared as high as 130 fatalities in a single day. Christmas saw a slackening of the fury, and by February of the following year the ten-month microbic assault had
spent itself, but not before enjoying a devastating success. To
read *The Plague* is to infer that not only Tarrou's interest,
but *the* interest in life is the death penalty. The novel, with
its fictive story of a plague, is a study of the meaning of death,

* *The Rebel,* translated by Anthony Bower (New York: Alfred A. Knopf,
1954).

a series of reflections on its source, and a consideration of the human responses it elicits. It is, above all, a study of man's rebellion "against his condition and against the whole of creation."

In virtually all of Camus's writings, man is cast primarily in the role of victim, though his antagonist, the victimizer, is variously identified. One allegation of Camus's "Letters to a German Friend" is that certain men victimize certain other men; that Germans, in blind servitude to fatherland and in preferring a "politics of reality" to a "politics of honor," an opting for national solitude rather than human solidarity, have wantonly sacrificed Frenchmen.* In *The Stranger* it is the rigidly conventional society of men which decrees that their world has no place for outsiders like Meursault. And Tarrou tells how he was first shocked into recognition of injustice when a court of law pronounced the death sentence upon a pathetic criminal. At other times Camus scores a god cruel and insatiable as man's awful antagonist. The rebel, he writes in his treatise on rebellion, not only defines the human condition as "a mass death sentence," but goes on to denounce "God as the father of death and as the supreme outrage."

But mankind's major antagonist in *The Plague* is not other men, even though Tarrou does affirm human guilt, finding germs in men's wills as well as in the Oranian air. Nor is it a supreme being, whether of satanic or divine essence, though the Jesuit priest, Father Paneloux, interprets the epidemic during its early stages as God's scourge, hopefully a redemptive one in its ultimate effect upon erring men. In *The Plague* the antagonist is, above all, a natural germ, advancing and retreating with what seems a total arbitrariness. Such is the belief of Dr. Rieux, who is at the novel's center and whose judgments most pervasively illuminate its pages. To him man's great enemy is an abiding quality of the physi-

* *Resistance, Rebellion, and Death,* translated by Justin O'Brien (New York: Alfred A. Knopf, 1961).

cal universe, a destructive force of the created order, an adversary which may withdraw from the world temporarily, only to return again. It is consequently not surprising that he defines his medical vocation as a "fighting against creation as he found it." He is chief spokesman for the Camus who, as early as *The Myth,* writes of man and the world being bound "one to the other as only hatred can weld two creatures together."

The Plague on its narrative level is a dramatic, imaginary account of a particular pestilence at a particular time in a particular place. The novel is also symbolic, with the plague representing, as I have suggested, different forces to different characters, the most articulate of whom are Tarrou, Paneloux, and Rieux—social philosopher, scholar-priest, and medical doctor. In one of his extended conversations with Rieux, Tarrou, describing his sense of the plague's omnipresence, voices one of the novel's most illuminating passages:

Each of us has the plague within him; no one, no one on earth is free from it. And I know, too, that we must keep endless watch on ourselves lest in a careless moment we breathe in somebody's face and fasten the infection on him. What's natural is the microbe. All the rest—health, integrity, purity (if you like)—is a product of the human will, of a vigilance that must never falter. The good man, the man who infects hardly anyone, is the man who has the fewest lapses of attention. And it needs tremendous will-power, a never-ending tension of the mind, to avoid such lapses.

Tarrou has traveled a long road to reach this conviction, a journey beginning at the age of seventeen when he observed his father, a prosecuting attorney, clamoring in court for the death sentence for an alleged criminal. Tarrou saw the man not as an abstract defendant who owed society his life, but as a man of flesh and blood, pitiful and terrified. His initial nausea at the horror and injustice of deliberately and legally calling for the murder of another human being—a preview, incidentally, of Camus's later *Reflections on the Guillotine*—stays with him. Haunted by thoughts of the trial, he becomes increasingly persuaded that the whole social order is based on the death sentence and that the established order breeds a competitiveness among men to see who can kill most extensively. Against this order he sets himself, knowing that his alternative is a tacit acceptance of and willing participation in its destructiveness. Thus the plague is for him not only a germ invading the human bloodstream, but a moral stain in the human will. And since he, like all men, has the plague within him, he must be constantly careful and vigilant, making of himself "a man who infects hardly anyone . . . who has the fewest lapses of attention." The main alternative—to join forces with the pestilence and thus to side with injustice rather than justice—he of course rejects. A third category, "that of the true healers," he believes far beyond the capacity of most men. Tarrou's position, incidentally, lends support to the argument that the plague symbolizes, among other things, the German Occupation of France in the 1940s and the French Resistance to it, a theme acknowledged by Camus to form a part of his intention. Yet *The Plague* as a whole emphasizes not so much a conflict between human forces of good and evil as the courageous though ultimately vanquished resistance of human beings to an inhuman universe. As even Tarrou puts it, "What's natural is the microbe." And it is the cruel sport of the microbe which dominates the ten months of the novel's action.

III

The climactic event of *The Plague* is a child's death, a most persuasive example of life's absurdity. Toward the end of October, with thousands already dead and nothing yet serving to stem the plague's force, Jacques Philippe Othon, young son of an Oranian magistrate, falls desperately ill. The decision is made to administer a new serum. It is unavailing; the boy's dying is torturous and seemingly interminable. Among those at his side are Father Paneloux and Dr. Rieux, prototypes of the Christian and the rebel. Attention to their responses to the death goes far in illustrating the two possible worlds (of grace and of rebellion) of the human mind proposed by Camus in *The Rebel,* and illustrates also two widely divergent interpretations of man's relationship to the physical universe.

A good introduction to the distinction between the worlds of grace and of rebellion as they appear in *The Plague* is found in Camus's reflections, in *The Rebel,* on Ivan Karamazov, who also is confronted with the death of a child. Ivan also must choose between the two worlds: he could in faith accept the death as a mark of God's righteous, if mysterious, ways, or he could in rebellion pronounce both the death and God's ways as unjust and unacceptable. He chooses the latter, simultaneously acknowledging, and determining to rebel against, a created order stained by suffering and evil. In his rebellion he refuses his own salvation:

Ivan incarnates the refusal of salvation. Faith leads to immortal life. But faith presumes the acceptance of the mystery and of evil, and resignation to injustice. The man who is prevented by the suffering of children from accepting faith will certainly not accept eternal life. Under these conditions, even if eternal life existed, Ivan would refuse it. He rejects this bargain. He would accept grace only unconditionally, and that is why he makes his own conditions. Rebellion wants all or nothing.

Father Paneloux does not side with Ivan—or with Dr. Rieux either. The philosophical tension in *The Plague* derives largely from the opposing views of the Jesuit priest and the medical doctor. Paneloux makes the leap of faith which is not the denial of absurdity but a transcending of it; in so doing he represents the Christian response, the philosophical suicide with which Camus long quarreled. And since Camus's convictions about the relationship between man and the physical world gain clarity in his very rejection of the religious position, his portrayal of Paneloux, as well as the many other evidences of his critical interest in Christianity, is, in the context of this chapter, of considerable significance. Nowhere is he more derisive of Christianity than in his caricatures of examining magistrate and prison chaplain in *The Stranger*, written contemporaneously with *The Myth of Sisyphus*, in which the leap of faith is seen primarily as an eluding of a truth which might invite despair, as a negating of reason, as a bypassing of an absurdity which demands confrontation. But Camus recognizes distinctions among Christians, as his unqualifiedly expressed affection and respect for the Resistance journalist and Christian René Leynaud and his candid affection of tone in addressing the Dominicans of the Monastery of Latour-Maubourg clearly show. Asserting to the Dominicans that he shares their revulsion from evil, but not their hope, he proclaims his continuing struggle "against this universe in which children suffer and die." He enumerates some of Christendom's more egregious crimes of omission and commission, warning that if the Church continues to pay only lip service to lofty ideals, then "Christians will live and Christianity will die." It is, indeed, not unusual for individual men to rise well above the lowest common denominators of the institutions they serve. Father Paneloux, I believe, is just such a man. Camus's largely sympathetic portrayal of him (critics are in sharp disagreement on this matter) is perhaps accounted for by the acknowledgment of his essay "Why Spain?" that, in *The Plague*, he "had to do justice to those of . . . [his] Christian friends whom . . . [he] met during the Occupation in a combat that was just."

Paneloux's allegiance to the world of the sacred or of grace is made clear through two sermons, through his response to the young Othon's death, and through his own way of death. The first sermon, delivered some six weeks after the plague's inception, proclaims to the people of Oran that they deserve their calamity, as the Egyptian Pharaoh had deserved his. The Oranians have rested secure in the belief that they can sin as they please, confident that a latter-day repentance will wash them clean. And God, chastising whom he loves, has loosed his wrath that his children may take warning, change their ways, and be receptive to the salvation willed for them. The sermon's conclusion is summed up by the narrator:

Never more intensely than today had he, Father Paneloux, felt the immanence of divine succor and Christian hope granted to all alike. He hoped against hope that, despite all the horrors of these dark days, despite the groans of men and women in agony, our fellow citizens would offer up to heaven that one prayer which is truly Christian, a prayer of love. And God would see to the rest.

Yet Paneloux is set off from Rieux not so much in terms of action as of philosophic or theological belief. The priest goes well beyond the final prescription of his first sermon—to pray and leave the rest to God—and thus refutes Camus's contention in *The Rebel* that "subservience to faith leads to the neglect of deeds." Paneloux's joining one of the sanitary squads and his later work at the quarantine station, probably the most dangerous post of all, bear ample testimony to his active participation in the fight against the plague. On the other hand, nothing shows more clearly the differing metaphysical premises of Rieux and Paneloux than their opposing responses to the death of the child. Rieux leaves the scene of death enraged—at the suffering of the child, at the absurd injustice of the suffering, at Paneloux's acceptance of a scheme of things in which suffering and injustice have their place. To the priest's plea that suffering is revolting because it is beyond human understanding and that men should perhaps love what they cannot understand, Rieux responds as Ivan Karamazov might have: "No, Father. I've a very different idea of love. And until my dying day I shall refuse to love a scheme of things in which children are put to torture." And Paneloux's reply is, at the time, a puzzling one: "Ah, doctor . . . I've just realized what is meant by 'grace.' "

Paneloux's second sermon, preached shortly after his confrontation with Rieux, evinces the deeper reflectiveness growing out of his close exposure to misery and death. Still insistent that all trials work toward the ultimate good of the faithful, he now acknowledges that nothing demands more of an accounting than a child's suffering, the response to which is the very measure and crux of a man's faith. Like Ivan, he finds no room for compromise; faith, like rebellion, demands all or nothing. Since acceptance of a child's death as a justifiable part of the divine order is the utmost test of a man's belief, to accept is to believe everything; to reject, to believe nothing. And acceptance means to Paneloux not merely resignation or humility but the actual willing of the suffering, since it is God's will. The sermon also goes beyond the priest's earlier injunction to offer a prayer and depend on God to "see to the rest." It urges the Oranians to take proper medical precautions, struggle against the pestilence, and do the good they can. They must, in addition, "hold fast, trusting in the divine goodness, even as to the deaths of little children, and not seeking personal respite," and their decision, finally, must be the choice "either to hate God or to love God." Paneloux is calling for a perfection of the will, a surrendering it into harmony with the will of God—even to willing the suffering of children.

From the second sermon we may infer how Paneloux reached his understanding of grace by means of the child's death. Many of the world's events are easily intelligible to the human mind and accepted by it. But there comes an event, most particularly the death of a child, which defies understanding. We stand before it in its mysterious horror, plumb the depths of our minds and hearts, and yet find it absolutely unacceptable, for it makes no sense before any human court of inquiry or justice. So both Ivan Karamazov and Bernard Rieux discovered, and so, importantly, does Father Paneloux. Yet he also discovers that the *unacceptable,* the death of a child, is in fact *acceptable* to him. Out of this paradox he concludes that only an act of God, which is the gift of grace, could have brought him to a position which no act of human will or understanding can attain. That he can accept the *humanly* unacceptable is to him evidence of the *superhuman* grace of God: thus he can believe everything and love God. Relevant is an observation attributed to the religious existentialist Leo Chestov and quoted by Camus in *The Myth of Sisyphus*: "The only true solution [to the greatest dilemmas] . . . is precisely where human judgment sees no solution. Otherwise, what need would we have of God? We turn toward God only to obtain the impossible. As for the possible, men suffice."

Paneloux's faith leads also to his own manner of facing death. Falling ill himself, his quiescence answers negatively the question of an essay he is currently writing, "Is a Priest Justified in Consulting a Doctor?" It is Tarrou who explains why it is illogical for a priest to summon a doctor. From his experience of once knowing a priest who lost his faith through seeing a soldier who had been blinded, Tarrou concludes: "When an innocent youth can have his eyes destroyed, a Christian should either lose his faith or consent to having his eyes destroyed. Paneloux declines to lose his faith, and he will go through with it to the end." Tarrou is correct. Paneloux, suddenly stricken, refuses to avail himself of the medical aid he commended to others. In his dying as in his living, he commends himself to God's grace alone.

Paneloux does not view the plague as evidence of a hostile or an indifferent natural order and does not, like the rebel, "protest against his condition and against the whole of creation." He interprets the plague as a scourge of God necessary in a created order made imperfect by man's sinfulness, and he is led to succor its victims and yet to surrender himself to its sickle, since such is God's will.

IV

Yet *The Plague* is not Paneloux's book, but Rieux's. The doctor is the main protagonist, narrator, and Camus's most fully drawn portrait of the metaphysical rebel, defined as one who *does* protest the human condition and the whole of creation. Rieux's first extended protest against the world's absurd injustice is his conversation with Tarrou after Paneloux's first sermon. Finding no evidence of Paneloux's redemptive God, he sees only some silent cosmic force indifferent to a world order shaped by death and the attendant human anguish. Rieux would fight against this order of things, against the microbe which, as Tarrou later asserts, is the very basis of the natural world. Yet Rieux conceives rebellion not primarily as a negative fighting *against* something, but a positive struggle *for* human dignity and solidarity. *The Plague* is a chronicle of the rebel's endurance, his refusal to bend to the annihilation of physical suicide or the, to him, illusory escape of philosophical suicide. Rieux is the perfect example of a man who acknowledges and confronts the absurd in order to resist it. His struggle is characterized by, as Camus expressed it in *The Myth,* "a total absence of hope (which has nothing to do with despair), a continual rejection (which must not be confused with renunciation), and a conscious dissatisfaction (which must not be compared to immature unrest)."

Rieux affirms twice in *The Plague* that his main aim in life is simply to do his job. Finding the world unacceptable as it is, the rebel's job is to do well the task at which God (if there is a God) has failed, or to fill the vacuum which God's withdrawal has effected. He is not content to infer, with the religious existentialists described in *The Myth,* another life in which the absurdities of this life will be swallowed up in victory. Nor is he willing, like Paneloux, to surrender himself passively to death. Affirming that "the earth remains our first and our last love," the rebel remains attentive only to the here and now. He will become a god to this earth, trying to wrest from its ruins some measure of the good life, an intention made clear through the inferences Camus draws from the metaphysical position of Kirilov, protagonist of Dostoevsky's *The Possessed:* "If God exists, all depends on him and we can do nothing against his will. If he does not exist, everything depends on us. For Kirilov, as for Nietzsche, to kill god is to become god oneself; it is to realize on this earth the eternal life of which the Gospel speaks." Thus a new church is born, an earthly institution without God. When the unbelieving Tarrou confesses to Rieux his desire to become a saint without God, he is perhaps professing allegiance to such a church.

Rieux expresses his sickness of the world, his fondness for his fellows, his contempt for injustice and compromise with the truth. In defining his medical vocation as "fighting against creation as he found it," he gives a wonderfully precise description of the rebel's calling. He rejects the created order as it is and tries to bring a portion of justice and happiness to a world whose collective human agony is to him enraging. Demonstrating, throughout the ten frightful months of the plague, those qualities of endurance, courage, and compassion so dear to Camus himself, he bears witness to a love of life even under the prevailingly desperate conditions. Rieux's doing his job, as he puts it, seemingly without temptation of either physical or philosophical suicide, carries the implication that this life is worth living and possesses its own meaning quite apart from any appeal to immortality.

Rieux's devotion to life is but one example of Camus's many tributes to the beauties and joys of this earth. Typical is *The Myth*'s epigraph from Pindar: "O my soul, do not aspire to immortal life, but exhaust the limits of the possible." Equally life-affirming is the Hölderlin epigraph to *The Rebel*: "And openly I pledged my heart to the grave and suffering land, and often in the consecrated night, I promised to love her faithfully until death, unafraid, with her heavy burden of fatality, and never to despise a single one of her enigmas. Thus did I join myself to her with a mortal cord." The marvelously sensuous essay "Summer in Algiers" proposes that man's greatest sin may lie in his attentiveness to another life and a consequent neglect of "the implacable grandeur" of this one. A memorable paragraph from "The Minotaur" refers to one of Flaubert's friends, whose last words—"Close the window; it's too beautiful"—imply that death's real agony lies in a man's approaching oblivion to the wonders of this earth. And the one phenomenon to which Meursault, the usually indifferent protagonist of *The Stranger*, remains consistently responsive is the beauty of the natural universe. Sensitive as Camus was to the absurd injustices of this life with its death-inducing microbes, he could at the same time love its terrain. In the essay "Return to Tipasa," recording his gratitude for being able "to welcome equally what delights and what crushes," he goes on to say that there "is thus a will to live without rejecting anything of life, which is the virtue I honor most in this world."

Dr. Rieux shares with his literary creator a capacity for delight. Even in the bleak November of the plague, he and Tarrou have their moment of rejoicing. It comes upon them just after Tarrou's autobiographical excursion relating his first direct awareness of the death sentence, his increasing apprehension that the whole world order is based on this sentence, and his decision to side not with the destructive powers but with their victims. Sober as the occasion is, both men realize that not every moment of their lives can be spent fighting the pestilence—indeed, that one reason for fighting it is that those who survive may enjoy both the physical universe and the company of each other. On that November evening joy comes to Rieux and Tarrou through a swim in the waters of Oran's harbor. In spite of the sad tenor of their recent discourse, of the pall that overlies the city, of the air's stale and fetid smell, they find in the rise and fall of the sea, the boundless darkness, and the gnarled rocks a source of strange happiness. They swim in concert, oblivious for the moment, through their oneness with the water and with each other, to the plague's presence. This brief interlude, representing the rebel's life at its best, is a persuasive reminder that death is to be resisted by all of man's powers. Yet the swim, like all earthly happiness, must come to an end, as the microbe, which for Tarrou is at the heart of the natural world, will finally obliterate the last of every man's joys. But even though all men share the ultimate fate of death, each man is measured and judged by the way he lives his few allotted days. A few months after the swim and shortly before the plague's retreat, the dying Tarrou, who seems to have come close to his goal of being "a saint without God," makes clear that there are good ways and bad of fighting a losing battle: "I don't want to die, and I shall put up a fight. But if I lose the match, I want to make a good end of it." His words reflect a sentiment of Obermann, quoted as epigraph of the fourth of Camus's "Letters to a German Friend": "Man is mortal. That may be; but let us die resisting; and if our lot is complete annihilation, let us not behave in such a way that it seems justice!"

Rieux knows that man's utmost resistance can only diminish suffering, not eradicate it, and only delay death, not prevent it. As he listens to the exultant cries which greet the lifting of Oran's quarantine and the uniting of loved ones, he knows that mankind will never enjoy a lasting victory. For though the plague has withdrawn, as plagues have done throughout history, it will lie dormant, certain to return and strike down rats and men again. In "Return to Tipasa" Camus lays claim to a strength which, he writes, "helps me to accept *what is* when once I have admitted that I cannot change it." Rieux possesses the same strength, a lucid recognition of what he believes to be the basic, unalterable conditions under which life must be lived. Acknowledging that he cannot change the fact of the plague and that he must live within the rules of its game and end the loser, he is determined, like Obermann and Tarrou, to make a real fight of it. And in so doing he exemplifies the implacable nobility of the rebel at his best.

We will recall that Paneloux, in his first sermon, interprets the plague as a mode of God's love, summoning Oranians to conviction of sin, repentance, and eternal life. Rieux too sees the plague as a force for good in that, like most catastrophes, it spurs men to transcend their usual selves. Such an elevating influence is found, for example, in the case of the Parisian journalist Raymond Rambert, who, quarantined in Oran far away from his loved one in France, first makes every attempt, legal and illegal, to escape the city. But when it seems, midway through the epidemic, that he can successfully bribe his way out, he decides that his proper place is by Rieux's side, his first business to continue his fight against the pestilence. And the once dull and lusterless M. Othon, the magistrate whose son suffers so miserable a death, chooses after his loss to work in the quarantine camp, where he meets his own death, a better man than he had been before the plague's inception. Nor should the seemingly insignificant Joseph Grand, self-demanding prose stylist, municipal clerk who charts the number of plague deaths, and secretary to Rieux's sanitary squads, be overlooked. Unpromising as he seems for a heroic role, he becomes under the adverse conditions of the pestilence a hero in his unfailing devotion to his self-assigned tasks. Only Cottard behaves abominably under the plague's influence. Cowering in Oran as law's fugitive, he welcomes an epidemic which delays his arrest and makes possible his black-market activity. The plague's end also brings to an end his sanity and his life. But Cottard's behavior is exceptional, serving as foil to the attitudes and actions of the novel's major characters. Under stress of the ten-month catastrophe these characters bear witness to the truth of Rieux's observations that "men are more good than bad," and that "there are more things to admire in men than to despise."

The most beneficent effect of the plague is the solidarity it engenders among those who suffer its presence. If, in Oran, the epidemic leads first to the city's exile from the outside world, it leads then to a solidarity among those of the exiled bound by common rebellion. That Camus views solitude as a miserable ordeal is evident in many of his writings and leads him in one of his political essays to urge a renaissance of that compassionate "feeling for man, without which the world can never be but a vast solitude." Solidarity, on the other hand, is for him the highest human good. It is a condition that may be found between two persons or among many. Rambert exemplifies both aspects, certainly bound to his sweetheart and yet constrained to defer their reunion until the Oranians need his ministrations no longer. And no one is more imbued with a passion for solidarity than Rieux himself. His swim with Tarrou is for both of them evidence of the possible unity between two persons. "Neither had said a word," we are told of them after the event, "but they were conscious of being perfectly at one, and the memory of this night would be cherished by them both." And no one gives more of himself to the stricken community than Rieux. Indeed, nothing is more inspiring in *The Plague* than the solidarity which the collective suffering elicits. Rieux, Tarrou, and Paneloux, despite their differing metaphysical persuasions, have in common their complete giving of themselves to others. Love for other men, whether motivated by grace or rebellion, by divine or humanitarian impulse, would seem on this earth to manifest itself in much the same manner. To observe simply the actions of Rieux and Paneloux, and be deaf to their words, would lead to the belief that their hearts beat almost as one. And their conversation, following upon the death of young Othon and illuminating the wide disparity between their responses to his suffering, ends with Rieux's expressed conviction that what unites them outweighs what divides them: "And whether you wish it or not," he tells the priest, "we're allies, facing them [death and disease] and fighting them together. . . . So you see . . . God Himself can't part us now."

It is remarkable that Camus, in his appraisal of man's condition, can begin where he begins and yet end where he ends. He begins with the fact of absurdity, the conviction that the disparity "between the mind that desires and the world that disappoints" is immense—that the thoughtful man yearns for life, yet knows the inevitability of death; longs for a friendly, solicitous universe, yet senses only its oscillation between indifference and hostility; wishes a distinct humanity, yet observes his mechanical rigidity. Even though we may believe, with Rieux and Sisyphus, that ultimate victory is never ours, Camus calls us to eschew physical suicide and to live without appeal to the leap of faith which graces the religious existentialist. With all this, there is nothing of despair in the literary portraits of Tarrou and Rieux, both of whom share their author's basic metaphysical position. Their conviction of ultimate defeat, far from breeding in them an apathy or a bitterness toward life, persuades them that they must give full devotion to man's only certainty, his brief sojourn on earth. A major distinction between the position of Camus and Rieux and that of men of religious faith is well put in the address to the Dominican monks: "If Christianity is pessimistic as to man, it is optimistic as to human destiny. Well, I can say that, pessimistic as to human destiny, I am optimistic as to man." Camus, with Prometheus, would side with men over the gods. And if he begins with what at first may seem the black despair of absurdity, he ends with an affirmation of the noble heights to which the rebellious man may aspire. Dr. Bernard Rieux is Camus's most inspiring testimony to the grandeur of man. If God is in fact dead, it is comforting to believe that men like Rieux may live.

V

The Plague celebrates the joys which occasionally blossom even in a world where sorrow comes more easily. It affirms that even under an unjust and oppressive order of things, men —individually and in community—may forge their own rich measure of justice and liberty. Whereas Conrad's *Nostromo* makes a strong case for man's collective guilt, *The Plague* largely stresses his collective innocence; and whereas *Nostromo* insinuates a natural order which seems hostile only when provoked, *The Plague* judges that order inherently malignant, its death sentence mysterious, irrational, arbitrary, and certain. *The Plague* is in the mode of Greek tragedy, disclosing the struggle of men against destiny in an action that first arouses and then purges our emotions of pity and fear. The plight of Rieux and his fellow Oranians first excites our pity, and we stand terrified before the fact of a plague which, in its symbolic implications, encompasses a far larger territory than one North African city. But when we discover how men at their best may respond to the worst that can befall them, our painful feelings are expelled. For though we are reminded again that all men must die, we are reminded too that a man may choose how he will traverse the period of his short years toward death, and how he will face death when it comes. When we leave Rieux at the end of his narrative, we know that still to feel pity and fear for him would be sheer presumption. He has advanced beyond our pity, an emotion transformed to awed admiration. And we need no longer fear for a man who has met and stood firm against cataclysmic forces. The reader of *The Plague*, as of an Aristotelian tragedy, having witnessed a man who has confronted destiny with courage and dignity, may put aside his own self-pity and fear and be humbly proud to be a man.

The Plague answers affirmatively a question posed in *The Rebel:* whether it is "possible to find a rule of conduct outside the realm of religion and its absolute values." If a man chooses, or is chosen for, the world of rebellion rather than the world of grace, he will find a noble and inspiring call to life in *The Plague*. The microbe may be the most persistent fact of the natural order, and man's rebellion, no matter how rigorously pursued, will finally fall to its poison. But what a grand fight unfolds along the way; in its majesty lies the rebel's hope.

"For Everything There Is a Season"

*Everything has its time.**

"Health and illness, that is the difference."

"I thought—I thought—there was nothing else coming."

"When the house is finished, death comes."

I

In October of 1835 the Buddenbrook family and a few close relatives and friends, celebrating a housewarming party at their new home on Meng Street, paused in the dinner conversation, "while the company looked down at their plates and pondered on the fortunes of the brilliant family who had built and lived in the house and then, broken and impoverished, had left it." The Ratenkamp family, at the height of their business success late in the seventeenth century, had built the house, but their firm had over the years undergone a gradual deterioration, culminating, just two decades before the present party, in Dietrich Ratenkamp's disastrous choice

---

* *Buddenbrooks* by Thomas Mann, translated by H. T. Lowe-Porter (New York: Alfred A. Knopf, 1924). Renewal copyright 1952 by Alfred A. Knopf, Inc. Reprinted by permission of the publisher. The novel was first published in 1901.

of a business partner. The firm ruined and the family broken, their house passed on to the Buddenbrooks, whose turn it now is for fortune's smile. The Johann Buddenbrook who, in 1768, founded the prosperous grain business of his family, is dead, but the three living generations of the family are present: the son of the founder, also Johann, a vigorous, high-spirited man in his seventies who guides the firm with wonderfully confident assurance; his son and business partner, the consul Johann, in his forties; and the consul's three children—Tom, who is nine or ten; Antonie, eight; Christian, seven. The Buddenbrooks have not only replaced the Raten-kamps as residents of Meng Street, but, more importantly, supplanted them at the top of fortune's slowly turning wheel. For such, Thomas Mann's *Buddenbrook*s would seem to affirm, is the way of some mysterious but certain cosmic or historical devolution and evolution.

Buddenbrooks is the grand, massive chronicle of the fall of the family and firm of Buddenbrook, a fall which, as with the Ratenkamps, apparently nothing—not even the tragically noble resistance of the later, adult Thomas Buddenbrook—could stay. In the course of the novel we come sadly to learn that, as the Ratenkamps gave way to the Buddenbrooks, so, only decades after the housewarming party, the Buddenbrooks give way to their parvenu rivals, the Hagenströms, who, comfortably settled in the same Meng Street house in the 1870s, may well with their dinner guests have paused and pondered the fortunes and misfortunes of the once brilliant Buddenbrooks who had lived in the house, left it, and fallen to death and decay. There might even be a trilogy—*Ratenkamps, Buddenbrooks, Hagenströms*—and the series could go on. But one novel suffices, for in the Buddenbrook family portrait we find what is to Mann the life process, the ever-recurring cycle of rise and decline. *Buddenbrooks,* like most of Mann's writings including *The Magic Mountain* and the best of the short stories, has about it the odor of mortality, not simply of individuals but of family and firm, the three being inextricably bound. When the novel's action ends in the autumn of 1877, forty-two years after its beginning, there is no one left to perpetuate the name of Buddenbrook and the firm has been liquidated. The pattern of decline is seen even in the life spans of the male Buddenbrooks. The elder Johann lives into his seventies; his son the consul dies at about sixty; Thomas at about fifty; Hanno, son of Thomas and last frail family hope, at sixteen. The undependable, hypochondriacal Christian simply does not count.

To contrast the robust, patriarchal Johann of Part 1 of the novel with the dying Hanno of Part 11 is to know in its fullness the family's decline. The early chapters also let go certain straws in the wind which presage the fall to come, straws seen largely in differences of attitude between Johann and the younger members of his family, particularly his dreamier, more serious, more pious son, the consul. Johann knows how to direct the course of life's events through his strong, though by no means unattractive will, knows how to act decisively and put first things first. Impatient with expenditures of time and effort on matters unrelated to family comfort and business prosperity, he refuses to be distracted from these goals by immoderate interest in other things—in religion, for example, or in knowledge for its own sake, or in the arts. He gently chides Tony's sober catechetical struggle and is annoyed by her, to him, time-wasting effort to distinguish between the effects of thunder and lightning. Certainly he must have been uneasy with the consul's religious sentimentality and would doubtless have given little encouragement, had he lived to know them, to Tom's later ecstatic reflections on death and immortality. Though he plays on the flute that "airy, charming little melody" which cheers his guests, he would have judged insidious and debilitating the passion for music which later inspires his great-grandson Hanno. But it is in his persistent, if on the whole mild, disagreements with his son that we find the most marked evidence of the change in generations. When the consul, reflecting on Dietrich Ratenkamp's

calamitous selection of a business partner, assigns the choice
to "fate," "destiny," "inexorable necessity," Johann, convinced
that man is master of fate, abruptly cuts off his son's musings.
He affirms the greatness of Napoleon, who to the consul was
a butcher. The consul's "practical ideals" are to him sentimental dreams. The elder Johann wishes to impress his will
even upon his garden by giving it formal order and shape,
while his son holds a very different view: "I have a feeling that
I belong to nature and not she to me." And when the consul
calls upon God's help, Johann shows a distinct preference for
his own. Johann is a forthright, independent, self-willed merchant, confident in his control over life's flow and faithful to
the admonition of his father: "My son, attend with zeal to thy
business by day; but do none that hinders thee from thy sleep
by night."

Johann is a worthy successor to the best of the Ratenkamps, but his family, following his death, gradually loses itself in the reflectiveness that breeds indecision and the love
of the arts that breeds decay. The fall of the Buddenbrooks
is the product of many immediate factors, among them faulty
judgment, sheer bad luck, unsalutary marriages, a change in
the cultural tradition with its movement from burgher to
bourgeois values. Yet all of them are part of a cosmic plan
decreeing that, though not all families know moments of
glory, those who do will inevitably come to know moments of
bitter, sorrowful defeat. *Buddenbrooks* is not a novel of discrete individuals, each fending for himself and going his own
way, but of a family, the actions of each of whose members are
felt by the whole. And viewed from the reader's Olympian
vantage point, it is a novel in which the family does not act
so much as it is acted upon. The book's dramatic action is the
Buddenbrook struggle—comic, tragic, and pathetic by turns—
against the same relentless forces that felled the Ratenkamps
before them and will fell the Hagenströms after them. At the
center of the action—or passion—are Johann's grandchildren:
Thomas, Antonie, Christian.

I I

Nowhere in literature or life, I believe, can there be found a person of stronger family loyalty than Tony Buddenbrook. There is hardly an action she takes of which she could not say, "I owe that to my family and the firm," words which she does say—it matters little about what—while still a schoolgirl. And for her, to be for means also to be against: fidelity to the Buddenbrooks means also a fight, a losing one, to the finish against the upstart Hagenströms. The pathos of her entire life springs from her misguided zeal for family, her readiness to allow what is mistakenly deemed the Buddenbrook welfare to prevail against her better intuitive judgment. She presents herself as a willing sacrifice to family and firm, as her two marriages so well exemplify.

Nothing is more determinative in directing the adult course of Tony's life than her marriage to that unctuous, obsequious fraud Herr Bendix Grünlich, whose first visit to the Buddenbrooks on a June afternoon in 1845 is drawn with a Dickensian precision and flavor. During this meeting and ensuing ones, Tony's every instinct rebels against her repulsive suitor, but her wise resistance to his entreaties to marry him and, more importantly, to her father's near insistence that she do so finally collapses. The successive evocations to surrender are clearly marked. Early in the courtship Tony reflects that her marriage should be "commensurate with the position of the family and the firm." Her mother, echoing her father, defines the proposed liaison as "exactly the marriage which duty and vocation prescribe." And Tom, in mistaken belief that Grünlich is wealthy, mounts the attack on Tony by enumerating the recent Hagenström successes and then saying to her: "If you want to balance the scale with the Hagenströms, you'd better marry Grünlich." It seems, briefly, as if Tony's idyllic weeks at Travemünde and her tender affection for the poor and idealistic young medical student Morten Schwarzkopf may put off disaster. But the consul, to whom Tony writes of her hopes with Morten, knows exactly how and where to apply the pressure. "We are not," he replies, "free, separate, and independent entities, but like links in a chain, and we could not by any means be what we are without those who went before us and showed us the way, by following the straight and narrow path, not looking to right or left." The simile of links and chains is decisive. With it in mind Tony, upon her return home, opens the large copybook that chronicles from the sixteenth century the family fortunes and misfortunes, accidents and illnesses, births and marriages and deaths, and she inscribes on its pages the record of her betrothal, on September 22, 1845, to Herr Grünlich, imagined a strong link for the Buddenbrook chain. A few months later, as the consul is bidding farewell to his daughter and newly acquired son-in-law at the beginning of their wedding trip, Tony leans over to her father and, in a few whispered words, implies the whole reason for and basis of her marriage: "Are you satisfied with me?"

Neither the consul's initial satisfaction nor the birth of Erica Grünlich is sufficient to sustain the marriage. With the eventual discovery that Grünlich's poor management has led him to insolvency and that he had married largely for the substantial attendant dowry with which to see him out of his prior financial difficulties, Tony decides to leave her husband. Of the many reasons for doing so, none is more persuasive than her father's testimony that to bail Grünlich out of his present difficulties would be detrimental to the Buddenbrook firm. As for the firm's sake she was willing to marry, for its sake she is willing to divorce. But the disastrous effects of that first marriage extend well beyond its four-year duration. An unsuccessful union, Tony believes, is a blot on the family escutcheon, and amendment lies only in a second, and this time successful one. It is a fateful trip to Munich which brings her into the company of the gauche Herr Alois Permaneder, who has little to recommend him to her except his familiarity with the name of the Buddenbrook firm and his speaking of it in terms of respect. Permaneder, who would once have elicited only Tony's ridicule, now is seen by her as the link so necessary for her family chain. As she confides to her former governess, Ida Jungmann, "This engagement to Alois . . . isn't really a question of my happiness at all. I am making this second marriage with my eyes open, to make good the mistake of my first one, as a duty which I owe our name." Permaneder, unfortunately, thinks considerably less of her name, as he finally shows in climaxing an argument by calling her a "filthy sprat-eating slut," thus bringing to an end two years of a marriage which occasioned Tony few joys. And as the years pass, it becomes increasingly evident that the first meeting with Grünlich sparked a whole series of repercussions which blight Tony's life. Had the Buddenbrooks but known, the name Tony Schwarzkopf might have served them better, almost certainly much longer.

In its consistency, Tony's ill fortune brings the reader close to tedium and annoyance. But if we come to learn, from the entrance of Grünlich into her life, that fortune always works against her, we learn too of her striking powers of adaptability and recuperation. At times, it is true, she resembles nothing more than a chameleon, particularly as she rather sententiously repeats through years of her life Morten's earlier expressed views on the nutritive benefits of honey, on the triviality of the popular and conservative German newspapers, on the idiocy and wretchedness of the nobility. At other times, however, she goes well beyond the chameleonlike, showing what seems a near-stoic strength. From her two unhappy marriages, as from that of her daughter Erica; from the sale of her precious Meng Street home—and to the Hagenströms at that; from the liquidation of the Buddenbrook firm; and from the steady parade of family deaths, each successive one more agonizing than the last—from all of these Tony bounds back with remarkable resilience. She has the rare ability to savor each new condition in life as it comes to her, a trait sometimes seeming to bespeak a docile shallowness, but more often a capacity to accept what she cannot change. Hateful as Grünlich's advances are, Tony derives from the role of sought-after an exhilarating sense of importance. Unpleasing as the dissolutions of her marriages are, she plays to the hilt the role of experienced divorcée who, as she never tires of saying, is no longer the silly goose that she was. Saddening as the family deaths are, she feels a warm sense of prominence as she helps make funeral arrangements and later takes part in settlement of the estate. The role itself, through the playing of which she would make a weighty impression on others as on herself, is both removed from the gravity of the life situation and more real to her than reality itself. The reason for her predictable responses is, I think, made clear. If the elder Johann saw himself as director of life's actions, and the consul was disposed to see God as prime mover, Tony looks to neither herself nor to God, but to the corporate entity of family.

Her strongly developed family sense [we are told] was instinctively hostile to conceptions of free will and self-development; it inclined her rather to recognize and accept her own characteristics wholesale, with fatalistic indifference and toleration. She had, unconsciously, the feeling that any trait of hers, no matter of what kind, was a family tradition and therefore worthy of respect.

Nothing could better account for Tony's wholehearted fidelity (with, admittedly, its moments of foolishness) to the center of her world.

As the novel ends in the autumn of 1877 the few remaining Buddenbrooks gather once again, this time to know that there is a wealth of sad retrospect, but little in prospect for them. And it is the fifty-year-old Antonie Buddenbrook Grünlich Permaneder who plays the major role in perpetuating the memory of a past splendor. She will continue to play hostess to the family remnant, and they will continue to read, but only nostalgically, from the notebook recording the rise and fall of some three centuries of Buddenbrooks. The overflowing abundance of loyalty and good will which Tony has always possessed has not been enough to sustain the House of Buddenbrook, which must go the way of all houses. For every dynasty must fall, one differing from others only in terms of its own peculiar road to decay. Tony's disappointed hopes are perfectly mirrored in a brief parabolic tale she tells Morten Schwarzkopf during her blissful Travemünde visit in 1845, and which she repeats about thirty years later to little Hanno: "I used to be frightfully stupid, you know," she tells Morten. "I wanted the bright star out of the jelly-fish, so I brought a lot home in my pocket-handkerchief and put them on the balcony, to dry in the sunshine. When I looked at them again, of course there was just a big wet spot that smelled of seaweed."

III

If Tony is not one to sustain family prosperity and prestige, her brother Christian, whose talents are those of mimic, raconteur, and bon vivant, is far less able to do so. Of the stability necessary for business success he knows nothing; his innumerable psychophysical ailments, whether real or imagined, prevent him from putting in a good month's work at any time in his life. His tactlessness is profound, as he is forever in the wrong places with the wrong people and saying the wrong thing. When his self-pity is not overriding, he wins the reader's pity, as he on occasion gives evidence of a sweet and thoughtful disposition that gains him little in his society. To his brother Tom, who is constantly financing his business failures and bohemian tastes, Christian is a persistent thorn. His unorthodox actions and careless words are constant threats to the firm's good name and lead Tom, in one of their many and inevitable arguments, to brand him "a growth, a fester, on the body of our family." Going his own errant way, Christian, after fathering the third of Aline Puvogel's illegitimate children, marries her and is shortly thereafter committed to an asylum.

I V

In the fall of 1875 a weary, nerve-racked Thomas Buddenbrook, mere months from his death, is urged by his doctor to seek rest at Travemünde, where he is occasionally visited by Tony. At one autumn twilight as they gaze seaward, Tom tells his sister that his younger preference for mountain over sea has changed and that a person reveals much of himself through his ways of viewing each:

The real difference is in the look with which one pays homage to the one and to the other. It is a strong, challenging gaze, full of enterprise, that can soar from peak to peak; but the eyes that rest on the wide ocean and are soothed by the sight of its waves rolling on forever, mystically, relentlessly, are those that are already wearied by looking too deep into the solemn perplexities of life.—Health and illness, that is the difference. The man whose strength is unexhausted climbs boldly into the lofty multiplicity of the mountain heights. But it is when one is worn out with turning one's eyes inward upon the bewildering complexity of the human heart, that one finds peace in resting them on the wideness of the sea.

Thomas had not always been bound to the sea, and it is his struggle to stay with the mountains that gives to *Buddenbrooks* its tragic dimension. He is the novel's pivotal character in that the Buddenbrook future lies in his capacity to manage the firm and to provide the male heir who may succeed him in this task. Thus it is he who, to a degree unparalleled by the other members of his family, pits himself against the destroying cosmic forces which turn fortune's wheel. More than this, Thomas, to a larger degree than anyone else, is conscious of what is transpiring and of his own precise and painful place in the disintegrating process. He possesses neither the inherent strength of his grandfather (whose vitality enabled him to the end of his life to climb "the lofty multiplicity of the mountain heights") nor the sustaining support of sister, brother, wife, or son. Tony is quite correct when, toward the end of 1859, after returning home from the fiasco with Permaneder, she tells her brother: "You must go on alone now. . . . There's nothing good to be looked for from Christian, and I am finished. . . . Now you stand quite alone, and upon you it depends to keep up the honour and dignity of the family. May God help you in the task."

It seems, over the course of the next few years, that Tony's hopes are well founded. In mid-1856, Tom had met Fräulein Gerda Arnoldsen, a stunning woman and superb musician, one of Tony's schoolmates of a decade and a half earlier. The dowry which graced their marriage early in 1857 was substantial, enough, in Tom's judgment, to make Hermann Hagenström blink, and certainly markedly to increase the capital of the Buddenbrook firm. In the spring of 1861 the anxiously awaited male heir is born. To this personal felicity is added a singular civic and political honor, Thomas's election early in 1862 to a senatorship, a post whose eminence exceeds that won by any former Buddenbrook and, importantly, an election in which his defeated rival is the rising Hermann Hagenström. The firm, to whose control Thomas had succeeded in the mid-1850s and brought "a fresher and more enterprising spirit," is by the early 1860s enjoying a business "as brilliant as ever it had been in his grandfather's day." Such success leads the senator in 1863 to lay plans for the building of the most luxurious home for miles around. When in June of 1864 Tom, Gerda, and son Hanno (christened Johann) move into their elaborate mansion on Fishers' Lane, it seems as if an earlier prophecy of Tony's has indeed come true. At the end of the christening party for the long-awaited infant Johann in the spring of 1861, Tony had remarked to Tom: "It has been a lovely day, Tom. I am happier than I have been for years. We Buddenbrooks aren't quite at the last gasp yet, thank God, and whoever thinks we are is mightily mistaken. Now that we have little Johann—it is so beautiful that he is christened

Johann—it looks to me as if quite a new day will dawn for us all!" The "new day," however, is but specious and short-lived. The gods who rule over *Buddenbrooks* have their little jests.

Tom's failure, despite his frequently manful resistance, is ordained. In the first place, he lacks the sustaining energy necessary to meet the endless demands of business and civic duties. "Health and illness," as he tells Tony, "that is the difference." We are constantly apprised of his own poor health —of his bad teeth from childhood, of nervousness, hemorrhages, and chills while still in his twenties. At thirty-seven he begins to lose "his elasticity"; at forty-three he is "an old, worn-out man"; at forty-eight he begins to feel the approach of death, to come two years later. He sets himself rigidly against every evidence of physical decline. He is always a stickler for convention and respectability, and "his first law," we are told, is "to preserve 'the *dehors.*' " Yet his scrupulous attention to dress, largely a matter of propriety in his earlier years, becomes increasingly a method of veiling the growing decay of his body. Just as he constantly masks his real feelings through tense, unrelaxed control of facial muscles, so does he belie his wretched physical health by most careful devotion to wardrobe. His dressing room comes to harbor more and more of his waking hours as he is bent, whatever the cost in time and effort, on staying, if not physical decline itself, at least its advertisement to the outside world. He is only in his mid-forties when juxtaposition of his descending business fortunes and ascending personal fastidiousness leads to the sad, witty jest that "Thomas Buddenbrook's function on 'Change . . . [is] now largely decorative!'

Not only does Tom lack the physical energy to pursue his desired ends; he receives little help from his family. As we have seen, Tony, despite every effort, can furnish only moral support, with Christian failing even in that virtue. Gerda brings not only wealth and beauty into the Buddenbrook family, but two other qualities—a disposition to illness and a passion for music—both disastrous. The blue shadows around her eyes, presaging the headaches and vapors which are constantly to assail her, make it clear that the Buddenbrook lineage will not gain from her the physical vitality so desperately needed. Of her exceptional musical talents Grandfather Johann would have disapproved, as Tom himself later comes to do. She, and even more particularly her son Hanno, who shares her devotion to music, are fine evidence of a trend noted by Tonio Kröger, protagonist of one of Mann's most brilliant short stories: "The kingdom of art increases and that of health and innocence declines on this earth." As Tom quickly ages, Gerda, despite her physical lassitude, remains virtually unchanged. Never close to her husband, she finally brings him to agony through her musical afternoons with Herr Lieutenant von Throta. In Gerda Tom finds little of the helpmate. Nor does she produce for him an heir who will eventually lighten his burdens.

Hanno inherits his father's bad teeth, his mother's blue shadows and passion for music. He nearly dies at birth, finds mere survival a struggle throughout his infancy, is slow to walk and to talk. He never acquires either the strength or the taste for the usual round of daily living and, as a young boy, carries his timorous, unhappy waking life into his dreams. Once, as Tony stood over the restlessly sleeping child, "from time to time a pained expression mounted over the little face, beginning with a trembling of the chin, making the lips and the delicate nostrils quiver and the muscles of the narrow forehead contract. The long dark eyelashes did not hide the blue shadows that lay in the corners of the eyes." He is only eight when he comes upon the family notebook and finds it opened at the family tree. He sees his own name, the last on the list, picks up a ruler and pen, and draws a double line across the page. When his father later upbraids him for his action, Hanno replies with the wisdom of babes and sucklings: "I thought—I thought—there was nothing else coming." But Tom, deaf to such wisdom and slow to understand that his son is simply unable to engage life, wages a desperately losing battle to make of Hanno a worthy heir. He tries to transform him from passion for music to interest in business, forever seeking to bend him from his natural inclinations and to redirect his way. In time Tom, coming to represent to his son all those expectations which the young boy cannot fulfill, serves as constant and dreaded reminder to Hanno of his limitations, his falling short of the kind of person his father would have him be. Hanno is bullied by Tom at home, by his teachers at school, by the Hagenström boys at play. His dying of typhoid fever in his sixteenth year is physically agonizing, but at least it is the last agony.

There is every outer evidence that Tom reaches his peak of success in the years 1856–64, from the time of his meeting Gerda to their moving into the new house on Fishers' Lane. Yet no one of the happy prospects of those years fulfills its imagined promise. Gerda never becomes a Buddenbrook in more than name and Hanno is not destined to carry on that name. The senatorship, prestigious as it is, is a terrible drain on Tom's already low energy. He forever regrets the building of his expensive house which, he feels, heralded the beginning of various business reversals. More than this, he is perceptive enough to realize that what might be considered as his two major achievements—the thriving business and the election to the Senate, both in the early 1860s—are not really his at all, but are indebted to the momentum given by earlier generations.

As early as 1858 Thomas confesses to his barber friend Herr Wenzel, who has just complimented him on a speech to the Assembly: "I can only be grateful that my Father, Grandfather, and great-Grandfather prepared the way for me, and that I inherited so much of the respect and confidence they received from the town; for without it I could not move as I am now able to." A few years later Thomas's senatorial victory over Hermann Hagenström is attributed not only to certain inherent abilities but to the Buddenbrook tradition, clearly on the wane, which he inherits. Hagenström has no "tradition" in the sense of past roots. He is honored for his own intrinsic powers; for his success in pushing ahead, even if at times with elbows more than with courtesy; for his open-minded flexibility. The narrator is quite explicit on this point: "Thomas Buddenbrook's prestige was of a different kind [from Hagenström's]. People honoured in him not only his own personality, but the personalities of his father, grandfather, and great-grandfather as well: quite apart from his own business and public achievement, he was the representative of a hundred years of honourable tradition."

Nothing more poignantly conveys Tom's sense of his own failure, of his ushering out rather than ushering in an illustrious family, than a conversation he has with Tony in July, 1864, a month after he, Gerda, and the three-year-old Hanno moved into their new home. It is the conversation of a tired man, one who already would prefer the vista of the sea to a vista of the mountains. He avers that pleasure has left his life, that he feels older than his years, and that, confronted by the mounting urgency of business affairs, he is losing his grip, is inadequate to his task. He defines success—the very kind, incidentally, that Grandfather Johann knew so well—as a man's consciousness that he is, through his own existence, exerting pressure on the life about him, as a man's conviction that he can adapt life to his own ends. But for Tom such inner power is ebbing; his influence is giving way to the more magnetic attraction of Hagenström. Seeing himself in a grievous, humiliating role, that of the beginning of the end, Tom concludes his painful discourse to Tony:

Often and often, in these days, I have thought of a Turkish proverb; it says, "When the house is finished, death comes." It doesn't need to be death. But the decline, the falling-off, the beginning of the end. You know, Tony . . . when Hanno was christened, you said: "It looks as if quite a new life would dawn for us all!" I can still hear you say it, and I thought then that you were right, for I was elected Senator, and was fortunate in my business, and this house seemed to spring up out of the ground. But the "Senator" and this house are superficial after all. I know, from life and from history, something you have not thought of: often, the outward and visible material signs and symbols of happiness and success only show themselves when the process of decline has already set in. The outer manifestations take time—like the light of that star up there, which may in reality be already quenched, when it looks to us to be shining its brightest.

The "house," not only Tom's new one on Fishers' Lane, but the considerably older House of Buddenbrook, *is* nearly finished, and the decline has set in. The firm's success in the early 1860s and Tom's election to the Senate are but outward and visible signs of a power which was at its height some three or four decades earlier, when Grandfather Johann presided over the Buddenbrook fortunes, moved into the Meng Street house, and, at the time of the housewarming, showed what a star is like when it truly shines at its brightest. Tom, on the other hand, lives largely on reflected glory, with even this soon to be extinguished. Given the philosophy of history out of which the novel is conceived, the Buddenbrook family, having risen to an impressive success, must sooner or later fall. And as various members of the family were sustaining links in its rise, so various other members—beginning with Consul Johann, father of the three children—are contributing links to its fall. When the consul dies in 1855, his children, hopefully with the help of their spouses and, later, their own children, are left to carry on. Of the lot Tom alone, and he only through the grimmest of efforts, can delay the evil day. In his growing recognition of his predicament and willing determination to do battle against it, Tom becomes a tragic, not merely pathetic, protagonist.

Tom recognizes in himself a conflict between two natures, the practical and the aesthetic, which can live together but temporarily and even then only under the most uneasy terms. He is a microcosmic reflection of Mann's view that the worlds of business and of art are mutually antagonistic, just as the generations of Buddenbrooks, in their succession, substantiate Tonio Kröger's observation that health gives way to art. We find Tom in his mid-twenties writing to his mother of his courtship of Gerda and pleased to note that he can hold his own with her in discussions of painting and literature, if not music. A dozen years later he reflects with nostalgic yearning on his three preceding male generations, knowing that they "were practical men, more naturally, more vigorously, more impeccably practical than he was himself." It is not that Tom is totally lacking in business acumen, but that it simply does not embrace his whole nature or sit on him so comfortably as it did on his ancestors. And throughout his adult years, the presence of Christian persistently evidences the danger of giving way to the lure of the impractical. Christian embodies those qualities which Tom sets himself to eschew: excessive preoccupation with the arts, especially music and the theater, and an intensive preoccupation with self leading to hypochondria and lack of manly self-control. Even before his marriage Tom makes clear to Tony his antipathy to Christian's ways and his own determination to avoid them:

I have thought a great deal about this curious and useless self-preoccupation, because I had once an inclination to it myself. But I observed that it made me unsteady, hare-brained, and incapable— and control, equilibrium, is, at least for me, the important thing. There will always be men who are justified in this interest in themselves, this detailed observation of their own emotions; poets who can express with clarity and beauty their privileged inner life, and thereby enrich the emotional world of other people. But the likes of us are simple merchants, my child; our self-observations are decidedly inconsiderable. We can sometimes go so far as to say that the sound of orchestra instruments gives us unspeakable pleasure, and that we sometimes do not dare try to swallow [both references to Christian]—but it would be much better, deuce take it, if we sat down and accomplished something, as our fathers did before us.

Tom's frequently frenzied reactions to Christian's indolence spring not only from disgust with his brother's ways and the possibility of their bringing scandal to family and firm, but also from his constant fear of becoming more like his brother. Some years after the above-quoted remarks to Tony, when he and Christian are in that violent, distasteful argument about the division of their mother's estate, Tom admits how deeply his own, often bitter, words and actions have been but reactions to Christian. "I have become what I am," he tells his younger brother, "because I did not want to become what you are. If I have inwardly shrunk from you, it has been because I needed to guard myself—your being, and your existence, are a danger to me—that is the truth."

Tom's adult life is a lonely battle. There is no one within the firm to whom he can turn for any substantial business help; and with the exception of Tony, who is at least sympathetic, there is no one within his family to whom he can turn for personal solace. He can chide Christian—without result; he can seek to transform Hanno—also without result. With Gerda he can only remain silent as she loses herself in her music and the company of Herr von Throta. The consequence is the building of a terrible inner pressure which, except for occasional confessions to Tony and fulminations against Christian, has no release. That Tom retains the control he does over his near-bursting emotional agony is in itself a remarkable feat. Finally, reaching his late forties and the realization that little more is to be expected of this life, he senses that it is time to prepare himself for another one. Never moved by the orthodox faith of his parents, he has, up to this time, rested in the belief that he will, after physical death, live on in his descendants, as his ancestors live on in him. But now he questions the accuracy of such a belief, indeed even its desirability, for Hanno is a weak vessel to hold his father's immortality. By chance he comes one day upon a book whose chapter "On Death, and Its Relation to Our Personal Immortality" serves, briefly at least, as a catharsis for all the pressures, fears, and anxieties that have harassed his recent years. Under the essay's immediate, hypnotic spell Thomas feels the ecstasy of what is to him a revealed truth hitherto undreamed of by him: life is eternal, and death, far from being an end or dissolution or mere living on in the still living, is the greatest of joys, a putting off of a physical frame which is but an encumbrance and a taking on of a freedom and bliss unimagined in this earthly

life. Death is a passing not into a son, but into all those blessed
ones who have ever lived and died. The Thomas who goes on
to reflect upon the redemptive words bears little resemblance
to the man whose nearly half century of life has been spread
before us:

Have I ever hated life—pure, strong, relentless life? Folly and mis-
conception! I have but hated myself, because I could not bear it.
I love you, I love you all, you blessed, and soon, soon, I shall cease
to be cut off from you all by the narrow bonds of myself; soon will
that in me which loves you be free and be in and with you—in and
with you all.

That Tom's instant conversion is the product of desperation seems likely. The ecstatic moments, moreover, are short,
the essay never reread. Thomas, not one long to forget his
earthly responsibilities, returns from spiritual reverie to practical business: he draws up his will. And shortly thereafter,
while immaculately dressed in accordance with that strict law
of his life to keep up appearances, he is felled by a stroke in the
public streets, his blood soon mingling with the mud and slush
of the wet pavement. It is the final humiliating irony, a man
of lifelong personal fastidiousness making his last public appearance lying bloodied in a gutter. Thomas, fortunately,
apparently never regains the consciousness to share this knowledge. With him dies the firm, liquidated through the terms of
his will after something over a century of life. And but a year
or so later, in the spring of 1877, death comes to the sixteen-
year-old Hanno. In the following autumn, forty-two years after
the Meng Street housewarming which showed the Buddenbrooks at the height of health and prosperity, the novel ends,
as the small remnant of a once great family meets to dream of
a great past.

V

Thomas Mann's *Buddenbrooks* shares with Conrad's *Nostromo*
and Camus's *The Plague* the theme of man's yearnings being

thwarted by natural forces. Of the three authors Conrad alone would seem to hold man largely responsible for his disappointments and downfall, as mankind upsets the world's balance by unrestrainedly encroaching on nature's proper domain, going beyond a proper stewardship and moving to tyrannic usurpation of the natural order of creation. Camus, on the other hand, sees man primarily as innocent victim, destroyed by the absurd injustice of a hostile or an indifferent universe, and yet, at his best, fighting his assailant to his own last breath. Thomas Mann is somewhat more relaxed than either Conrad or Camus. He neither, on the one hand, sees men as unrestrained trespassers upon a natural order; nor, on the other, views them as victims of a deliberately malignant order. Perhaps the most precise expression of his view is contained in the words of the consul, Tom's father, at the housewarming party in 1835: "I have a feeling that I belong to nature and not she to me." The actions and passions of Mann's characters, some fortunate and others not, seem governed by a historical or natural determinism, a cyclical process through which families and firms move from dust to dust. The Buddenbrooks, like the Ratenkamps before them and the Hagenströms after them, rise out of nothingness, enjoy a fine burst of creative activity, and then fall again into nothingness. The fortunate are blessed with practical acumen, healthful energy, worldly success; the unfortunate are plagued by devotion to the arts, enervating sickness, a fading from the scene. In some mysterious way the beginning of every distinguished family contains the seeds of its own gradually begotten destruction.

In *Buddenbrooks* it is Thomas who suffers the main brunt of the turning of fortune's wheel. Grandfather Johann is the button of fortune's cap; Tony's response to life's vicissitudes is summed up by variations on the theme of her words, "It *is to be!*" Hanno, it seems, welcomes the end of his struggle. Thomas alone offers resistance to a decline which Johann predates, Tony accepts, and Hanno embraces. He is most aware of his family's deteriorating condition and of his role within it. Modestly equipped as he is to do battle, he does the most that any man can do: he makes the best of what he has. Thomas Mann, in the great family novel which is *Buddenbrooks,* is asserting a philosophy of both history and man. His greatest sympathy and affection are with the man who, finding himself at the most crucial moment of fortune's descent, rallies his best forces in a losing battle. In *Buddenbrooks* that man is Thomas Buddenbrook.

Introduction

Since novels, like plays, habitually present men in action, and almost invariably in action with other men, we may ask if the heading "Man and Other Men" serves any categorizing purpose. I think it does. For in fiction at least, the prime mover or movers of a protagonist's action and passion are not always other men. Joyce's Stephen Dedalus and Sartre's Antoine Roquentin are cases in point. Both men, it is true, are in varying degrees affected by other persons and affect them in turn. Yet in their respective novels each makes his own way in relative independence of other individual persons. Stephen is in constant interaction with Irish culture and Roquentin with French bourgeois society, yet neither experiences any enduring human relationship. Each looks within himself to determine that calling which will enable him to fly by his inhibiting nets or to rise above his Nausea. Even Ellison's invisible man, so persistently confronted by hostile persons representing various American power structures, is chiefly motivated by a determination to find his own nature; he too looks inward in order to discover a subsequent action proper to him.

Nor is the first cause of human action in *Nostromo, The Plague,* or *Buddenbrooks* a man's relationship with other men. In *Nostromo* the obsession with San Tomé, for whatever reason, determines more than anything else the comings and goings of men. And had Dr. Rieux not found the physical universe unacceptable, he would not have become the rebellious doctor, "fighting against creation as he found it," a rebellion which in turn led to his sense and practice of solidarity with other men. Even Thomas Buddenbrook, protagonist of a novel which in some ways seems to place greatest emphasis on the interplay of human relationships, is finally moved not so much by other men as by the inexorable flow of historical cycles.

To a greater extent than any other twentieth-century novelist D. H. Lawrence, I believe, conceives characters who move or are moved almost exclusively in conjunction with other persons, usually with one other person (at a time, at least) and usually with one of the opposite sex. The Lawrence protagonist does not concentrate on introspective guidance to the extent of a Dedalus or a Roquentin. And even though his being in or out of step with a certain cosmic harmony is a matter of considerable importance, he is not seen as one whose fate is largely determined by anything resembling the lure of silver, or a germ, or a historical determinism. To Lawrence relationships among men are of supreme importance. Of *The Rainbow* and of the novels of George Orwell and Virginia Woolf to be discussed in this section, I will say more in a moment.

How can we distinguish among human relationships or pass judgment upon any one of them? Can it be said that one is better, more desirable, more gratifying than another? If so, what is the measure of a good or a bad relationship? A safe beginning is to affirm that the most cherished is that embodying a mutuality of love between or among persons. The main alternative to a person's loving another is not his hating another but his loving himself. Self-love leads, inevitably, to self-serving—or, perhaps more precisely, to seeing the function of others as that of serving one's own self. "Love does not insist," St. Paul wrote to the Corinthians, "on its own way." Self-love does insist on its own way; it is assertive, expressing itself not in cherishing another but in seeking to gain power over him.

Martin Buber has given most precise phrasing to the two kinds of relationships of which I am now speaking: I-it and I-Thou. The former designates the situation in which a human being comports himself as if he is the only person existing in a universe otherwise inhabited by a host of things or its. To that person other men and women are seen as existing solely for his own personal comfort and advantage: a waitress to serve him, a bus driver to transport him, parents to provide for him, a wife to solace him, children to obey him. He seeks power over others that he may wield them to his advantage; he sees himself as the only I in a world of its. The alternative is to view another as an end in himself, as a human being created in God's image and sensitive to life's joys and sorrows; it is to respond to him not as an objective it but a personal Thou. An "I-Thou" relationship embraces a mutuality of feeling and concern; it is an outgoing, unselfish not-insisting-on-its-own-way; it is to respond to another much as one responds to himself. A literary work focusing beautifully on the polarities of human relationships is T. S. Eliot's *The Cocktail Party*. Celia Coplestone is most graced with the love which selflessly reaches out to other persons, all the way to her crucifixion near an ant-hill "for a handful of plague-stricken natives." The early relationship of Edward and Lavinia Chamberlayne, on the other hand, is a superb example of a two-way "I-it" relationship. Through the wise ministrations of their guardian, however, they move toward a compatibility which will never reach, but at least approaches, Celia's purity of heart.

Lawrence is acutely aware of the frequency with which people mistake the passion for power for the passion of love. No other writer of my acquaintance is so obsessed with the quest for a loving relationship between a man and a woman and few others are so grievously convinced of the supreme difficulty, the near impossibility, of attaining such a relationship. Lawrence's earliest major novel, *Sons and Lovers,* sets the stage. Mrs. Morel's love for her son Paul is terribly possessive, crippling him in relationships with women of his own age. To the spiritually oriented Miriam Leivers, who wishes union with his soul but not his body, Paul can often be nothing but cruel. He comes to view Clara Dawes as a body which may gratify him, not as a person with whom he may live harmoniously. *Sons and Lovers* is, from beginning to end, a chronicle of frustrated human relationships in which the characters experience little but the depression of loneliness. In *The Rainbow* the generations of Brangwens which span the novel's ample chronology struggle, with varying degrees of failure, in quest of the kind of man-woman relationship obviously so dear to Lawrence himself. But what little tenderness exists in *The Rainbow* is quite overshadowed by Anna Brangwen's "victory" in her power struggle with her husband Will, and by Ursula Brangwen's psychic destruction of Anton Skrebensky. Throughout Lawrence's fiction, whatever the degree of a man's or a woman's success or failure, its determinant rests largely on the individual's relationships with other women or men.

As Lawrence is aware of the awful power that one person may exert over another, George Orwell is aware of the awful power that a community of men may exert over individual men. If the fabulous horror and grotesque humor of *Animal Farm* fail to penetrate some of its readers, certainly the terror of *1984* does not fail. We see on the one hand a small group of rulers, symbolized by the invisible Big Brother and represented by the all too visible O'Brien, who are absolutely devoted to the quest for personal power. Most political philosophers, from Plato to the present, have accepted the necessity of a power residing in the state, but a power to be used benignly for the good of individual citizens. In the nightmare world of *1984* the rulers are interested exclusively in personal power, whatever torture or humiliation must be visited upon others in order to realize it. Not only does the protagonist, Winston Smith, fall victim to such a manic lust; in the process he betrays Julia, the only person he has ever loved. One large dimension of the novel's terror lies in the fact that those who carry to its extreme an "I-it" response to other people have the power to destroy the only relationship, that between Winston and Julia, which approached an "I-Thou" dimension.

Lawrence concentrates largely on the relationships between two persons; Orwell on the relationship between a political juggernaut and an individual person. Virginia Woolf's *Mrs. Dalloway* focuses on the relationship between one woman and the members of a small community of persons who are her family, friends, and acquaintances. Few literary characters are more impressed by or responsive to their manifold and diverse relationships to other human beings than is Clarissa Dalloway. No character is more sensitive to or grateful for such relationships than she. We accompany her through a June day in 1923 as she, now in her early fifties, looks back to her youthful days of three decades earlier when she formed most of her friendships which still endure, responds to the present day which leads to her climactic evening party, and thinks forward to the day when she will no longer be among the living in the flesh, but will nonetheless remain among them in the spirit. To Clarissa nothing approaches in importance her empathetic feelings not only toward those whom she knows, but also toward those whom she may only see in passing, or even to those whom she may never see. No one is more compassionate, if not passionate, of heart than Clarissa, and in no literary character have I felt such warm and tender sensibilities toward others. Clarissa is the supremely grateful woman, and from gratitude spring most of those human attributes that make a person loving and lovable. In a three-chapter discourse on the relationships between one human being and others, the most solacing conclusion must be the portrait of Clarissa Dalloway.

The Paradisal Quest

It was the unknown, the unexplored, the undiscovered upon whose shore she had landed, alone, after crossing the void, the darkness which washed the New World and the Old.*

She saw in the rainbow the earth's new architecture, the old, brittle corruption of houses and factories swept away, the world built up in a living fabric of Truth, fitting to the over-arching heaven.

I

The fictional characters of D. H. Lawrence—among them persons so diverse as Paul Morel in *Sons and Lovers,* Ursula Brangwen in *The Rainbow* and *Women in Love,* Rupert Birkin in *Women in Love,* and Lady Chatterley—all seek that human relationship which is a mutually fulfilling giving and receiving and which enables two persons to glimpse paradise. For all of Lawrence's fiction the opening words of *Lady Chatterley's Lover*—"Ours is essentially a tragic age"—may serve as epigraph, for the disparity between hope and realization, though of different degrees in different novels, is usually considerable. Lawrence seems to know, theoretically, what would make for the ideal human life, but also to believe that its attainment is virtually impossible, at least under the condi-

* *The Rainbow* by D. H. Lawrence (New York: Viking, 1961). Copyright 1915 by David Herbert Lawrence; copyright 1943 by Frieda Lawrence. Reprinted by permission of the publisher. The novel was first published in 1915.

tions in which life is now lived. In his expository essays he writes at length of how we have brought this tragic age upon ourselves and his mythology of our fall from presumably happier days is of extended and mystical proportions. An exchange, early in *Women in Love*, between the two male protagonists, Rupert Birkin and Gerald Crich, assumes the "fall" and points, if briefly, to at least the first, and for the moment perhaps the only, step we may take to attempt a regaining of our long-lost sense of fulfillment. Birkin is speaking:

"The old ideals are dead as nails—nothing there. It seems to me there remains only this perfect union with a woman—sort of ultimate marriage—and there isn't anything else."

"And you mean if there isn't the woman, there's nothing?" said Gerald.

"Pretty well that—seeing there's no God."

"Then we're hard put to it," said Gerald. . . .

"You think it's heavy odds against us?" said Birkin.

"If we've got to make our life up out of a woman, one woman, woman only, yes, I do," said Gerald. "I don't believe I shall ever make up *my* life, at that rate."

Birkin watched him almost angrily.

"You are a born unbeliever," he said.

On the one hand I think it can be said that Lawrence's novels are largely studies in human failure at life's most intimate level, the relationship between individual man and individual woman. On the other, it can be argued that Lawrence's men and women, paired as they almost invariably are, exemplify a failure of relationship no greater than, indeed considerably less than that of the men and women who live through the pages of most other novels. Roquentin and Anny, Charles and Emilia Gould, Tony Buddenbrook and Grünlich and Permaneder, Thomas Buddenbrook and Gerda—to mention some of the couples who have figured in earlier chapters —none of them begins to know the intensity and complexity of the male-female relationship experienced by innumerable Lawrencian characters. But for Sartre and Conrad and Mann, as for most twentieth-century novelists, such relationship is neither understood nor deemed crucial to nearly the degree that it is understood and deemed crucial by Lawrence. And to him the relationship between a man and a woman is crucial because its success is the absolutely ground basis for the paradisal quest which informs the whole of his own life and that of his fiction as well. Stephen Dedalus, Antoine Roquentin, and the invisible man, for example, can each in his own way attain success outside any bond with a woman—or a man either, for that matter. And failure, finally, for the Goulds and the Buddenbrooks is determined by far more than incomplete or unsatisfying relationships between husbands and wives. But no Lawrence character, man or woman, can know success apart from a woman or man, and his failure is almost invariably determined by an imperfect human relationship. For Lawrence the road to paradise must travel through a relationship difficult to define: it is a most graciously given and received harmony, understanding, conjunction, fulfillment between a man and a woman. If it is at all accurate to say that Lawrence's novels are in some ways studies in human failure at life's most intimate level, it is largely because Lawrence and his characters have such fantastically high goals. And indeed, a failure to Lawrence might be to many a novelist a marked success.

I I

Lawrence's *The Rainbow* begins in Edenic setting; moves successively through three intimate male-female relationships, the first most gratifying and the last least so; and ends with a vision of the rainbow, harbinger of hope. The novel's action begins in the mid-nineteenth century. Its narrative is of the Brangwen family, which for over two hundred years has dwelt on the Marsh Farm, close to the border of Derbyshire and Nottinghamshire. As the opening, pastoral-infused paragraphs reveal, the Brangwens have for generations lived in closest communion with the land, knowing the constant presence of

heaven and earth, thrilling to the new begetting of each recurring spring, exposed to the sun and the wind, opening and
planting the soil, watching the crops grow, milking the cows,
and mounting the horses. The lives of the Brangwen men have
merged indissolubly with the whole cosmic landscape in solacing, life-giving and life-receiving intimacy. For them this life,
this harmonious interaction with the living universe, is enough.
But while their lives and ambitions are contentedly confined
to the Marsh Farm garden of paradise, their wives restlessly
look outward to what they envisage as a world of knowledge
and culture. In the neighboring village of Cossethay it is the
vicar who, with his educated ways and facile urbanity, strikes
the women as a happy model for their own children. With a
touch of condescension for their husbands, who live as one with
soil and beasts, they yearn for a "higher form of being," for a
life informed more by subtlety of mind, less by things of earth.
And they have their way. As the Brangwens move on toward
the end of the nineteenth century and, particularly in *Women
in Love* (chronological sequel to *The Rainbow*), into the
twentieth, the visions of their women, tantalized by curiosity
concerning what lies beyond their knowledge, take form, their
dreams becoming reality. The family's movement is gradually
but surely away from Marsh Farm, spiritually and psychically
as well as geographically, and by the time we hear the last of
the Brangwens at the end of *Women in Love*, the sisters Ursula
and Gudrun, great-granddaughters of the Alfred Brangwens
who mark *The Rainbow*'s beginning, have reached a worldliness beyond the wildest imagination of earlier generations.

We catch but a glimpse, at the novel's beginning, of the
Alfred Brangwens, who, about 1840, see the construction of a
canal across their lands for the benefit of the new collieries,
soon to be followed by a nearby railroad. The pastoral wonder
of Marsh Farm is thus invaded by the clamor of industry, and
man's easy intercourse with the cosmic order, his blood-intimacy with the earth, is threatened. But if the Brangwen male
loses something of his treasured way of life, the Brangwen

female finds the outer, foreign world which she has sought now brought closer to her once more circumscribed existence. Thus the Alfred Brangwens are the last of their kind. Bearing their four sons and two daughters, they live in that healthy relationship which enables each simultaneously to keep his own rich identity and yet know a life-giving connection with the other. "Two very separate beings," they are called, "vitally connected, knowing nothing of each other, yet living in their separate ways from one root." It is their youngest son, Tom, who dominates the early section of the novel, and who, though remaining on Marsh Farm, takes that first large stride into the unknown so intriguing to the Brangwen women.

The Brangwen distaff side has contributed much to the making of Tom. At the age of twenty-four, on a jaunt to the town of Matlock, he meets an attractive young lady, who, briefly abandoned by her male escort, showers rather generously the gifts of her female company upon him. Deciding to stay over in Matlock that he may see more of her, Tom observes the girl and her now returned companion in the hotel later in the evening. The man is a foreigner, largely unattractive, yet fascinating in his foreignness to Tom, who views him almost as one from another planet. We are told that the meeting with this man from the outside world is perhaps even more significant for Tom than his blood-rousing experience with the girl. Tom dwells long upon the strangeness and its distance from his own life, and, held in tension between desires for unknown and known, grows angry under the opposite attractions of two seemingly disparate, mutually exclusive worlds. "He wanted to go away—right away," we are told. "He dreamed of foreign parts. But somehow he had no contact with them. And it was a very strong root which held him to the Marsh, to his own house and land."

Four years later circumstances provide an unexpected solution to the problem, as it chances that Tom need not desert Marsh Farm to savor the foreign. He meets the widowed Lydia Lensky, a Pole who, with her four-year-old daughter

Anna, has recently come as housekeeper to the neighboring vicarage. It takes only a passing of Tom and Lydia on a country road to elicit from him a "That's her," as he knows in the excitement of pain and joy that the outside world has come to him. Lydia's foreignness is to him a matter of deep satisfaction and certainly no barrier to intimacy. "She was strange, from far off, yet so intimate. She was from far away, a presence, so close to his soul." Their marriage, soon accomplished, should have pleased the generations of Brangwen women, for Lydia brings to the once enclosed farm an urbanity which it had never known. In four years Tom has moved from his wild curiosity at Matlock to its gratification through Lydia.

From its beginning the relationship of Tom and Lydia, like that of most Lawrence couples, is a passionate shuttling between attraction and repulsion, renewal and destruction, love and hate. Yet Tom never loses his conviction that Lydia alone can bring him to human completion, that without her he is nothing. With her first pregnancy and the crisis consequent upon her absorption with her growing womb and its later happy issue, an absorption to the neglect of husband, Tom turns to the child Anna. She becomes a near surrogate for Lydia herself, as father and stepchild enjoy tender mutual devotion and are seldom apart. The period of marital hostility runs its course, and the coming together again of Tom and Lydia brings with it an ecstatic intensity unknown to the early days of their marriage. Their renewal brings them to paradise, or at least to its gates, and through its description, conveyed in religious imagery, we come to feel the wondrousness attending the most fulfilling conjunction of man and woman, wherein each finds in and through the other his salvation. The new coming together is "the entry into another circle of existence . . . the baptism to another life . . . the complete confirmation." Each is an open doorway to the other, the ensuing outer light illuminating their faces, each now knowing "the transfiguration, glorification, the admission." The Lord takes up his abode on Marsh Farm, touching not only

Tom and Lydia, but Anna too, whose soul finds peace in the rays of her parents' love for each other. The rainbow, which will shine for Ursula at the novel's end, arches the Tom Brangwens:

Anna's soul was put at peace between them. She looked from one to the other, and she saw them established to her safety, and she was free. She played between the pillar of fire and the pillar of cloud in confidence, having the assurance on her right hand and the assurance on her left. She was no longer called upon to uphold with her childish might the broken end of the arch. Her father and her mother now met to the span of the heavens, and she, the child, was free to play in the space beneath, between.

Thus at the age of thirty, the time of his newfound marital bliss, Tom would seem to have little more to ask from life. Fifteen years later he is somewhat less certain of the extent of his triumph. Anna is about to be married, a fact to which Tom's emotions do not respond with full grace and generosity, as he laments the loss of their own earlier bonds and feels, as he has for some time, a jealousy of Anna's growing into another kind of love. His reflections at the wedding's approach are desolate, those of an aging man who not only is losing his daughter but is suddenly aware that his own life, outside his consummate relationship with Lydia, has been somehow lacking:

Was his life nothing? Had he nothing to show, no work? He did not count his work, anybody could have done it. What had he known, but the long, marital embrace with his wife! Curious, that this was what his life amounted to! At any rate, it was something, it was eternal. He would say so to anybody, and be proud of it. He lay with his wife in his arms, and she was still his fulfilment, just the same as ever. And that was the be-all and the end-all. Yes, and he was proud of it.

Tom's musings (there will be later, similar ones by his nephew and son-in-law, Will) are on a subject figuring prominently in Lawrence's essays as well as his fiction. His most explicit remarks are in "The Birth of Sex," a chapter of *Fantasia of the Unconscious*, published in 1922. The argument, in brief, is that beyond sexual fulfillment lies the crown of man's endeavor, his purposive activity in the world of mankind. Sexual consummation, no end in itself, is nevertheless the great renewing, vitalizing act, man's enabling means to leave his home and enter into the collective activity of society, then to return home, then to go forth again in a cycle of existence. To realize the wholeness of his creative nature, a man must thus move from a continuing passion with one woman to a passionate communal activity dedicated to some chosen social purpose:

> This meeting of many in one great passionate purpose is not sex, and should never be confused with sex. It is a great motion in the opposite direction. And I am sure that the ultimate, greatest desire in man is this desire for great *purposive* activity. When man loses his deep sense of purposive, creative activity, he feels lost, and is lost. When he makes the sexual consummation the supreme consummation, even in his *secret* soul, he falls into the beginnings of despair. When he makes woman, or the woman and child the great centre of life and of life-significance, he falls into the beginnings of despair.

Tom has succeeded magnificently in the first step of the process, without which any going into the world would be doomed to sterility. But he has rested in the first stage without summoning or finding energy for the second. That Lawrence does not offer satisfying examples, in *The Rainbow* or elsewhere, of men who move from gratifying marriage to rich purposive activity seems to me clear. The material success of a Gerald Crich or a Lord Chatterley is to Lawrence of brutal, insensitive proportions, the product of men who have not, really, known women. Perhaps the Oliver Mellors whom we leave at the end of *Lady Chatterley's Lover* will go on, in and through marriage to Constance Chatterley, to the purposive activity of farming. And perhaps Birkin, beyond the action of *Women in Love,* will return to fruitful work as administrator of schools. But certainly not in Tom Brangwen, or in the fictive lifetimes of Mellors, Birkin, or other male protagonists, do we find the carrying through of the collective activity so important to Lawrence. The reason perhaps is that, in an essentially tragic age, no man attains the height of personal and social fulfillment. And so Tom Brangwen, expressing pleasure and pride in his marital happiness, yet feels a certain emptiness.

III

Anna, at twenty, marries Will Brangwen, son of Tom's older brother Alfred. As Lydia represented the outside world to Tom, so Will represents the outside world to Anna, who has grown up on Marsh Farm. The second marriage is less successful than the first, and for a variety of reasons, among them Anna's and Will's mutual lust for power over each other and their strain of sadism, qualities found in many of Lawrence's characters. The marriage begins in comedy, its early weeks in Yew Cottage spent in that prodigal attentiveness to sex which underlies much of the comic genre. Such a life of vigorous leisure, quite cut off from the world that goes about its daily affairs outside their dwelling, seems to Will, in those brief intervals between caresses, just a little unmanly and shameful, at odds with some vague sense of a man's duty. But these intermittent prickings of conscience are no match for Anna's indolent, luxurious attraction. And so the "Tablets of Stone" which have previously guided Will's sense of responsible conduct are splintered, and the two blissfully careless lovers resemble "two burning bushes that . . . [are] not consumed." When Anna, however, at last temporarily surfeited and ready to glimpse the outside world again, decides to give a tea party, Will, learning his utter dependence on her every moment of time, bitterly resists such an incursion. In the ensuing fiery battle of words and tears, Will loses the first of his many marital battles.

The tracing of their marriage testifies to the brutal, violent power of which Lawrence believed women capable. It is true that Lawrence's women are provoked, that their men are sometimes disposed more to demand submission than to seek harmonious conjunction. It seems to me equally true that, in the pitched battle which marriage becomes in so many of Lawrence's novels, the woman almost always conquers, hollow though her victory usually is. Gertrude Morel and Clara Dawes in *Sons and Lovers* master and subdue their husbands; Gudrun Brangwen is, in *Women in Love,* instrumental to Gerald Crich's disintegration and death. And perhaps no other Lawrence novel draws more vividly woman's dreadful power over man than *The Rainbow.* Even in their successful marriage Lydia is stronger than Tom; Ursula is later completely to unman Anton Skrebensky; and despite the novel's assertion that Anna and Will are well matched, Anna is clearly dominant. The impressive and rather terrifying chapter "Anna Victrix," covering the period from the marriage to the birth of Ursula, is well named. Anna's victory is conveyed not only through the chapter's title and action but through one of its major images as well. At the chapter's beginning Yew Cottage is designated as the ark in the flood, an ark inhabited solely by Anna and Will, to whom all the outside world, in its virtual nonexistence to them, might just as well be drowned. But as the days progress it is no longer the jointly and happily occupied Cottage which is the ark: it is Anna who alone becomes the ark, with Will a drowning man in total dependence upon a woman who knows how to hate and despise as well as love him.

After the comic interlude of honeymoon, there is little of joyful giving and taking in their marriage. Will, first thwarted by Anna's readiness to move from marriage bed to social context, becomes a desperate man. Out of the humiliation of his initial defeat, he seems to take pleasure in hurting Anna, wishing completely to absorb her, to make her "the extension of his will," to have "her in his power." He comes to see her as necessary to his existence, but certainly at the cost of his own separate identity, which, in Lawrence's view, every person must maintain by the side of his simultaneously and mutually enjoyed harmony with the person closest to him. And the more Will recognizes his dependence, the more he knows his impotence:

And upon what could he stand, save upon a woman? Was he then like the old man of the seas, impotent to move save upon the back of another life? Was he impotent, or a cripple, or a defective, or a fragment?

It was black, mad, shameful torture, the frenzy of fear, the frenzy of desire, and the horrible, grasping back-wash of shame.

But Anna wants *her* way, and she has the weapons largely to get it. From the tea party contention on, she seeks, and for the most part gains, control not only over Will's comings and goings, but over his thoughts and attitudes as well. She is enraged, for example, by her husband's religious mysticism, by the thoughtless rapture with which he attends services or contemplates the rich symbols and architectural beauties of a chapel or cathedral. Instead of leaving him to the secure bliss of his religious temperament, she jeeringly demands of him rational explanations of doctrines, symbols, sacraments: to her a lamb is a silly animal and pictures of the Pietà are simply loathsome. With each assault on his active and his contemplative life Will seems to lose a little more ground to a woman who knows when to advance and when to withdraw, when to be petulant and when to be tearful, and who exults in her triumphs which bring pain to her husband. A description of Anna's imperious mastery over her sewing machine serves well as oblique analogy to her dominion over Will: "But she was enjoying herself, she was triumphant and happy as the darting needle danced ecstatically down a hem, drawing the stuff along under its vivid stabbing, irresistibly. She made the machine hum. She stopped it imperiously, her fingers were deft and swift and mistress."

As Anna's pregnancy with Ursula advances, Will becomes increasingly cast off from his sustaining ark. But painful as his solitude is, it forces him to turn to himself and to find that at least a part of him, small as it is, can maintain a manful, independent, separate identity. And so in a sense Anna's cruelty has the beneficent effect of giving Will back to himself in a way necessary to his sustaining a narrow degree of dignified personal survival:

> She had given him a new, deeper freedom. . . . He had come into his own existence. He was born for a second time, born at last unto himself. . . . Now at last he had a separate identity, he existed alone, even if he were not quite alone. Before he had only existed in so far as he had relations with another being. Now he had an absolute self—as well as a relative self.

This "absolute" self, however, develops very slowly in Will. Like his Uncle Tom before him, he has little part in that creative, communal activity which Lawrence believed important to a man. His world is predominantly matriarchal, as Anna continues to live rapturously in a constant glow of motherhood. Will does move a step forward when, after some six years of marriage, he and Anna rediscover each other sexually, entering violent intimacies which bring to him a new sense of manhood. "He had at length," we are told, "from his profound sensual activity, developed a real purposive self." But he is forty or more before he gives noticeable outward evidence of it, at that time going to the post of "Art and Handiwork Instructor for the County of Nottingham." To the end Anna remains "Anna Victrix," largely because she is "Mater Victrix," and she continues to feel more certain of her roots and her place in life than Will ever does. He is simply not man enough, not independent enough, to provide his half of the basis which makes for the good marriage and, in turn, the ideal life.

IV

The remainder of *The Rainbow* is Ursula's book and a continuation of the movement toward the outside world on which Brangwen women have long set their sights. The novel's movement is also toward vision of the rainbow, finally to be fully beheld by Ursula at the novel's end. We may recall the rainbow image overarching Tom, Lydia, and Anna when "the Lord took up his abode" on Marsh Farm, and Anna's "father and her mother . . . met to the span of the heavens, and she, the child, was free to play in the space beneath, between." We are told, at Ursula's birth, that Anna has some dim discernment of the hope and promise which lie ahead in some distant rainbow. The novel's scope takes us from the mid-nineteenth-century Marsh Farm, through several generations of a family moving geographically from the farm and humanly from its idyllic embrace and into discord, on to the symbolic rainbow which affirms a new covenant. The last movement, portraying the old order's utmost descent and death necessarily precedent to the rising issue of a new one, is played by Ursula and Anton Skrebensky, whom she meets when she is not quite sixteen and he twenty-one. Like other Lawrence couples, they endure oscillating passions, now loving, now despising, now hating; but whereas Tom and Lydia happily resolve their conflict on Marsh Farm, and Anna and Will come to at least a truce short of disaster, Ursula contributes to Anton's figurative death, as her sister Gudrun is later to contribute to Gerald Crich's literal death.

Ursula carries the Brangwen outer journey to its extremity. Two of the chapters relating her activities are appropriately entitled "The Widening Circle," and Skrebensky, like Lydia a Pole, embodies for her "a strong sense of the outer world." But in her case his is a world to be discarded, because, far from being a positive nurturing of her human development (as the world of Lydia was to Tom), it is a dead end. Her early hope that he might become to her as one of the Sons of God to one of the daughters of men is disappointed. Skrebensky is absolutely no match for Ursula; she is more woman than he is man, her will too strong for him. The sequence of their physical embraces, far from becoming a union of mutual giving and taking, becomes a series of agons, of battles for supremacy and to the death. A study of two crucial episodes in their lives is instructive.

The first takes place, only months after their initial meeting, at a dance celebrating the wedding of one of the Brangwens. As Ursula and Anton first dance they enjoy that ideal Lawrencian mode of being in union, but not fusion: "It was his will and her will locked in a trance of motion, two wills locked in one motion, yet never fusing, never yielding one to the other. It was a glaucous, intertwining, delicious flux and contest in flux." The distinction is of real importance. In both essays and fiction Lawrence repeatedly suggests that the perfect relationship between a man and a woman consists of their coming together in harmonious union while at the same time maintaining their separate identities. Lawrence calls for a dual separateness which, he believes, will nurture a mutual relationship much more fruitfully than will an absorbing of either person by the other. But Ursula and Anton are not long to sustain the equilibrium of their dance. They leave the gathering and walk toward the fields to the rising of the moon. It is an eerie scene, as Ursula becomes irresistibly attracted by the moon, whose presence becomes more desirable to her than that of Anton himself. She resents the burden of his physical attendance as an obstacle to her full and mystical lunar communion. Thus frustrated, she becomes enraged, oddly moved to tear things asunder, her hands feeling "like metal blades of destruction." She asks to be left alone and walks toward the moon, only to have the music call them back to the dance again. But the former happy locking of wills, the delicious equilibriating flux is no more. Anton now sees an Ursula strange to him, a young girl as "cold and hard and compact of brilliance as the moon itself, and beyond him as the moonlight was beyond him, never to be grasped or known." In desperation, he wishes only to "set a bond round her and compel her!" He is not to have his way. The dance over, Ursula again walks into the fields and toward the moon, seized by a curious lust to annihilate Skrebensky. Like some demon lover, she destroys him through what is generally thought a unifying, vitalizing act—a kiss:

> But hard and fierce she had fastened upon him, cold as the moon and burning as a fierce salt. Till gradually his warm, soft iron yielded, yielded, and she was there fierce, corrosive, seething with his destruction, seething like some cruel, corrosive salt around the last substance of his being, destroying him, destroying him in the kiss. And her soul crystallised with triumph, and his soul was dissolved with agony and annihilation. So she held him there, the victim, consumed, annihilated. She had triumphed: he was not any more.

It is appropriate that this terrible battle of wills, ending in female overcoming and complete separateness, takes place under the moon's dominance. The health of the earth, as Lawrence later affirms in *Fantasia of the Unconscious* (particularly in the chapter "Cosmological"), depends upon an equilibrium between the great, dual antipathetic polarities of the sun and the moon. The sun attracts the earth and all its creatures to a oneness which would obliterate all distinctions and reduce life to an innocuous mingling. The moon, on the other hand, Lawrence writes in the chapter "Sleep and Dreams," is "the declaration of our existence in separateness," is "the fierce centre of retraction," is she "who sullenly stands with her back to us, and refuses to meet and mingle." A crippling imbalance will result should the earth be attracted exclusively by either sun or moon. The same is true of persons, who should be led neither by the sun into an absorption of or by, or a fusion with, another, nor by the moon into a splintering, complete separateness. The moon which shines on the evening of the dance has no counterbalancing sun and thus embraces Ursula completely under its spell. When, as Lawrence writes, "a sort of daytime consciousness came back to her," it is too late. Not until Ursula meets Birkin in *Women in Love* will her balance be achieved. Of Skrebensky it can only be said that "the core was gone . . . as a distinct male he had no core. His triumphant, flaming, overweening heart of the intrinsic male would never beat again. . . . She had broken him."

Six years later, with Skrebensky on leave from military service in India, he and Ursula come together again, though Ursula deep in her intuitive being foresees only a temporary truce between enemies never to be reconciled. Their physical embraces continue more a struggle by each for personal power over the other than a meeting ground for union, largely because their relationship seems unable to move beyond its sexual basis. For beyond his sexual stamina, Anton is but an empty being quickly and wholly to be known by Ursula and soon to possess none of those mysteries intriguing to a woman who wishes to push back her horizon. "She knew him all round," the novel tells us, "not on any side did he lead into the unknown. Poignant, almost passionate appreciation she felt for him, but none of the dreadful wonder, none of the rich fear, the connection with the unknown, or the reverence of love." Anton, on his side, never breaks away from the limitation attributed to him earlier in the novel, his inability to move beyond the purely physical conjunction to a more total communion: "Why did he never really want a woman, not with the whole of him: never loved, never worshipped, only just physically wanted her." He is incapable both of embracing what the total person of Ursula has to offer and of offering Ursula all that her questing nature demands. It is no wonder that she tells her college friend Dorothy Russell that what might be called the "love" between her and Anton means nothing to her, that it "doesn't lead anywhere." It is only Birkin who can approximate a verbal expression of what Ursula is reaching toward. As he later tells her in the chapter "Mino" of *Women in Love*: "There is a beyond, in you, in me, which is further than love, beyond the scope, as stars are beyond the scope of vision, some of them." And again: "What I want is a strange conjunction with you . . . not meeting and mingling;—you are quite right:—but an equilibrium, a pure balance of two single beings:—as the stars balance each other."

As Anton, at twenty-one, was unable to love a woman wholly, so he remains at twenty-seven. And six years after that first moon-drenched evening, he and Ursula endure their last contest, this time at the sea's edge, the night again moon-filled. In this final agony Ursula is imaged as a bird of prey, her voice "like the voice of a harpy to him," "like the scream of gulls." In their embrace, "his heart . . . [melts] in fear from the fierce, beaked, harpy's kiss," as Ursula seems "to be pressing in her beaked mouth till she . . . [has] the heart of him." When Anton seeks to lead them into a dark hollow of the beach for the consummation, Ursula insists on lying "full under the moonshine." There they struggle in their separateness, until, in agony, Anton succumbs, giving "way as if dead." When it is all over, Skrebensky beats a hasty retreat to India, there to marry his colonel's daughter, who, we may be sure, falls far short of Ursula's awesome power and fierce demands.

Skrebensky gone, *The Rainbow* moves quickly to a conclusion which seems not fully to grow out of the novel's antecedent action. In the last chapter Ursula, pregnant (or at least believing she is), goes for an early autumn afternoon walk. Suddenly, whether in reality or in hallucination is difficult to say, some wildly rampant horses cut off her way, bursting and surging about her, persistent and terrifying in their presence. The episode's dramatic intensity is immense, shocking the bewildered Ursula, who returns home to a fortnight's serious illness. In her delirium she broods over the expected child, over Anton, over the frustrating failure of the whole relationship. Yet the illness, in all its unease, is purgative. Out of its wretchedness Ursula awakes to a new world, learning that there is to be no child and knowing that the husk of the old dispensation may be cast aside, leaving her very kernel free to take root in more nurturing soil. She has finally reached a far station of that journey first dreamed of by

the Brangwen women of generations back, and then begun
by Tom and carried on by Anna before her: "It was the unknown, the unexplored, the undiscovered upon whose shore
. . . [Ursula] had landed, alone, after crossing the void, the
darkness which washed the New World and the Old." In her
convalescence, as she looks from her window upon the passing
colliers, she senses a "new germination," a "new liberation,"
thus attributing to the world about her what is budding in
her own being. In all that she sees she both grasps and
gropes for "the creation of the living God, instead of the old,
hard barren form of bygone living." Still beholding the same
dead-spirited workers, their ugly homes, and the earth's corruption, she nevertheless now sees far more than a fallen
world. For her

the rainbow stood on the earth. She knew that the sordid people
who crept hard-scaled and separate on the face of the world's corruption were living still, that the rainbow was arched in their
blood and would quiver to life in their spirit, that they would cast
off their horny covering of disintegration, that new, clean, naked
bodies would issue to a new germination, to a new growth, rising
to the light and the wind and the clean rain of heaven. She saw in
the rainbow the earth's new architecture, the old, brittle corruption
of houses and factories swept away, the world built up in a living
fabric of Truth, fitting to the over-arching heaven.

V

I have remarked that the novel's conclusion—Ursula's vision
of the rainbow in particular—seems not fully convincing. Certainly we have been readied for the image itself. The entire
novel has pointed to it, as earlier Brangwens variously sense
the rainbow, the sign and seal of God's covenant with Noah
and every living creature that the world will never again experience so flesh-destroying a flood. The question is whether
Ursula's own past gives basis and occasion for the optimism
of her vision. I think not: her various interpersonal relationships, including her round of lesbianism (between the two

Skrebensky episodes) with her schoolmistress Winifred Inger, seem hardly sufficient ground for it. Yet if her final vision seems insufficiently rooted, unjustifiable in terms of her past, it is in fact a true promise of what awaits her in *Women in Love*. For she goes on to a new world, finding in Birkin a far stronger man than Skrebensky, and entering with him into the most fully drawn and satisfying love relationship of the whole Lawrencian canon.

It is important to note that the Brangwen journey in *The Rainbow* is not circular and that Ursula's concluding vision does not imply a regaining of the same paradise that has been lost. The novel's action coincides temporally with England's transition from a farming to an industrial culture, thus rendering virtually impossible a return to that "blood-intimacy" with the natural world known to earlier generations. We witness, during the period from the Alfred Brangwens to (in *Women in Love*) the Rupert Birkins, the growing pains attending a major cultural change. Lawrence writes not of an old order in the process of being recaptured but of a reaching toward a new one, different in kind from the formerly Edenic Marsh Farm and redolent not exclusively of the soil, but of the subtle introspective intricacies of the mind as well. For all his frequently expressed pastoral nostalgia, I really cannot conceive of Lawrence himself as willing to settle for the beautifully simple life of an Alfred Brangwen. Lawrence was and, I believe, chose to be an approximation of Rupert Birkin, who would not have exchanged his mental involutions for the Garden of Eden itself. *The Rainbow* is a story of transition, beginning with one kind of paradise, recognizing the impossibility of its return, and ending with hopeful vision of another kind of paradise which might issue from a new world.

We know too that the striving for an earthly paradise is a never-ending quest for a condition always on the far side of the horizon. Even Ursula and Birkin (and the Alfred Brangwens too, I suspect), with all their moments of bliss, experience the desolation of loneliness and misunderstanding. To

read a large body of Lawrence's fiction is to know that for
him our age is essentially a tragic one. Most of his characters
are considerably less successful and impressive than Ursula
and Rupert. Most of them, both the sensitive and the insensitive, have their strains of brutality. Most are hungry for
power, usually for power over another human being, most
frequently evidenced in a man-woman confrontation, or for
the kind of industrial power ruthlessly achieved by a Gerald
Crich or a Lord Chatterley. Such failures in human relationships are insuperable obstacles to the reaching of a paradise
which must rest so substantially on the love between a man
and a woman and a devotion to some selfless, communal,
purposive activity. There are, it is true, scattered and intermittent glimpses of paradise—sometimes through observation of the natural beauty and rhythm of the cosmos known
to the early Brangwen men, sometimes when a man and a
woman touch each other's deepest, most responsive self. But
as Oliver Mellors, lover of Lady Chatterley, realizes, every
man, even he who can at times come to know and be known
by a woman, must return to that persistent state, the common
denominator of all tragedy: aloneness. About midpoint in
his novel and after he has come to know Connie Chatterley's
love, Mellors meditates on the condition of life which pre-
dominates and spaces widely those moments of happy knowledge of another:

But he, the keeper, as the day grew, had realised: it's no good!
It's no good trying to get rid of your own aloneness. You've got to
stick to it all your life. Only at times, at times, the gap will be
filled in. At times! But you have to wait for the times. Accept your
own aloneness and stick to it, all your life. And then accept the
times when the gap is filled in, when they come. But they've got to
come. You can't force them.

Every man is an island, at least for most of life's moments.
Such is life's tragedy, that human condition which Lawrence
describes as vividly and poignantly as any writer I know.
We live, however, not for the tragedy, but for those intervals

"when the gap is filled in." The filling is usually accompanied by and accomplished through the bond of sexual relationship. But it does not always require such intimacy. It sometimes comes through a sympathetic word, perhaps between two persons just met and never to meet again; or through a meeting of eyes, those perhaps of persons never to meet in any other way; or through a stunning sense of nature's beauty. Such communions do occur and, for a time, comfortingly replace the dejection of loneliness. And such moments, not forgotten, bring us a sense of that paradise that *is* a man's relationship with another or with the living universe. These moments come rarely, and it is with incomparable brilliance that Lawrence illuminates this cornerstone of our tragedy. Yet his writings are always, finally, on this side of despair. The quest for paradise, both by Lawrence's more spirited characters and by ourselves, goes on. And Lawrence helps us savor those occasional moments of ecstasy which grace our search for earthly fulfillment.

The Demonic Comedy

*There will be no loyalty, except loyalty toward the Party. There will be no love, except the love of Big Brother.**

"I have not betrayed Julia."

"Do it to Julia! Do it to Julia! Not me! Julia! I don't care what you do to her. Tear her face off, strip her to the bones. Not me! Julia! Not me!"

I

The movement and events of D. H. Lawrence's *The Rainbow* are motivated largely by the relationships between individual men and individual women. George Orwell's *1984* is a study of man's relationship to his political community and his dehumanization through its dreadful power. Orwell's novel takes its place in a literary tradition beginning with Plato's *Republic* and enjoying two periods of particular prominence, the Renaissance and the past half-century. In this tradition, however, it is a long journey from the quest for justice of *The Republic* or the quest for rational behavior of Sir Thomas More's *Utopia* to the nihilism of *1984*. It is the journey from utopian literature to its anti-utopian counterpart.

Among the most important common denominators of *The Republic* and most of the Renaissance utopias is the

* *1984* by George Orwell (New York: Harcourt, Brace, 1949). Copyright 1949 by Harcourt, Brace and Company, Inc. Reprinted by permission of the publisher.

conviction that what benefits the larger community benefits the individual, that the state is the individual writ large, macrocosm to microcosm. The imaginary ideal states of the sixteenth and seventeenth centuries—utopias so diverse as More's, Thomas Lupton's *Siuqila,* Johann Andreae's *Christianopolis,* Campanella's *City of the Sun,* and Francis Bacon's *New Atlantis*—offer various orders of brave new worlds adorned with all kinds of economic, social, political, religious, and scientific achievements which their authors envisaged as the perhaps attainable or near-attainable goals of individual men and their communities. Though a reader may question some of the utopian goals or at least the proposed means of their attainment, he is invariably impressed by the underlying quest for a more gratifying life.

A utopia, of course, presents not what is but what may be or, at least, should be. Plato and More, for example, did not find in their own worlds the justice and rationality which their works celebrate. Yet in full awareness of human fallibility and of the lust for power corrupting to individual and state, they nevertheless envisaged a movement toward an ideal community serving the best interests of all men. For Orwell and other twentieth-century writers of what are called anti-utopias, such a happy concurrence of interest between individual men and the body politic seems nearly unthinkable. Both the Russian Eugene Zamiatin's *We* (1924) and Aldous Huxley's *Brave New World* (1932) satirize the utopian ideal, implying that the state of the future will serve its citizens only by reducing them to thoughtless automata deprived of those qualities considered essentially human. *1984* goes beyond satire, affirming a movement toward collectivism for its own sake and dependent upon the individual man's capitulation to its ruthlessly employed power. Plato's benignly wise philosopher-king becomes transmogrified into the O'Brien of *1984.*

Among anti-utopian novels it is important to distinguish between *We* and *Brave New World* on the one hand and *1984* on the other. The books of Zamiatin and Huxley have a full share of fantasy and humor, grim though the humor may be. They both successfully invite an occasional willing suspension of disbelief. Though their predictions are frightening, there are intervals of relief afforded by a satiric, sometimes comically exaggerated tone and by the reader's conviction that the authors are not always fully serious.

The philosophy of the United State, mythical country of *We,* is predicated, like that of Dostoevsky's Grand Inquisitor, on the belief that man must choose between freedom and happiness. The Grand Inquisitor begins with Christ and his rigorous call that each man choose freely and sufferingly to take up his cross. The Well-Doer, ruler of the United State, begins with Adam and Eve and the decision confronting them between remaining happily in the Garden or choosing freely to disobey their single charge. From the calamitous results of that early decision the Well-Doer is bent upon rescuing man, by force if necessary, and insists that man surrender to the United State his dearly bought freedom in exchange for an easy happiness. The perfect state will be achieved when every trace of individuality is dissolved (thus the title *We*), when men have no decisions to make, no thoughts to take, no deep emotions to feel. Ideally, the Well-Doer will ultimately hold court over subjects totally drained of personhood. Yet the reader seldom identifies with the characters, viewing them instead as exaggerated warnings or caricatures too far removed from reality to be accorded complete seriousness.

The political ambitions of *We,* presented in seriocomic tone, call for a repudiation of freedom and an acceptance of thoughtless, colorless contentment. *Brave New World* also exalts "happiness" over freedom. Life begins through rigidly controlled fertilization of eggs (there are no mothers) which produce masters and servants—the famous Bokanovsky process at its best engenders ninety-six identical twins (of the servant class) from a single egg. At infancy begins a meticulous conditioning, nowhere more effective than in its sleep-teaching, whereby young people absorb "suggestions," principles of indoctrination leading to the social stability so highly prized. Every person's sole devotion must be to the state and its ideals, and there are no wives, husbands, children, or parents to divert such loyalty. But the day comes when the community's ideals are challenged by the intrusive appearance of a man born and bred in another land, a land less brave, less new, more traditional. And the novel's concluding dialogue between this "savage" and Mustapha Mond, monarch of the newer order, makes clear the fundamental choice between a hard freedom and a characterless happiness. The savage rebel speaks first:

"But I don't want comfort. I want God, I want poetry, I want real danger, I want freedom, I want goodness. I want sin."

"In fact," said Mustapha Mond, "you're claiming the right to be unhappy."

"All right then," said the Savage defiantly, "I'm claiming the right to be unhappy."

"Not to mention the right to grow old and ugly and impotent; the right to have syphilis and cancer; the right to have too little to eat; the right to be lousy; the right to live in constant apprehension of what may happen tomorrow; the right to catch typhoid; the right to be tortured by unspeakable pains of every sort."

There was a long silence.

"I claim them all," said the Savage at last.

Mustapha Mond shrugged his shoulders. "You're welcome," he said.

Despite this moving dialogue *Brave New World,* like *We,* lacks the immediacy and verisimilitude necessary to evoke a reader's frightened, earnest attention. Not only do we not identify with the characters of either novel sufficiently to be moved at the deepest level of our being; we are not deceived by the satirically specious arguments of either novel that the health of their states and that of their individuals are interdependent. The utopias of Plato and More, on the other hand, in which a mutuality of welfare between state and individual is impressively argued, are truly brave new worlds; the anti-utopias of Zamiatin and Huxley are cleverly conceived, satirically distorted communities in which the state is king and man achieves a hollow harmony at the cost of everything human.

I I

George Orwell's *1984*, though anti-utopian like *We* and *Brave New World*, is markedly different from its predecessors. For one thing, its unbroken verisimilitude and absence of fantasy and satiric humor contribute to its thorough horror. For another, the rulers of the communities differ in their expressed aims. Both the Well-Doer and Mustapha Mond insist on the benevolence of their tyranny, affirming that their strict control is to the end of relieving the citizens of an onerous freedom and investing them with a carefree happiness. But when Orwell's protagonist, Winston Smith, stretched out before O'Brien in the torture chamber, opines that the Party employs its methods of extremity for the good of human beings who simply do not know how to govern themselves, O'Brien becomes infuriated. He is no Grand Inquisitor who sees man's choice to lie between freedom and happiness. He does not believe, like Plato and More, nor does he say he believes, like the Well-Doer or Mustapha Mond, that what is good for the state is good for the individual. The Party, he assures Winston, has no interest in individuals; its tyranny is a means to nothing except its own power and is for the sole gratification of those who hold this power. And the Party, we discover, has successfully evolved a mode of operation spelling the end of the individual, draining him of everything markedly *his*, and then absorbing the nothingness that remains into the fabric of its collectivism.

1984 is the most frightening novel of my reading experience, and for reasons going beyond its unrelievedly serious realism and O'Brien's chilling candor. Most depressingly the novel becomes, finally, a book without a hero and thus lacks the gratifying tragic implications of a work in which the protagonist dies at the moment of an otherwise noble triumph. William Golding's *Lord of the Flies* and Bernard Malamud's *The Fixer* are among the horrifying tales of our century, yet these novels have their heroes and near-heroes—Simon, Piggy, and Ralph in the former, Yakov Bok in the latter—and where there are heroes there is hope. Winston Smith and his world, however, are incapable of tragedy. In the essay "Lear, Tolstoy, and the Fool," Orwell asserts that there can be no tragedy without a belief in human dignity and an acceptance of the fact that virtue does not always triumph. "A tragic situation," he writes, "exists precisely when virtue does *not* triumph but when it is still felt that man is nobler than the forces which destroy him." Winston himself recognizes his own time's incapacity for tragedy: "Tragedy, he perceived, belonged to the ancient time, a time when there were still privacy, love, and friendship, and when the members of a family stood by one another without needing to know the reason." To live in a world beyond tragedy, empty of heroes and human dignity, where there is no Oedipus or Lear to rise above the very forces that destroy him, is horrible to contemplate. This is the world of *1984*.

Such a world, with its incapacity for tragedy and its quest for power for its own sake, may have begun to take shape in Orwell's mind during the 1930s, particularly through his response to the injustices and horrors of the Spanish Civil War. A decade or so later, in his essay "Writers and Leviathan," he states that his generation, as distinguished from that of his grandparents, has developed "an awareness of the enormous injustice and misery of the world, and a guilt-stricken feeling that one ought to be doing something about it, which makes a purely esthetic attitude towards life impossible." And in "Why I Write," he remarks that all of his writing after 1936 was directed against totalitarianism and that he was seeking to make political writing an art. With *Animal Farm* (1946), he tells us, he first tried "to fuse political purpose and artistic purpose into one whole." In *Animal Farm* there are certain adumbrations of *1984:* the pig Squealer can reputedly turn black into white; "history" is altered at will by the totalitarian regime of the Farm, as its rulers seek to induce a forgetfulness of earlier times, in their view so intolerable and in need of reconstruction; and there are political lies and forced confessions. *Animal Farm,* to be sure, is a grim book, yet it is only an appetizer to the horror of the later *1984*.

The aim of the Party which dominates the world of Winston Smith is absolute power. It must be said in O'Brien's behalf that he has, as Big Brother's prime minister, carried totalitarianism to a perfection hardly imaginable to a Hitler, Mussolini, or Stalin of half a century earlier. As I have remarked, O'Brien is fully conscious of and, to Winston, honest about his aim: the subjecting of every Party member, in terms of both outward behavior and inner feeling, to the desires of the Party. One need only read, as Winston does, *The Theory and Practice of Oligarchical Collectivism*—purportedly written by the Party's greatest enemy, Emmanuel Goldstein, but actually composed in part by O'Brien himself—to understand clearly the Party's hunger for power, its consciousness of aim, and its ineluctable determination to crush all opposition. In this context Winston makes his journey, moving from a time when tragedy, privacy, love, and friendship were still possible (a time, significantly, which dwells only in the depths of his memory), to a time when he has been emptied of every thought and emotion, and can, in his final moribund condition, love Big Brother. Winston's odyssey moves through four main stages: (1) the destruction of privacy, (2) the obliteration of memory of both personal and public history, (3) the narrowing of language and thought to virtual nothingness, and (4) the abolition of interpersonal fidelity and love. It is a major surgery which deprives man of absolutely everything that makes him man.

III

A first step toward control over any human being is the destruction of his privacy. In *We* a drawing of curtains is allowed only for coital refreshment, the indulgence of which is freely, frequently, and promiscuously granted through the female's obtaining of a promissory pink slip. In *Brave New World* desire for solitude is viewed as a deplorable breach of normal behavior. Only the world of *1984,* however, has advanced technologically to the telescreen, stationed in rooms public and private and enabling the Party bureaucracy to observe their subjects' every movement. Facial expressions, physical gestures, words spoken in sleep—all fall under watchful eye. Willfully to step beyond the range of telescreen is the crime of *ownlife.* To manifest incredulity, by even the slightest involuntary physiognomic expression, of some Party announcement, however absurd, is *facecrime.* The Party's protective armor of *crimestop* is evidence of its careful foresight: "Thoughts and actions which, when detected, mean certain death are not formally forbidden, and the endless purges, arrests, tortures, imprisonments, and vaporizations are not inflicted as punishments for crimes which have actually been committed, but are merely the wiping-out of persons who might perhaps commit a crime at some time in the future."

To be constantly under the attentive eye of another, to be forced to relinquish one's privacy, is a nightmarish and humiliating experience. Yet the Party goes beyond depriving a man of his *present ownlife;* it seeks also, through obliteration of his memory, to destroy his *past ownlife.* It would expunge both his personal memories, those most intimate, bittersweet reminiscences of family and home, and his more public memories, the objective facts of past history. For to live in a

terroristic state and yet recall a better life antecedent to its
formation is both to sense a fall from paradise and to yearn,
nostalgically, for its return. As Winston observes the barren
ugliness of London, he asks himself if life has always been so
drab and depressing. The Party's propaganda, of course, must
seek to assure him that London was once far worse—a corrupt
city of cruel capitalists who enslaved the populace. But there
is something deep in Winston's spirit and bones which instinctively protests this view. There come to him, at rare
intervals to be sure, sights and sounds and smells which kindle
deeply buried memories of a time when life dealt more gently
with persons. Most tenderly provoking is his recurring dream
of a pastoral landscape (one recalled later in his waking life
when he is in the country with Julia) which he defines as a
"Golden Country" from an idyllic past. The dream's warm,
sensuous evocation of natural loveliness is in keen contrast
to the bleak pallor of his present reality:

Suddenly he was standing on short springy turf, on a summer evening when the slanting rays of the sun gilded the ground. The
landscape he was looking at recurred so often in his dreams that he
was never fully certain whether or not he had seen it in the real
world. In his waking thoughts he called it the Golden Country. It
was an old, rabbit-bitten pasture, with a foot track wandering across
it and a molehill here and there. In the ragged hedge on the opposite side of the field the boughs of the elm trees were swaying very
faintly in the breeze, their leaves just stirring in dense masses like
women's hair. Somewhere near at hand, though out of sight, there
was a clear, slow-moving stream where dace were swimming in the
pools under the willow trees.

Beyond the dream there are other intimations of a happier past. The old room which Winston and Julia frequent
at Mr. Charrington's, and particularly its relic, a double bed,
stir ancestral memories in Winston. A rhyme about the bells
of St. Clement's and St. Martin's he recognizes as something
not new, but temporarily forgotten. Twice the aroma of
real coffee and once of chocolate evokes childhood days. But
it is the beautiful glass paperweight which above all is sym-

bol, surrogate, and microcosm of the past. With virtually
everything in London altered to render the past beyond recall, the paperweight remains a fact of history as yet inviolate
to the Party's ravagement. Within this artifact and its enclosed
coral flower time has come to a stop. In this precious memento
Winston sees the counterpart of the wonderfully solacing
life he has temporarily found with Julia in Mr. Charrington's
dwelling: "The paperweight was the room he was in, and the
coral was Julia's life and his own, fixed in a sort of eternity
at the heart of the crystal." When they are invaded by the
Thought Police, the paperweight's brutal smashing marks the
end of the last, small, cherished hold on a distant paradise.
Since happy memories, and all that excite them, dangerously
challenge the Party's claim to a present utopia, they must
be effaced.

The Party's assault on memory goes beyond that of personal reminiscence and embraces also that of the more public
life—of persons, places, and events of history. Such a totalitarian mode of operation is outlined in Orwell's essay "The
Prevention of Literature." Since a despotic state must maintain the illusion of infallibility, all its predictions must *seem*
to come true. If they in fact do not, then either the prediction
itself or its contravening facts must be denied: thus "history
is something to be created rather than learned." "Totalitarianism demands," Orwell continues, "the continuous alteration
of the past, and in the long run probably demands a disbelief
in the very existence of objective truth." The Party of *1984*
has learned its lesson well and gone about the task of creating
history with unparalleled thoroughness and ingenuity. For
example, a person inimical to its aims does not simply disappear, never again to be seen or heard. He is vaporized: his
existence is not ended—he simply never existed. Every written
reference to him is destroyed, and though he may linger for a
while in human memory, the memory is soon distrusted and,
like the man himself, soon vaporized. As Winston notes, it is
possible to create dead men, but not living ones. He vividly

recalls once holding a photograph of three men—Jones, Aaronson, and Rutherford—*after* their vaporization. With some degree of fear he had dropped the photograph into the convenient "memory hole," an expunging abyss. Later, the entire episode is dismissed by O'Brien as an example of Winston's defective memory. The ironically named memory hole is, moreover, the destructive depository for more than photographs; it also devours written records of unfulfilled predictions. Thus there is no objective external reality, since evidence observed by the physical senses is simply denied and, hopefully, forgotten. History is transformed from a true record of the past to a continual rewriting, a constant juggling of unfacts to protect the illusion of Party infallibility. The past becomes "whatever the Party chooses to make it." It is a major Party tenet that he who controls the past controls the future, and that he who controls the present controls the past. Since the Party clearly *does* control the present, it controls the past and future as well.

Party members are deprived not only of privacy and memory; a dual assault is made also on language and thought. Orwell's observation in his essay "Politics and the English Language"—that "if thought corrupts language, language can also corrupt thought"—is substantiated in *1984*. A man endowed with full powers of human consciousness, the Party knows, is a constant threat to its tyrannic ambitions. It knows too that language lies on both the near and the far side of thought, that it is necessary for both the conception and the communication of thought, and thus, that to cripple language is to cripple thought. The enabling (or disabling) instrument of such enfeeblement is the gradual transition from Oldspeak, language of the earlier part of the twentieth century, to Newspeak, which, by 2050, it is predicted, will be fully operative. Newspeak will have the incalculable advantage of making impossible all modes of thought except that amicable to Ingsoc, abbreviation of English Socialism. Its three carefully constructed vocabularies will be devoid of words that could form heretical thoughts or could express them if they could be formed. The A vocabulary, for example, is stripped of all those subtle nuances which make possible literature or a discussion possessing any degree of political or philosophical nicety. The B vocabulary, designed particularly for political usage, is so cleverly conceived that its very use imposes the desirable mental attitude upon its user. Its purpose is the utter subversion of what had formerly been thought the function of language, for it serves not to express, but to destroy the capacity to express, the complexity of the human mind. From it such words as "honor," "justice," "morality" have been removed by vaporization; all words expressing such concepts as liberty and equality are subsumed in the word *crimethink;* those expressive of such quaint mental powers as objectivity or rationality are designated solely as *oldthink.* Still other words—a good example is "Miniluv," for Ministry of Love, which has made of torture the finest of arts—designate the polar opposites of their former meanings. Thus Newspeak both narrows the range of language and furnishes a means of verbal communication devoid of an active, thinking human consciousness. One learns to "think" without taking thought, his words automatically accommodating themselves to Party orthodoxy. To such repression there will be an initial resistance by the intelligent Party member until he becomes indoctrinated through the art and science of *doublethink,* a feat of mental gymnastics enabling its practitioner to enjoy a simultaneity of consciousness and unconsciousness. To understand its mode of operation (it is kin to Sartre's concept of bad faith or self-deception) is to understand the Party's success in, among other things, the destruction of history and of every vestige of objective reality:

Doublethink means the power of holding two contradictory beliefs in one's mind simultaneously, and accepting both of them. . . . The process has to be conscious, or it would not be carried out with sufficient precision, but it also has to be unconscious, or it would bring with it a feeling of falsity and hence of guilt. *Doublethink* lies at the very heart of Ingsoc, since the essential act of the Party is to use conscious deception while retaining the firmness of purpose that goes with complete honesty. To tell deliberate lies while genuinely believing in them, to forget any fact that has become inconvenient, and then, when it becomes necessary again, to draw it back from oblivion for just so long as it is needed, to deny the existence of objective reality and all the while to take account of the reality which one denies—all this is indispensably necessary. . . . Ultimately, it is by means of *doublethink* that the Party has been able—and may, for all we know, continue to be able for thousands of years—to arrest the course of history.

Through its discouragement of privacy, obliteration of memory, and narrowing of language and thought, the Party has structured a logically sound *Summa Politica*. It is conceived out of the absolute lust for power, the attaining and maintaining of which demands the complete invasion of every fiber of a Party member's being. It moves surely from the destruction of a man's present *ownlife* to that of his past *ownlife*, as his body and mind fall under Party X-ray. Once his actions are spied and his memory expunged, he is fed a language whose meagerness is a bulwark against heretical lapsing. Should he be resistant to this new fetter, he is tamed through the anodyne of *doublethink*. There remains but the last and crowning step, yet to confront Winston after the three preliminary effronteries: the abolition of all interpersonal fidelity and love—and to this climactic assault we will soon come. But we already may acknowledge that Ingsoc is, to employ the mode of Newspeak, the bravest of brave new worlds.

IV

It is to this world that the novel introduces us on April 4, 1984—or so Winston thinks at least, though dates, like other "historical" facts, are uncertain. Winston is thirty-nine, living in a world divided among three vast powers: Oceania, Eurasia, Eastasia. His home is London, capital of Oceania, ruled by the four Ministries of Truth, Peace, Love, and Plenty, skilled respectively in the arts of falsehood, war, hate, and poverty. A member of the Party, which constitutes fifteen percent of Oceania's population, he works in the Ministry of Truth, "rectifying" former news items and feeding the memory hole references to "unpersons." His London is the epitome of drabness and joylessness: houses have rotted, plumbing is defective, air is polluted, Party members neither sing nor laugh with joy. Against his fetid, squalid environment, as well as the assaults on his privacy, memory, and flexibility of consciousness, Winston struggles with sufficient tenacity to embody the novel's sole hope of freedom. For a while it seems that *1984* may be moving toward a tragic, and therefore noble and dignified, conclusion, one in which Winston, maintaining to the end his manhood and spirited resistance to demonic forces, will die a hero. But the Party, finally, proves too resourceful and powerful, refusing to kill him while resistance remains. Instead of dying with his manhood intact, Winston lives physically but dies in every other sense. At the novel's end, loving Big Brother, he is reduced to a no-man, a vegetable. The last step in Winston's spiritual demise is the betrayal of the one person he loves, Julia.

The story of *1984* is relatively simple. Winston, horrified by Party methods (the novel opens amid orgiastic preparations for "Hate Week"), is set on its destruction. His initial step toward this hope is an eager searching for some knowledge of the past from which the Party claims to have rescued Oceania. Winston turns first to the working-class proles, so innocuous that they are permitted to live in their thoughtless freedom. To uncover in their minds some remembrance of a past happier than the present may inaugurate a more felicitous future, may stir the proles, comprising eighty-five percent of the population, to rebellion against the Party. But his visit to one of their pubs and conversation with one of their members reveals the futility of his strategy. His attempts to elicit from an old man some memory of social and economic conditions of an earlier generation are largely unavailing. The man asserts that the beer was better then, delights in reminiscence of fashionable top hats, recalls being pushed into the gutter by a gentleman, and—completely missing the serious intent of Winston's queries—goes on to discuss the compensations of old age. No hope, Winston learns, lies with the proles, preoccupied as they are with trivia and possessing no spark which may kindle rebellion.

Thus thwarted in his initial move toward the Party's overthrow, Winston settles temporarily for escape from its oppression and finds in his relationship with Julia a brief and luxurious interlude. Through their trysts, first in a pastoral setting recalling Winston's dream of the Golden Country, then in a deserted church, and still later in the seeming privacy and rare bliss of Mr. Charrington's rented room, they subvert every principle of Party discipline. And Julia would have forever rested content with their, to them, clandestine affront to the Party, which she hates not on large philosophical grounds but for its barrier to her personal interests and indulgences. As Winston astutely tells her: "You're only a rebel from the waist downwards." His own rebellious urge springs from heart and head as well. Disappointed in his conversation with the prole and unwilling simply to ignore the Party while enjoying Julia's favors, he plots another way of rebellion. He will confess his hopes to and seek an ally in that Party member who to him seems most charming, civilized, intelligent, and open to sympathetic conversation: O'Brien. There had been, Winston feels sure, fleeting moments of eye-to-eye confrontation with O'Brien which spoke a mutual understanding and suggested tacit complicity against a common oppressor. An appointment made, Winston and Julia visit O'Brien, divulge their hopes for rebellion, and argue a readiness to sacrifice their lives, to murder, to commit any atrocity whatsoever toward the Party's destruction. Only one demand is refused—the willingness to separate forever from each other. In a world of uncertainties, Winston and Julia hold most invulnerable their continued determination never voluntarily to part, and surely never to betray the other. Upon his absolute fidelity to Julia Winston stakes his whole personhood. It is here that the lines of potential tragedy are drawn. If Winston, despite all pressures, could maintain his fidelity to and love for Julia, he would, under terrible duress, either die a martyr or live a physically broken but spiritually whole person. Betrayal, on the other hand, is suicide of will and spirit. The novel's closing action makes sadly clear that the satanic O'Brien, incarnation of Party despotism, is more ingenious, ruthless, and persistent than the gods of Olympus who balked the Greek heroes. Greek Fate was never so cruel as Party determination. The recital of Winston's dehumanization is one of literature's most ghastly accomplishments.

Winston's climactic surrender takes place in the Ministry of Love, to which he has been removed after his arrest at Mr. Charrington's. In Room 101, torture chamber of the Ministry, he is confronted by the O'Brien in whom he had placed his trust and is paced through the three educative stages of learning about, understanding, and accepting the Party. The Party refuses to grant death to a man as long as he retains any vestige of resistance against its will, for martyrs are always possible rallying points of opposition to their killers. A Party enemy, as O'Brien puts it, must be "washed clean," "squeeze[d] . . . empty." He must be brought to the ultimate state of purgation described by O'Brien: "There will be no loyalty, except loyalty toward the Party. There will be no love, except the love of Big Brother." Thus Winston's ultimate struggle is set: he must "choose" between remaining loyal to and loving Julia or assuming loyalty to and love of Big Brother. Under the most intensive physical torture he is moved by O'Brien through the first two stages of his purgation. He learns how the Party works and comes to understand why it works as it does. He is persuaded that the Party can both "make the laws of nature" and "create human nature." Forcibly indoctrinated with *doublethink,* he is led to believe that two and two make five. He is, through incredible physical humiliations, reduced to a hideously distorted skeleton. But with all this, Winston maintains in his heart the love for Julia with which he began. O'Brien is speaking:

"We have beaten you, Winston. We have broken you up. You have seen what your body is like. Your mind is in the same state. I do not think there can be much pride left in you. You have been kicked and flogged and insulted, you have screamed with pain, you have rolled on the floor in your own blood and vomit. You have whimpered for mercy, you have betrayed everybody and everything. Can you think of a single degradation that has not happened to you?"

Winston had stopped weeping, though the tears were still oozing out of his eyes. He looked up at O'Brien.

"I have not betrayed Julia," he said.

O'Brien looked down at him thoughtfully. "No," he said. "no; that is perfectly true. You have not betrayed Julia."

Thus Winston has at this point come to a knowledge and an understanding of the Party, at the expense of both his body and his rational powers. But as long as his innermost being remains faithful to Julia he does not *accept* the Party. This third stage, however, the stage of acceptance, is not long in coming. Removed from the torture chamber, his defenses somewhat relaxed, Winston in an unguarded moment of sleep cries out his love for Julia. Returned to Room 101, he now learns its ultimate terror: it holds for every person what is for him the absolutely unendurable, what dissolves the strongest of human wills. For Winston the unendurable is rats. As a closed, rat-filled cage is masked over his face and its door about to be opened that the creatures may bore through his eyes, his cheeks, his tongue, Winston knows his one way of escape: "He must interpose another human being, the *body* of another human being, between himself and the rats." The last remnant of his personhood snaps as he cries, in final defeat: "Do it to Julia! Do it to Julia! Not me! Julia! I don't care what you do to her. Tear her face off, strip her to the bones. Not me! Julia! Not me!"

V

The intent of *1984* is to make clear the kind of society which would evolve with the perfection of totalitarianism. That Winston's home is London, not Moscow, suggests the entire world's vulnerability to such tyranny. The novel is a demonic apocalypse, predicting the end product of the world's political tendencies of the 1930s and 1940s should their drift go unchecked. Its movement, the reverse of Dante's *Divine Comedy*, is from a paradise lying in Winston's distant memory of a Golden Country where tragedy, privacy, love, and friendship were still options, through the purgatory of the Ministry of Love, to the hell of the closing pages where Winston scribbles "$2 + 2 = 5$" and knows that he loves Big Brother. Orwell's *1984* is thus a demonic comedy. It also makes full and appropriately ironic use of theological imagery. Big Brother is the hidden God, infallible and omnipotent; the source, in Newspeak's terms, of all knowledge, wisdom, happiness, and virtue; "a focusing point for love, fear, and reverence." O'Brien is priest: he promises to "save" Winston, to wash him clean and make him perfect; and he evokes from his victim something akin to worship. O'Brien, moreover, carries his promises to fulfillment, if we but remember that Newspeak provides the art of using words to express the polar opposite of what has customarily been expected of them: the final paradise of *1984* is the hell of common parlance, and Big Brother is Satan, with O'Brien his earthly surrogate. Orwell has conceived a perfect hell, a place for men who have surrendered their manhood and betrayed not only other men, but the image of God in which, before the Party relieved him of the prerogative of creation, they were created.

The novel *1984* is frightening not only in its prediction

of what will ensue should totalitarianism have its way. It is frightening in its intimation that all of us have a breaking point, whether or not it is ever tested. Unnerving also is the fact that Winston seems a man more courageous, more persistent, more resistant than most of us, and that even he calls for the intercession of Julia that he may be spared. Perhaps even more disconcerting in its implications about human nature is that Julia was not the first whom he would willingly sacrifice. Among his early and less happy dream-memories is one of his mother and sister sinking deep into a subterranean grave, a horror for which he bore the responsibility and for whose victims he refused to intercede:

He was out in the light and air while they were being sucked down to death, and they were down there *because* he was up here. He knew it and they knew it, and he could see the knowledge in their faces. There was no reproach either in their faces or in their hearts, only the knowledge that they must die in order that he might remain alive, and that this was part of the unavoidable order of things.

He could not remember what had happened, but he knew in his dream that in some way the lives of his mother and his sister had been sacrificed to his own.

While it is comforting to note that there were once two persons who readily sacrificed themselves for another, we should recall that Winston's mother and sister lived prior to the refined techniques of Room 101.

To reflect on Winston's odyssey through *1984* is to entertain the dreadful thought that there may be ingenious devices, real or potential, capable of subverting the love and fidelity of any man, of inducing him to sacrifice his parents, his wife, his children for his own self-preservation. George Orwell has shown what the collective state intent only on demonic power may do to individual men. He also occasions us to ask if our own last particle of decency is maintained only because we have not yet been touched to the quick.

The Soul's Sad Delight

*. . . how there is no death.**

. . . [a] secret deposit of exquisite moments.

. . . one must seek out the people who completed them; even the places.

. . . there being in her a thread of life which for toughness, endurance, power to overcome obstacles, and carry her triumphantly through he had never known the like of.

I

Virginia Woolf confesses to having read little of D. H. Lawrence and to falling short of keen enthusiasm for his work. We may assume her assent to his desire for fully harmonious relationships between men and women (her marriage to Leonard Woolf was uncommonly gratifying) and between mankind and the living universe, which she savored with an intensity equal to, though less frenetically expressed than, that of Lawrence. He is simply too explicitly prophetic for her taste. In "Notes on D. H. Lawrence," she remarks the admirable vividness of *Sons and Lovers,* particularly in its capturing "the rapture of physical being," but she complains that with Lawrence "[e]verything has a use, a meaning, is not

* *Mrs. Dalloway* by Virginia Woolf (New York: Harcourt, Brace, 1925). Copyright 1925 by Harcourt, Brace, Inc.; copyright 1953 by Leonard Woolf. Reprinted by permission of the publisher.

an end in itself." And after a reading of his letters she acknowledges, in her diary entry of October 2, 1932, that she is put off by his "repetition of one idea," that she does not want " 'a philosophy,' " and that his preaching "rasps" her. She then turns to more positive comment: "Art is being rid of all preaching: things in themselves: the sentence in itself beautiful: multitudinous seas; daffodils that come before the swallow dares: whereas Lawrence would only say what proved something."

A decade earlier, summing up in her diary entry of June 19, 1923, some of her hopes for a novel then in composition, Virginia Woolf had written: "I want to criticise the social system, and to show it at work, at its most intense." The novel, tentatively entitled *The Hours,* was published in 1925 as *Mrs. Dalloway.* From the brief statement of intent, a reader might anticipate in *Mrs. Dalloway* something akin to John Galsworthy's *The Forsyte Saga,* which had appeared the year before the notation; or perhaps in the tradition of H. G. Wells's novels of social criticism published during the 1890s and 1900s; or perhaps even similar to Lawrence's lamentations at what industrialism had done to the texture of human life. In any case, a fictional criticism of the social system seems at first glance counter to a novel whose art lies in its "being rid of all preaching." In fact, however, *Mrs. Dalloway* is both.

In *Mrs. Dalloway,* as in her other novels, Virginia Woolf above all bears witness to her world, but never confuses the role of witness with that of sociologist or preacher or philosopher. In "The Novels of Thomas Hardy," a commemorative essay following close upon his death, she quotes approvingly Hardy's remarks that a novel "is an impression, not an argument," and that "[u]nadjusted impressions have their value . . . the road to a true philosophy of life seems to lie in humbly recording diverse readings of its phenomena as they are forced upon us by chance and change." A novel is thus conceived not as an argument or theory which in turn generates characters to substantiate its theme. It is instead something "forced upon" its creator through his impressions and intuitions of the universe unfolding itself daily, and frequently contradictorily, before him. He is called upon first and always to observe the changing forms and motions of a human and natural world too diverse for reduction to the consistency of argumentative position. To life's protean phenomena he must be attentive, never imposing a facile, distorting structure on the rich fragments confronting him. The intention of *Mrs. Dalloway* is to bear witness to human beings and to the social impulses of the early 1920s, but neither to simplify them nor to proffer for their cure amelioratively practical prescriptions.

Virginia Woolf bears witness primarily to what is to her the ultimate reality—the human soul. In "The Russian Point of View," published in the same year as *Mrs. Dalloway,* she comments on the stories of Tchekov, observing that he is aware of social injustices without being a reformer, is interested in the mind without overemphasizing its importance. It is the soul's condition that most intrigues him, particularly in its relation to health and goodness, in its intrinsic illness and recuperative powers. "In reading Tchekov," she writes, "we find ourselves repeating the word 'soul' again and again. . . . Indeed, it is the soul that is the chief character in Russian fiction." The novels of Dostoevsky, she continues, "are composed purely and wholly of the stuff of the soul." Out of such vision and intensity there "tumbles upon us, hot, scalding, mixed, marvellous, terrible, oppressive—the human soul."

At the center of *Mrs. Dalloway* is the soul of Clarissa Dalloway. It is a force both centripetal and centrifugal, affecting all that falls within its orbit and absorbing gratefully all that touches its sensitive vision.

I I

Mrs. Dalloway is in part, as already mentioned, Virginia Woolf's express attempt "to criticise the social system, and to show it at work, at its most intense." The novel exemplifies its author's continuing interest in exploring both the souls of her characters and the soul of her time. Though its protagonists are from the upper middle class it presents virtually every manner of character, from prime minister to nursemaid, even if fleetingly in many cases. Like Joyce's *Ulysses, Mrs. Dalloway* encompasses but one day, in mid-June of 1923, which yet serves as microcosmic reflection of a London whose temperament and citizens still bear the scars of a world war. The day's passing is marked by the periodic tolling of Big Ben. The prevailing tone of frustration and sickness of heart broken only intermittently by gusts of joy and personal satisfaction is a mirror of Virginia Woolf's own response to life, of her will's persistent and sometimes successful struggle to find cause for exultation in a universe seemingly ruled by perverse gods. Beautifully expressive of that thin thread of happiness which may be salvaged from a world gone berserk is her diary notation for October 25, 1920: "Why is life so tragic; so like a little strip of pavement over an abyss. I look down; I feel giddy; I wonder how I am ever to walk to the end." And after enumerating some of the immediate causes, serious and less serious, of her melancholy, she continues: "Yet I'm persuaded that these are trivial things; it's life itself, I think sometimes, for us in our generation so tragic—no newspaper placard without its shriek of agony from someone. . . . Unhappiness is everywhere; just beyond the door; or stupidity, which is worse. . . . And with it all how happy I am—if it weren't for my feeling that it's a strip of pavement over an abyss." As the most cursory reading of her fiction would attest, moreover, she shares with the Russian novelists what she describes in "The Russian Point of View" as their "assumption that in a world bursting with misery the chief call upon us is to understand our fellow-suffers, 'and not with the mind—for it is easy with the mind—but with the heart. . . .'" Even the Miss Kilmans and the Hugh Whitbreads, those least attractive characters of the novel, elicit from us an occasional tender sentiment. Virginia

Woolf seldom relinquishes her gift of compassion and never forgets that human beings are not caricatures, but complex blends of courage and cowardice, generosity and selfishness, joys and sorrows, though the proportions differ.

The novel traces two main clusters of action, one climaxing in Clarissa Dalloway's party, the other in Septimus Warren Smith's suicide. From various of Virginia Woolf's diary entries we learn her anxiety lest the two actions fail to coalesce. But it can easily be argued that the suicide of the unbalanced Septimus does echo reverberantly into the Dalloway circle—that Peter Walsh is led to speculate on London's "civilisation" as he hears the screaming ambulance bearing Septimus, dead or dying; that Clarissa's party, toward which the whole day has been moving, encounters a momentary pall through news of the casualty; and that Clarissa herself, whose impressions and feelings throughout the day have noticeably much in common with those of the Septimus whom she knows not, is strangely moved by news of his death to thoughts of a bell which tolls not for him alone. The two major actions, despite the author's expressed anxieties, do coalesce. Beyond such relationship of action there is in *Mrs. Dalloway* a more comprehensive unifying principle. Instructive in this respect is Virginia Woolf's assertion in "The Novels of Turgenev" that the unity informing his works is one of emotion, not of events. From a central character emotions irradiate, touch upon and mingle with those of other characters, and blend with the cosmic presence. The reader, at the novel's end, feels "a sense of completeness," evoked not simply through unity of protagonist, or soundly played concords and discords among characters and events, but through the perfect emotional fusion of every element, animate and inanimate, of the novel's universe. In the novels of Turgenev, Virginia Woolf writes,

the individual never dominates; many other things seem to be going on at the same time. We hear the hum of life in the fields; a horse champs his bit; a butterfly circles and settles. And as we notice, without seeming to notice, life going on, we feel more intensely for the men and women themselves because they are not the whole of life, but only part of the whole. Something of this, of course, is due to the fact that Turgenev's people are profoundly conscious of their relation to things outside themselves.

The passage is in large part descriptive of *Mrs. Dalloway* as well. For though the novel is dominated by Clarissa's presence, it is also infused with the sights and sounds of a sprawling London whose motions—of flowers and trees, of clocks and jewels, of motor car and ambulance and aeroplane, of shops and homes, of all manner of persons—never cease. *Mrs. Dalloway* is the anatomy of an entire culture.

III

Of Virginia Woolf's many achievements in *Mrs. Dalloway*, perhaps most remarkable is her bringing together the diversity of its London—particularly its people, though its places as well—into so satisfying a unity. There are innumerable threads crisscrossing and zigzagging in ways sufficiently various to relate a person in some way even to those he may never see. Certainly one predominant unifying mode is the city's simultaneous concentration upon some single, central sound or sight. Many Londoners are within hearing of the Big Ben striking those hours (and its quarters) which pattern their day; and before the sound fades, its leaden circles finally dissolving in the air, it is shared by a now bustling, now quieted metropolis. More electrifyingly demanding of attention in the late forenoon of Clarissa Dalloway's June day are, first a motor car, and then an aeroplane, each of which provides a point of concentration for a heterogeneous citizenry. Shortly before the stroke of eleven, a shotlike noise draws manifold regard to a luxurious motor car whose punctured tire has detonated, and whose distinguished, aristocratic passenger peers briefly through its window before the blinds are drawn. This unifying center of attraction elicits myriad responses, as the explosion, the car's magnificence, and the imposing face radiate centrifugally to embrace persons who may never be related, one to the others, in any other way. To Edgar J. Watkiss it is "The Proime Minister's kyar." To the mad Septimus the sound is harbinger of the world's end, and he the sole obstacle to the approaching, final conflagration. To his wife Lucrezia and to Clarissa, who emerges from a shop with flowers for her party, the face which appeared fleetingly may well be the queen's. A little later the departing car inclines all eyes and ears in its direction and, proceeding down St. James's Street, it invites the inspection of those well-dressed men without whom London's business world would come to a halt, men who, "looking out, perceived instinctively that greatness was passing, and the pale light of the immortal presence fell upon them as it had fallen upon Clarissa Dalloway." There are those too who linger at the gates of Buckingham Palace—Sarah Bletchley, Emily Coates, a gentleman with an Aberdeen terrier, little Mr. Bowley—hoping for a glimpse of royalty and thrilling to the car's approach.

As suddenly as the car had gathered to itself the eyes, ears, and speculations of London, it passes on, replaced by sight and sound of an aeroplane puffing letters into the sky. Mrs. Coates thinks they spell one word, Mrs. Bletchley another, Mr. Bowley still another. Lucrezia, remembering Dr. Holmes's counsel that her husband be diverted from his ghastly, death-centered introspectiveness, calls his attention to the new phenomenon. And as the car had beaconed to Septimus the world's approaching end, the aeroplane bears its own mysterious message, whose beauty calls him to tears. To Septimus everything is rising and falling, thinning and thickening: trees, sparrows, fountains, sounds. All point unmistakably not to a passing motor car or a skywriting aeroplane, but to "the birth of a new religion" and to "how there is no death." To Mrs. Dempster the swooping, falling plane calls to mind her long attraction to foreign places, and desire to visit her missionary nephew. To Mr. Bentley, the plane is "a symbol . . . of man's soul." Thus centripetally drawn to the tolling of an hour, the passing of a car, the smoke-formed letters in the sky, London is transformed from an isolated assortment of discrete and lonely inhabitants to a society of man bound to man. Virginia Woolf's imagery is forever delicately cast in motions of procession and recession: sights and sounds rise, ripple, vibrate, agitate, graze, living out their moments which are pervasive if fleeting, to be dissolved only after they have performed their ministry of effecting a unity among seemingly quite disparate elements.

The soul of London is composed of the souls of its people. And in *Mrs. Dalloway* it is above all the soul of Clarissa which touches upon, directly and indirectly, the souls of other persons, thus weaving, visibly and invisibly, those threads that bind. Writing on August 2, 1924, of the developing Clarissa, Virginia Woolf observes: "But oh the delicacy and complexity of the soul—for haven't I begun to tap her and listen to her breathing after all?" To the novel's individual souls we may now turn, beginning with that of Septimus Smith, who may at first glance seem so remote from Clarissa and who yet, in impulse and sensitivity, bears her close kinship. *Mrs. Dalloway's* inclusion of a man driven mad by the war and its memories is, moreover, quite appropriate to the novel's total portrait; he substantiates well the truth of the avowal, "so prying and insidious were the fingers of the European War."

Septimus has, on that June day of his suicide, been married some four or five years to the Milanese Lucrezia, whom he had met in his loneliness shortly after the war. His insanity springs from the death, just before the Armistice, of his officer and closest friend, Evans. The loss, first rendering Septimus numb and insensitive ("he could not feel"), has now led to visions and hallucinations making normal social intercourse impossible. Visited periodically by the ghostly Evans, Septimus is convinced that he too has returned from death to life, this time as the very Lord to whom has been revealed all truth and meaning—that "trees are alive," that "there is no crime," that there is "love, universal love" —revelations which he must in turn make known to the world. Yet the world to which Septimus has returned from the war seems at almost every point to contradict his visions, and certainly to have changed drastically in just a few short years. For he had, in youthful idealism, gone "to France to save an England which consisted almost entirely of Shakespeare's plays and Miss Isabel Pole [his affectionate literary mentor] in a green dress walking in a square." But by the time of his homecoming even Shakespeare—or was it Septimus?—had changed. Beauty of language had been transformed to loathing of humanity, song to dirge, and celebration of human grandeur to "the putting on of clothes, the getting of children, the sordidity of the mouth and the belly!" Septimus, contemplating death and reflecting on the obtuse Dr. Holmes and the arrogant Dr. Bradshaw, both of whom to him seem more intent on his misery than on his cure, now sees human nature as "the repulsive brute, with the blood-red nostrils." It is, finally, Dr. Holmes, playing well the brutal image attributed to him, who drives Septimus to his fatal leap. And the death of Septimus has, like Big Ben, its own vibrant ripples that stir the soul of Clarissa Dalloway, whose thoughts also embrace Shakespeare and death on that day of suicide.

Clarissa's relations with what we may call the Dalloway circle are, of course, much closer than her invisible ties with Septimus. Each member of her circle labors under his or her own peculiar sickness of soul, though a lesser sickness than that of Septimus. And as we come to know Clarissa and those closest to her on that June day, we learn also of the time, some three decades earlier, when she and they formed their friendships and loves at Bourton, her family home. Her husband Richard, Peter Walsh, Sally Seton, Hugh Whitbread— all of them knew Bourton. And now, still pale from a recent illness, just turned fifty-one, and rather sadly impressed with the condition of middle age, Clarissa nevertheless wakes to the day of her party in buoyant spirits. She has scarcely risen before her thoughts turn back to Bourton where, at eighteen, she had made the choice—to marry Richard Dalloway rather than Peter Walsh—which has largely determined her life. To know some of the events of the early 1890s is to understand better the small society we meet in 1923. And to observe that society, however small, is to recognize the successful issue of Virginia Woolf's stated intention "to criticise the social system, and to show it at work, at its most intense."

We come to know, rather well, three women (not counting Clarissa) representing widely divergent modes of life, none of them better than Sally Seton, unexpected guest at the party. Sally, extraordinarily attractive and rather impoverished (even to the necessity of pawning her ruby ring, gift of a French ancestor who had known Marie Antoinette), had found her way to Bourton over thirty years ago. It was she who, once having forgotten her sponge, had run naked through the halls of Bourton; who had smoked cigars; who had known something about sex and had discussed with Clarissa the catastrophe that marriage, any marriage, is; who, with shocking effect, had reported the slightest of assaults made upon her by the sedate Hugh Whitbread; who had once kissed Clarissa on the lips; and whose presence had inspired in Clarissa a feeling proclaimed by Othello—"if it were now to die 'twere now to be most happy." Sally's return to the Dalloway circle some thirty years later, a Sally now somewhat less lustrous and lovely (middle age works simultaneously among contemporaries), is the return of a woman who has used her idiosyncratic charms well—if it is well to be married to "a bald man with a large buttonhole who owned, it was said, cotton mills at Manchester"; to have conceived five boys, all enormous and at least some of whom at Eton with cases of mumps; to have "myriads of servants, miles of conservatories"; to have an income of ten thousand pounds a year and be in a position to neither know nor care whether the stated income is before or after taxes. Sally Seton, now Lady Rosseter, once rich in her poverty, seems now somewhat poor in her wealth.

To Miss Kilman, who never knew Bourton but now tutors Clarissa's daughter Elizabeth, no richness of person, position, or possession has been granted. She, though to a lesser extent than Septimus, has also felt the war's dispossessiveness. Just launched, less than a decade earlier, on her career at Miss Dolby's school, her German origin (Kilman had once been Kiehlman) caused her dismissal, for Miss Dolby was careful and patriotic if not charitable. Later, through Richard Dalloway's kindness, she had come to Elizabeth as tutor; and through God's grace, "Our Lord had come to her." As the Lord comes first with her, she is desperately anxious to come first with Elizabeth, to draw her from her mother's influence. Miss Kilman is one of those rare persons who can move Clarissa to ugly thoughts, the only person who can stir the "brutal monster" of hate in Clarissa's soul. Clarissa resents Miss Kilman's closeted prayer meetings with Elizabeth, her embittered pride in her poverty (worn mackintosh and all), her formidable and sinister bearing as she stands "with the power and taciturnity of some prehistoric monster armoured for primeval warfare." But Miss Kilman's defensive attitude, as well as her self-pity, has its reasons ("Never," she feels, "would she come first with any one"), and we are moved to compassion in knowing that eating, which she accomplishes rather untidily, is just about the only pleasure that a hostile or indifferent world provides her. If Sally Lady Rosseter is the poor little rich girl who makes it with a bald husband, five enormous sons, servants, conservatories, and ten thousand a year (before or after taxes), Miss Kilman, who never smoked cigars or ran naked through corridors or knew about sex, makes it not at all. The anxieties and longings of her sad soul are most poignantly expressed as her beloved Elizabeth is about to take leave following their afternoon tea together:

She was about to split asunder, she felt. The agony was so terrific. If she could grasp her, if she could clasp her, if she could make her hers absolutely and forever and then die; that was all she wanted. But to sit here, unable to think of anything to say; to see Elizabeth turning against her; to be felt repulsive even by her—it was too much; she could not stand it. The thick fingers curled inwards.

And then there is Lady Bruton, to the manor born as Sally was not, and born to lead, as Miss Kilman was not. At sixty-two she can look back to a series of triumphs, personal and political. It was perhaps on her advice, certainly with her knowledge, that General Sir Talbot Moore had once issued the telegram ordering the advance of British troops. If Miss Kilman is formidable in her way, Lady Bruton is more formidable in her own. "She should," we are told, "have been a general of dragoons herself." No woman, we are also told, could better "have worn the helmet and shot the arrow . . . have led troops to attack, ruled with indomitable justice barbarian hordes and lain under a shield noseless in a church, or made a green grass mound on some primeval hillside" than Millicent Bruton. On this June day she uses her power and position to summon Richard Dalloway and Hugh Whitbread to lunch at her home where, postprandially, Hugh, who possesses the highest skill in letter-writing, if in little else, drafts to the *Times* an epistle promoting her "project for emigrating young people of both sexes born of respectable parents and setting them up with a fair prospect of doing well in Canada." The portraits of Sally Seton, Miss Kilman, and Lady Bruton are not only exquisitely conceived in themselves. They serve to convey with fine economy the sense of the larger order of society in which they live, a sense supplemented not only, of course, by Clarissa, but by—to refer only to some of the female company of the novel—the maid Lucy, the florist Miss Pym, Miss Bletchley and Miss Coates and Miss Dempster, the secretary Milly Brush, Lady Bradshaw, the old lady whose house faces the Dalloways', the coming-of-age Elizabeth, the bereaved Lucrezia Smith.

Men also inhabit Clarissa's world, and we must infer
that, of the three who habitually visited Bourton over thirty
years ago—Richard Dalloway, Hugh Whitbread, and Peter
Walsh—Richard was a wise choice for marriage. Possessed of
a warm though rather dispassionate heart, he was kind to the
once jobless Miss Kilman, is sympathetic toward the unfortunate Armenians (or was it the Albanians?), and is attentive
at the party to the otherwise ignored Ellie Henderson. Clarissa,
chiding herself for doing things to enhance her attractiveness
to others, notes that the self-effacing Richard "did things for
themselves," and Peter Walsh finds him, of all the men at
the party, "the most disinterested." Yet Richard has not quite
the mind or the heart to achieve greatness as statesman or
husband: Sally had predicted that his "second-class brain"
would forever keep him short of a cabinet post; and we
see that his greatest effort could not bring him on that June
day to say to Clarissa, in so many words, "I love you." Peter,
who lost Clarissa to Richard, passes sound judgment when
he reflects of Richard: "He was a thorough good sort; a bit
limited; a bit thick in the head; yes; but a thorough good
sort." And Sally Seton's last remark about him is equally perceptive: "What does the brain matter . . . compared with
the heart?"

Hugh Whitbread comes out considerably less well than
Richard. As far back as Bourton Sally had enragedly told
him he "represented all that was most detestable in British
middle-class life," and had later remarked to Peter that
Hugh had read, thought, felt nothing. And Peter, thirty years
later, finds him a snob, a prig, and further characterizes him
with keen acerbity: "And he'd found his job—married his
Honourable Evelyn; got some little post at Court, looked
after the King's cellars, polished the Imperial shoe-buckles,
went about in knee-breeches and lace ruffles." Should we be
inclined to attribute such judgments to the sharpness of
tongue habitual to Sally and Peter, we need only observe Hugh

at Mr. Dubonnet's jewelry shop to witness the lengths to which pomposity and arrogance may go.

Peter Walsh is, to define him most precisely, the man who did not win the hand of Clarissa Parry. His life's failures —he himself recognizes that "his whole life . . . [has] been a failure"—are many: he has failed at Oxford, lost Clarissa to Richard partly by default, been a poor socialist, never carried out his writing plans, married and lost one woman, and is, in June of 1923, contemplating and not contemplating marriage to the wife of a major and the mother of two, a woman who inspires in his flickering heart more jealousy than love. He is fighting a middle age which has, in fact, advanced him little beyond adolescence. Over fifty, he on the same day weeps uncontrollably into Clarissa's lap and tracks a young lady through the streets of London, fantasying a meeting which never comes off. We pity him, this "solitary traveller," in his rationalization that he no longer needs people ("one doesn't want people after fifty," he reflects), knowing as we do that he will always need others to fill the vacancies in his own person. Peter is a man who does little and says much, frequently in derision of those who have come to better terms with life than he. Yet we are indebted to him for giving us a fuller portrait of Clarissa Parry Dalloway than we would have without him. And we must admit that, with all his fickleness and vacillation, he is constant in one respect—his thirty-odd-year devotion to Clarissa. Though his judgments of her may occasionally be harsh (she had, after all, passed him by for Richard), he loves her to the full capacity of his mercurial and less than profound passion. He constantly scolds her—by word, by glance, by thought—but for every observed or imagined defect or defection (except perhaps her marriage to Richard), he finds a counterbalancing virtue.

The faults Peter has always attributed to Clarissa are perhaps without exception characteristics he has seen as preventing his possession of her. He has found her cold, heartless, prudish, rigid, unyielding, and never more so than when she rejected him for the more conventional and more dependable Richard. It was at Bourton on a summer day early in the 1890s that Peter first ascribed to Clarissa a phrase he recalls again in 1923: "The death of the soul." He had pronounced it following upon a relatively trivial incident. But the remark, made on the very day of Richard's first visit to Bourton, was prophetically timed, for both he and Sally came to see Richard as a man whose marriage to Clarissa would "stifle her soul . . . make a mere hostess of her, encourage her worldliness." And none of Peter's disparaging charges against Clarissa was more cuttingly offered, upsettingly received, and long remembered than the comment that "she had the makings of the perfect hostess," a complaint springing in large part from his besetting jealousy and his bitter unwillingness to share her with anyone else. But the remark was ostensibly meant to imply a frivolity in Clarissa, a preference for parties over the more serious pursuits of life. Even so, Peter later acknowledges (at least to himself) her perfect manners and social instincts, her making of her home a meeting place where time and again she would "take some raw youth, twist him, turn him, wake him up; set him going." And despite all his ill-tempered criticisms he finds in Clarissa "a thread of life which for toughness, endurance, power to overcome obstacles, and carry her triumphantly through he had never known the like of."

Of all Peter's reflections and meditations upon Clarissa, most illuminating is a theory he made up to account for her behavior, which to him is bred of skepticism and humanity. Perhaps, he theorizes, Clarissa might even say to herself:

As we are a doomed race, chained to a sinking ship . . . as the whole thing is a bad joke, let us, at any rate, do our part; mitigate the sufferings of our fellow-prisoners . . . decorate the dungeon with flowers and air-cushions; be as decent as we possibly can. Those ruffians, the Gods, shan't have it all their own way,—her notion being that the Gods, who never lost a chance of hurting, thwarting and spoiling human lives were seriously put out if, all the same, you behaved like a lady. . . . Later [after the horrible death of her sister] she wasn't so positive perhaps; she thought there were no Gods; no one was to blame; and so she evolved this atheist's religion of doing good for the sake of goodness.

Clarissa knows that Peter knows her well, and she is discomforted as he chides her openly or stands in gloomy, silent disapproval at her party. She can bear the disapproval, believing she half deserves it. It is Peter's total possessiveness that had been too much for her and had really disqualified him for marriage. He has never had any sense of the sanctity of privacy, could not hold back in Bourton days from prying toward the innermost secrecies of her soul, was arrogant in his demands that she commit herself wholly to him. Richard, on the other hand, has always granted the independence she needs. There is in people, Clarissa reflects, a dignity, a solitude, "even between husband and wife a gulf; and that one must respect." Peter would have offended persons less fastidious than Clarissa, and she was more fastidious than most, certainly in sexual matters. She is frequently imaged as a nun, unable to "dispel a virginity preserved through childbirth which clung to her like a sheet," and her response to Peter's recent involvement with the major's wife is perhaps excessive. She does not see the liaison for what it is—infantile, pathetic, halfhearted, as must be expected of a stunted man; rather, she sees his "love" (the sentiment, not the woman) as "that monster," and thinks of his passion as "[h]orrible" and "[d]egrading."

Clarissa, it is true, falls short (as, indeed, does Peter!) of enjoying that blood-intimacy with another person so precious to Lawrence. Yet she savors virtually every motion of her universe, admittedly narrow though it may in some ways be. Hardly a quality of her everyday world fails to make its impression upon, and to lay claim to the gratitude of, her soul. For her, the variegated sights and sounds of life, her dogs and canaries, her servants, above all her husband Richard—these are among those unnumbered blessings which comprise for her a "secret deposit of exquisite moments." And though some of her reasons for devotion to the role of perfect hostess may be self-indulgent, the overwhelmingly informing reason springs from her humane gratitude. Her parties are to her, above all, repayments, tokens of appreciation, offerings to a bountiful, if godless, universe and to its human inhabitants. This world of persons, places, and things she loves; and such love occasions not only her bursts of thankfulness, but her painful reflections that she must some day leave behind a world so good. On this June day of 1923 Clarissa looks back to a youthful Bourton, looks presently upon a middle-aged Mrs. Richard Dalloway no longer Clarissa Parry, and sees in Lady Bruton, ten years her senior, the harbinger of her own steady lockstep toward life's end. Clarissa, we are told,

feared time itself, and read on Lady Bruton's face, as if it had been a dial cut in impassive stone, the dwindling of life; how year by year her share was sliced; how little the margin that remained was capable any longer of stretching, of absorbing, as in the youthful years, the colours, salts, tones of existence, so that she filled the room she entered, and felt often as she stood hesitating one moment on the threshold of her drawing-room, an exquisite suspense, such as might stay a diver before plunging while the sea darkens and brightens beneath him, and the waves which threaten to break, but only gently split their surface, roll and conceal and encrust as they just turn over the weeds with pearl.

It is no wonder that Clarissa's party is for her a matter of great importance, one of the summits of a life which will inevitably give way to death.

I V

Clarissa's day begins and ends on thoughts of death, such meditations providing still another binding of the novel's abundant diversity. As Clarissa walks to the flower shop on that bright June morning and rejoices in what she sees, she reflects that she will some day see and rejoice no more. But she has come to believe, so organic is her sense of the whole created order, that to die is not to die, and that she will survive in all the persons she knows and does not know, even in the trees and houses that line her daily walks. She recalls, as Septimus does later, those lines from Shakespeare's *Cymbeline*, sung by Guiderius as the presumably dead Imogen is borne before him: "Fear no more the heat o' the sun / Nor the furious winter's rages." Death is, as the song goes on to say, a "quiet consummation." Clarissa looks beyond death to her continuing presence in a world she loves so well. For she has, as we learn later from Peter's retrospective musings, a theory which both affirms immortality of a sort and serves to overcome her sadness at not knowing, and not being known by, other persons so intimately as she could wish. In order for any person to know any other person and to survive beyond death, she believes,

one must seek out the people who completed them; even the places. Odd affinities she had with people she had never spoken to, some woman in the street, some man behind a counter—even trees, or barns. It ended in a transcendental theory which, with her horror of death, allowed her to believe, or say that she believed (for all her scepticism), that since our apparitions, the part of us which appears, are so momentary compared with the other, the unseen part of us, which spreads wide, the unseen might survive, be recovered somehow attached to this person or that, or even haunting certain places after death . . . perhaps—perhaps.

It is more than perhaps, for the apparition of Septimus Smith, now dead, spreads to Clarissa's party and attaches itself to a truly "perfect hostess," perfect enough to empathize with the dead as well as the living. The Bradshaws, whom Clarissa has the good taste to dislike, arrive late, bringing with them news of Septimus. With remarkable sensitivity Clarissa reenacts the death: the ground flashes up to her as it had to the plunging Septimus; the rusty spikes pierce her body; the dull thud impacts her ears. And with keen intuition she asks herself if the "obscurely evil" Sir William Bradshaw —who, we may recall, invoked "proportion" but actually worshiped "conversion," that wicked power of bending another to one's own will—if he might not have outrageously forced the soul of Septimus; she wonders "if this young man had gone to him, and Sir William had impressed him, like that, with his power, might he not then have said (indeed she felt it now), Life is made intolerable; they make life intolerable, men like that?" Most importantly, Clarissa, who knows that every person is bound to every other person, knows too that she, as well as Dr. Bradshaw, shares the guilt for Septimus's death:

> Somehow it was her disaster—her disgrace. It was her punishment to see sink and disappear here a man, there a woman, in this profound darkness, and she forced to stand here in her evening dress. She had schemed; she had pilfered. She was never wholly admirable. She had wanted success. Lady Bexborough and the rest of it. And once she had walked on the terrace at Bourton.

As Clarissa's party and *Mrs. Dalloway* reach their ends, we feel the rich satisfaction of having come to know the most delicately traced lineaments of human souls and a societal soul as well. We feel too the satisfaction of resolution, a feeling that the novel is complete and self-contained, not petitioning us, as Virginia Woolf (in "Mr. Bennett and Mrs. Brown") affirms of the major Edwardian novels, "to do something—to join a society, or, more desperately, to write a cheque." We are simply asked to bear witness to the "true reality" of which Virginia Woolf speaks in her diary notation of June 19, 1923. In *Mrs. Dalloway* the true reality is above all Clarissa's soul, reflecting upon itself, other souls, and the physical world in which she rejoices. If in the novels of Lawrence it would seem, almost without exception, that every man is an island, it would seem in the fiction of Virginia Woolf that no man is so. In her essay "The Russian Point of View," she remarks that with Dostoevsky the story of a bank clerk, so simple at first glance, in fact irradiates in such a way that a host of persons are touched and affected by one of his seemingly most insignificant actions. So it is with *Mrs. Dalloway*, which persuades us that the society of man, seemingly so fractured, is in reality possessed of a most wondrous organic wholeness. At its center is Clarissa, whose heart embraces the whole world of the seen and the unseen.

PART FOUR

MAN AND GOD

Introduction

Introduction

Great religious literature, in any orthodox or traditional sense, has not flourished during the twentieth century. Of the literature of commitment, however, of works embracing what Paul Tillich called ultimate concerns, there has been no dearth. Examples are many: Lawrence painstakingly affirms the splendor of the earth and its creatures; Sartre devotes himself to the cause of a human freedom which distinguishes man from the rest of the animate and inanimate universe; Camus urges against life's absurdity a rebellion which nurtures the highest human value, solidarity among men. The committed works of Sartre and Camus, certainly *Nausea* and *The Plague,* are of course repudiations of biblical teachings. To Sartre, assent to the biblical proclamation of a God who creates man is the death of human choice and its attendant freedom; to Camus, biblical faith breeds, indeed *is,* the philosophical suicide which prevents rebellious opposition to the world's absurdity. At the same time Sartre, Camus, and other dissenters are strongly influenced by the biblical tradition, though in a negative sense. It is almost impossible for any strongly committed literature to bypass the Bible, largely because its teaching is so deeply ingrained in Western thought and, equally important, because it is so basically concerned with matters of good and evil, freedom and bondage, life and death. The Bible calls upon its readers to take a position for or against virtually everything of human significance; it thus remains a norm for or against which the committed person in Western culture takes his stand. Alfred North Whitehead remarked that the history of philosophy is a series of footnotes to Plato. The history of that literature which plumbs most deeply man's nature and destiny is a series of footnotes to the Bible, viewed as either model or target.

The common denominator of traditional religious literature I would define as the acceptance, by the writer and at least some of his characters, of the presence of God's grace in and beyond history. Grace is the biblical God's will and power to give man (1) a sense of the disparity between human sinfulness and divine righteousness, and (2) a conviction that his sins will be forgiven if, in contrition and to the full extent of his will, he resolves to surrender himself to God's lordship. The final power of grace is to redeem man from the bondage and absurdity of history and bring him to a condition or community purged of every misery and impurity, and knowing only love. One element of grace is the gift of faith, which rests beyond the grasp of reason and of those human senses which make known matters of knowledge. For the fruits of grace, if apprehended at all, are apprehended through Paul's dark glass, eluding every power of man's rational and sensuous perception. Grace, as well as the God who offers it, is a mystery; it is also the absolute ground of biblical thought.

To acknowledge a belief in God's grace is to acknowledge a conviction of man's sin (his contravening of God's will) and his guilt (his responsibility for such contravention). Camus acknowledges neither, seeing man as an innocent victim of hostile or indifferent forces against which he should fight a courageous, though ultimately losing, battle. For Camus there is no beneficent God whose justice man violates or whose gifts he receives. Sartre sees man as a victim of his own apathy, pusillanimity, and unimaginativeness. In Sartre's world there is no gift of grace or of any other kind— unless it be the original nothingness which enables each man to create himself. According to biblical thought, on the other hand, man in choosing to sin, to assert his own will against God's, introduces guilt into the world, so weakening himself that he can be redeemed only by a gift beyond his power and deserts, God's grace. Since medieval times it has not been unusual for Christians to view the fall as to a degree fortunate, since man's compounded sin and guilt have been the continuing occasions for the outpouring of God's grace. Milton's Adam gratefully summarizes this paradoxical argument:

> O goodness infinite, goodness immense!
> That all this good of evil shall produce,
> And evil turn to good; more wonderful
> Than that which by creation first brought forth
> Light out of darkness! full of doubt I stand,
> Whether I should repent me now of sin
> By me done and occasioned, or rejoice
> Much more, that much more good thereof shall spring,
> To God more glory, more good will to men
> From God, and over wrath grace shall abound.
> *(Paradise Lost,* XII, 469–78)

It is not surprising that relatively few distinguished twentieth-century literary works present characters of biblical faith who have both the intellectual and emotional assent of their authors. A period's literature reflects a period's assumptions, attitudes, beliefs—its predominating style of life. To contrast the subject matter and themes of, say, the metaphysical poets or Milton or Bunyan with those of the more eminent writers of the present age is to remark the vast difference between the seventeenth-century disposition toward religious matters and our own. Sartre is intent upon writing God's obituary in large letters, and Camus's Dr. Rieux (who speaks for his author) argues that if there is a God it might be better for him "if we refuse to believe in Him and struggle with all our might against death, without raising our eyes toward the heaven where He sits in silence." And for many of our contemporaries, God, if alive at all, is deemed hardly a major factor in man's daily thoughts, decisions, and aspirations; such writers seem content to let the matter of God's life or death pass unobserved.

The three novels I have chosen to discuss in this final

section are in their religious natures quite diverse. I sought first a novelist who represented a quite explicit religious position. Georges Bernanos, Graham Greene, François Mauriac, and Charles Williams came immediately to mind. The reasons for my choice of Mauriac are at least three: his novels intrigue me; their religious orthodoxy has been hostilely questioned by Christians and non-Christians; such criticism impelled Mauriac to write various expository, "apologetic" essays which illuminate beautifully his sense of the relationship between his faith and his fiction. Mauriac's *Woman of the Pharisees* gives clear expression to his conviction of the presence of God's grace in and beyond history. The novel's dramatic tension is both interpersonal and intrapersonal. The former is the conflict between Madame Brigitte Pian, vivid embodiment of that pharisaical temperament whose punctiliously narrow devotion to legal proscription at first shuts out the light of compassion and sensibility, and the Abbé Calou, curé of Balzac, whose saintliness is as tenaciously rigorous as Brigitte's pharisaism. There is also the conflict within Madame Pian, whose fiendish propensities gradually give way to the promptings of the Holy Spirit. At first bound to the demonic emotions of hate, suspicion, selfishness, and self-righteousness, she is then through the instrumentality of the curé brought by slow stages to the recognition that it is God's grace, not a corrupted human will, which engenders the love that defines true righteousness. In the tradition of the medieval morality play, *Woman of the Pharisees* presents the conflict of good and evil for the possession of a human soul.

Franz Kafka's *The Castle* is a more ambiguous, less explicitly and traditionally religious novel than *Woman of the Pharisees*. Madame Pian knew perfectly well the object of her desire—the biblical God's grace—though she had a distorted sense of the channel which carries that grace to the human soul. But the heart's desire of K., *The Castle's* protagonist, like that of Samuel Beckett's Vladimir and Estragon, is but dimly discerned; though deeply desired, it remains largely undefined. It is true that *The Castle* has frequently been read as a search for biblical grace and its issuing salvation. Max Brod, Kafka's friend, literary executor, biographer, and critic, viewed the novel in this way. Camus, in his essay on Kafka, writes that *The Castle* "is first of all the individual adventure of a soul in quest of its grace"; that for its author there "is nothing that is not God's"; and that the novel is an example of the evasive leap of faith. Thomas Mann, in his homage to Kafka prefacing the definitive English edition of *The Castle*, also affirms the novel's biblical basis: "For it is plain that regular life in a community, the ceaseless struggle to become 'a native,' is simply the technique for improving K.'s relations with the 'Castle,' or rather to set up relations with it: to attain nearer, in other words, to God and to a state of grace." But I find it difficult to interpret *The Castle* in so explicitly a biblical context, or to equate the dim, undefined object of K.'s persistent search with the grace toward which and by which a Mauriac or Bernanos or Greene protagonist moves and is moved. More helpful, I think, than the suggestions of Brod, Camus, and Mann are those of Eugène Ionesco in his essay "By Way of Postscript," found in *Notes and Counter Notes*:

[The] theme of man astray in the labyrinth, without a guiding thread, is primordial, as we know, in Kafka's work: if man has no guiding thread, it is because he no longer really wanted one. Hence his feeling of guilt, his anguish, the absurdity of history. Anything without a goal is absurd: and this ultimate goal can only be found outside history, it ought to guide the history of mankind, in other words give it meaning. Whether we like it or not, this reveals the profoundly religious character of all Kafka's work; when man is cut off from his religious or metaphysical roots, he is lost, all his struggles become senseless, futile and oppressive.

But why in Kafka does man suffer? Because in the last resort he exists for something other than material comfort or the ephemeral: his true vocation, from which he has turned aside, must lie in his quest for the imperishable. It is the world unsanctified that is denounced by Kafka; and this is exactly what is meant by a world without Goal; in the dark labyrinth of the world, man now reaches out only unconsciously and gropingly for a lost dimension that has completely vanished from sight.

It is this "lost dimension," something less precise than the biblical concept of grace, for which K. is groping. Any attempt to define his quest in terms of the familiar imposes a restriction on the rich—and tantalizing—openness of Kafka's world.

Hermann Broch's *The Sleepwalkers* is fiction, philosophy of history, and apocalypse. On its strictly narrative level it portrays the disintegration of Germany from 1888 to 1918, largely through three protagonists whose life styles are defined, respectively, as romantic, anarchistic, and realistic (the last given a particular Brochian meaning). It is one of Broch's major achievements that his characters and their short eras can symbolize centuries of religious history without losing in any way their vivid flesh-and-blood credibility as individual figures and periods. Broch's narrative is a microcosmic reflection of Western civilization's collapse of values, from the time of their zenith during the great Thomistic synthesis in the late Middle Ages to their near nadir at the time of the novel's closing action. History's unfolding Broch interprets as movement from a theocentric culture in which man's every act and belief was judged in terms of its apparent proximity to God's will, to an anthropocentric culture in which man pursues, irrespective of all else, what seems to be his immediate self-interest. The catastrophic turning point in Western civilization was the Protestant Reformation, whose history has been a persistent slope toward the now near complete reign of Antichrist, a time whose fullness will be marked by every man's "realistically" seeking only his own interest. But even as we now prepare for the Antichrist's coming in fullness, we are given hope through Broch's apocalyptic promise of a reversal of the past seven centuries' ebbing tide and a return of Christianity as life's center. As both work of art and theocentric philosophy of history, Hermann Broch's *The Sleepwalkers* is a vast, exciting achievement.

The Mysteries of Evil
and Grace

Brigitte Pian . . . [found] each day ever stronger rea-
sons for thanking her Creator that He had made her
*so admirable a person.**

For the first time, the impulse of gratitude that set her
in the presence of God had in it something of a tender-
ness at once humble and very human.

It had been revealed to her that our Father does not
ask us to give a scrupulous account of what merits
we can claim. She understood at last that it is not
our deserts that matter but our love.

I

We are indebted to some of François Mauriac's more disap-
proving critics for many of his revealing, and sometimes defensive, remarks about his fiction and his faith. Representative
of such criticism is the comment of Georges Bernanos, quoted
in Mauriac's *Mémoires Intérieurs* and comparing his fiction
"to a cellar, the walls of which are sweating with moral anguish." The eloquent simile is understandable: the Mauriac

---

* *Woman of the Pharisees* by François Mauriac, translated by Gerard
Hopkins (New York: Henry Holt, 1946). Copyright 1946 by Henry Holt
and Company, Inc. Reprinted by permission of the publisher. The novel
was first published in 1941.

reader, quickly surfeited with accounts of man's sin, wretchedness, and obsessive propensity toward bringing suffering upon
others (even upon himself), must look far for examples of
happy and loving human relationships. But Mauriac is
charged with more than a blindness to the generally pur-
ported joys and redemptive qualities of the religious life: he
is accused of a perverted fascination with the subtle, demonic
delights of sin, a perversion thought more likely to tempt
than to inspire his readers. Such criticism has been made by
various Christians, but no criticism has been more personally
directed, or more smartingly received, than that of André
Gide, who argued a great gulf between Mauriac the accomplished writer and Mauriac the professing Christian. In a
letter to Mauriac, Gide writes:

. . . what you are searching for is the *permission* . . . to be a
Catholic without having to burn your books; and it is this that makes
you write them in such a way that you will not have to disown them
on account of your Catholicism. This reassuring compromise, which
allows you to love God without losing sight of Mammon, causes you
anguish of conscience and at the same time gives a great appeal to
your face and great savour to your writings; and it ought to delight
those who, while abhorring sin, would hate not to be able to give
a lot of thought to it. You know, moreover, what the effect would
be on literature and especially on your own; and you are not
sufficiently Christian to cease to be a writer. Your particular art is
to make accomplices of your readers. The object of your novels is
not so much to bring sinners to Christianity as to remind Christians
that there is something on earth besides heaven.

Once I wrote—to the great indignation of certain people—"It
is fine sentiments that go to make bad literature." Your literature is
excellent, my dear Mauriac. Doubtless if I were more of a Christian
I should be less your disciple.

In his book of essays entitled *God and Mammon,* in which
Gide's letter is quoted, Mauriac seeks to counter the imputa-
tion that, under the guise of a Christian position, he derives
from his excursions into the more salacious aspects of human
behavior a certain forbidden joy, one generously shared with

his readers. Whether or not Mauriac's self-defense is in practice substantiated by his novels, it is theoretically impeccable.
The novel, he affirms, is above all a study of human nature
and must portray man as he is, not as the writer wishes he
were. More than this, the novelist's art (certainly that of the
Christian writer) "is concentrated on reaching the secret
source of the greatest sins." To write of sin and probe its
sources is hardly to commend it. In *God and Mammon* and
other writings, Mauriac argues the indefensibility of a literature which promotes a spurious optimism and confuses itself
with moral homily. His major goal is an accurate reflection
of the fallen creatures of this world, showing both the condition of the man at least temporarily beyond the touch of
God's grace and the transfiguration following upon the renewed flowing of that grace.

To read Mauriac's fiction is to find grounds both for his
detractors' arguments and for his self-defense. Though his
novels observe no depravity unobserved by the Bible, their
composite picture of depravity is less leavened by evidences
of tenderness. His analyses of man's fallen nature, of the
sources and workings of sin, are brilliant, though most readers
are inclined to sense an imbalance, an excessive grimness, in
his view of humanity. Mauriac, of course, sees his view as grim
but hardly distorted: in life itself he finds the quality of purity
in few individual hearts and of impurity in the large body of
mankind. In *The Son of Man,* for example, he acknowledges
the presence of saints, while at the same time insisting that
the world at large has remained obdurate to them: "The
course of history," he writes, "has not been influenced by the
saints. They have acted upon hearts and souls; but history has
remained criminal." From a Frenchman who endured two
world wars on his own soil such judgment is not surprising.
We find among the essays comprising *Cain, Where Is Your
Brother?* reflections on Buchenwald, Auschwitz, Ravensbrueck,
and Dachau. The Allied advance into Germany late in World

War II was to Mauriac a descent into hell and brought into sharp focus the concentration camps' incredible atrocities: "We . . . [saw] with our own eyes, heard with our own ears, the witnesses of the most extensive outrage which the dignity of man has ever suffered since there have been men on earth who killed each other."

Through his attempt to portray mankind as he sees it, Mauriac, I believe, seeks to protect his readers from the self-deception of wishful thinking without casting them into despair. He wishes both to dissuade men from what he believes is their mistaken view that Satan no longer exists, and to persuade them that Satan's net is not so thickly woven as to prevent escape for those persons given the faith to accept the faith. In *The Son of Man* he writes that Christians of the twentieth century, like those of the first, are called upon "to persevere in the faith in a world without faith, to remain pure in a society delivered to all manner of covetousness." And in this respect his tribute in *Letters on Art and Literature* to Georges Bernanos (of whose work he *might* have said what Bernanos said of his own—that it resembles "a cellar, the walls of which are sweating with moral anguish") is relevant:

If you were to ask me what I admire most about him, I would say that it is his faith, the fact that he never doubted God's mercy, although he was face to face with evil; that his work bears witness to the love of the Creator for His creatures; that in this murderous world in which he lived (and in which we continue to live), where this divine love is insulted, rejected, held in contempt by many, and completely ignored by many more, he held fast; that he did not lose heart when for him holiness remained crucified on the very brink of despair.

Mauriac's words about Bernanos are equally applicable to himself. Face to face with the evils of a century lacerated by the most devastating conflicts in history and with the sins and crimes of his fictional characters, Mauriac yet believes that there remains a remnant of men who bear witness to their creation in God's image and to the continuing presence of his grace. The binding force between God and man is manifested above all in the Incarnation, the God-man, Jesus Christ, the living promise that life has a purpose and man a destiny beyond the human frailties which Mauriac so persistently underscores in his fiction. When, Mauriac writes in *The Son of Man,* our bitterness and disgust with the world's travail threatens to reduce us to sheer contempt for man, then

we must remember that Christ was a man like us and that He loved us. If He was one of us, then every man, no matter how miserable he be, has a capacity for God. Since the Lord belonged carnally to the human race, we must not despair of a humanity sanctified and glorified by Him; if He loved us, it is because in spite of so many crimes we are worthy of being loved.

II

Woman of the Pharisees (1941) is one of Mauriac's most explicitly religious novels, its protagonist, Madame Brigitte Pian, owing her epithet to the Lucan parable of the Pharisee and the publican. The novel's narrator and one of its main characters is Brigitte's stepson, Louis Pian, a schoolboy of thirteen at the beginning of the novel's action. The story, the central part of which encompasses a period of about three years early in this century, is told retrospectively, as the narrator looks back over a span of decades. The tone is striking in its quality of bittersweet nostalgia, of remembrance of things past, which marks a large body of Mauriac's fiction and of which *The Desert of Love,* narrated by the embittered Raymond Courrèges, is perhaps the best example. Such a retrospective point of view carries the advantage of a double focus or temporal pattern: the past, with all the richly sensuous responses of a young boy to the events of his youth; and the present, the mature and sympathetic vantage point of an older man reflecting on his adolescent anguish. The book is cast in the form not of a novel conceived by an omnipotent author, but of a memoir composed by one of the main participants in the events recounted. Louis Pian, like the narrator of Mauriac's

The Knot of Vipers, at various times disclaims the use of invention, insisting that he is not novelist but historian or biographer. He once confesses a repugnance to the events he records, remarking at the same time that professional novelists usually eschew such repellent material. "But," he continues, "those who turn their backs on fiction, and set out to follow up the destinies of persons with whom they have actually been connected, are forever coming on the traces of these miseries and aberrations of the flesh." Mauriac, having elected not to adopt the third-person omniscient viewpoint, feels called upon to account for his narrator's widely ranged and subtly detailed knowledge of events unwitnessed by him and of psychological intricacies of minds not his own. And so Louis Pian tells us early that he is "the sort of man who keeps old papers." These include a diary of the pathetic Monsieur Puybaraud; copious writings of Abbé Calou, curé of Balzac, including one entire volume devoted to that most distressing evening and night in the lives of Jean de Mirbel and his mother, the countess; and a variety of letters from Abbé Calou, the countess, and the vengeful Hortense Voyod. Over the period of years after the novel's primary action, moreover, Louis has conversed reminiscently with other actors of those unhappy times, thus adding to his knowledge.

Woman of the Pharisees is indebted in title and theme to one of the Bible's most familiar parables; it also bears some relationship to the early Christian morality plays, with their disposition toward rather rigidly simplified division between good and evil. At the novel's center is Madame Pian, to Mauriac the embodiment of the faith's greatest threat—pharisaism. Thus she is, through most of the action, the force of evil, countered by the novel's greatest force for good, the curé, Monsieur Calou. Brigitte's pharisaism works toward the misery, sometimes the destruction, of most of the characters: her stepchildren, Louis and Michèle; Jean de Mirbel; Monsieur Puybaraud and his wife Octavia; her own husband; and the Abbé Calou himself. The curé works selflessly in behalf of

Louis, Michèle, and Jean, and, with largest measure of success and through the grace of God, is instrumental in awakening Brigitte to the self-knowledge prerequisite to her remorse, contrition, and salvation.

As almost any evil when disguised is more poisonous than the most heinous crimes when recognized as such, so the pharisaism of Brigitte is more insidious than the frivolous carnality of the Countess de Mirbel or the depraved vengefulness of Hortense Voyod. It is the juxtaposition of Brigitte's "reputation for shining virtue," her being regarded as a "reg'lar Mother of the Church," with her hypocrisy that makes for her particularly virulent influence and demonic power. The novel is the story of her regeneration, inspired by the life of, nurtured by the ministrations of, and enlightened by the spiritual counseling of the Abbé Calou. The novel is also the story of how destructive the hardness of a pharisaic heart, smugly following the letter of the law while remaining blind to its spirit, may be on the lives of those who live within its orbit. To come to know the power of such a heart we may begin with attention to Brigitte's three young victims: Jean de Mirbel and Michèle and Louis Pian. Relevant to their characterization is a remark of Mauriac's in *Words of Faith:* "A child's dream is the keystone of all my books: children love and exchange their first kisses, and for the first time experience loneliness."

The loneliness and misery of Jean de Mirbel began well before his meeting with Brigitte. His father dead, Jean had long been at the mercy of his guardian uncle, the Comte de Mirbel, whose cruelty is neurotic, and of a mother whose devotion to sensuality makes her careless of and insensitive to her son's adoration. Even before the novel's beginning Jean's anguished cries, evoked by the whippings celebrating his uncle's visits to the school Jean attended with Louis Pian, were well known. The comte's decision to place Jean under the summer care and tutorship of Monsieur Calou, whose presbytery is near the Pian home in Larjuzon, stems from his mistaken belief that the abbé is a stern disciplinarian who will

break Jean's spirited temperament. For Jean, however, his
uncle's ill will is far less ravaging than the sight, shortly after
he came to Larjuzon, of his mother and her lover etched in a
window at the Hotel Garbet. By the time Brigitte becomes an
important factor in Jean's life, he sees his chaste, reciprocated
love for Michèle Pian as the only hope of his otherwise
wretched, lonely life. And when Brigitte, moved to action by
the scandalmongering of the Vignottes, decrees that her step-
daughter neither see nor correspond with Jean, he loses for a
crucial period the one person who might have saved him from
the despair eventuating in his capitulation to Madame Voyod.
More than this, Brigitte's interdiction leads to her battle of
wills with the curé, who, seeing in Michèle's love for Jean the
boy's greatest hope for salvation, is induced to transgress the
spirit of Brigitte's prohibition of correspondence.

It is Brigitte's pathological abhorrence of sex that leads
her to forbid the meetings of Jean and Michèle, and leads
them, in turn, into the worst miseries of their adolescence. Of
love Brigitte knows nothing—at least until late in her life; of
a deeply seductive carnal impulse in virtually everyone except
herself she seems reasonably sure. It thus takes little from the
Vignottes to persuade her that the fourteen-year-old Michèle
and the sixteen-year-old Jean, when left alone, indulge in
wicked intimacies. She is quite blind to the real qualities in
Michèle, who, as Louis tells us, is "one of those human beings
whose temperaments are so surely balanced, their hearts so
pure, that their instincts are almost always at one with their
duty, so that their natural inclinations lead them to do precisely what God expects of them." The best impulses of both
Jean and Michèle are, however, consistently thwarted or
blocked by Brigitte, who, in separating the two young people,
deprives them both of what each needs most—as Monsieur
Calou so well recognizes.

Brigitte's third young victim is her stepson, Louis, who is
only a little less scarred than Jean and Michèle by the events of
adolescence. On occasion he allies himself with his stepmother

in the perpetration of evil. As a young boy, for example, he shares with her an eager interest in the scandalous, and he is treacherously led on by her to reveal what decency would judge confidential. His first sense of guilt, for which he forever feels the pain of remorse, springs from his telling Brigitte (with her own malign encouragement) of the letter which he has, presumably in confidence, mailed for Monsieur Puybaraud to his beloved Octavia. And he knows even then, in his thirteen-year-old wisdom, that it is but a feigned innocence with which he imparts the information leading to ultimate consequences of so grievous a nature, and that he is led on by a sense of self-importance and by an impulse to shock and scandalize. He recognizes too his poisonous strain of jealousy—"that mental and emotional pain which was to infect my whole existence"—which wracks him as he observes the growing mutual affection of Jean and Michèle, both of whom he wishes only for himself. Knowing his stepmother as he does, it is with comforting malice that he tells her of his sister's and friend's desire to be alone together, thus bringing to them, as he had brought to Monsieur Puybaraud, Brigitte's meddling action. Indeed, the whole novel conveys the titillating allure of scandal: that of the Countess de Mirbel, of the first Madame Pian, of Monsieur Puybaraud and Octavia Tronche, of Jean and Michèle, and Jean and Madame Voyod, and, later, even of Brigitte herself and the sexagenarian Dr. Gellis. "Scandal" is, in the novel's sick world, of very inclusive definition. But Louis, with his occasional malignant jealousy and debased taste for scandal, at the same time knows his own evil and possesses a sure instinct for what is good. He reflects accurately on himself when he writes: "From the lives of a very small number of human beings I have derived an idea of what happiness might be in this world if it were based on generosity and love."

Among this small number Louis may have been thinking foremost of the Abbé Calou, embodiment of Mauriac's contention in *Letters on Art and Literature* that "a priest's most

effective sermon has always been his own life." The curé is the
novel's healing force, its vessel of grace, and therefore inevitably incurs the wrathful opposition of a pharisaical temperament knowing only self-indulgence and passion for power. As
the battle lines between Monsieur Calou and Brigitte are
drawn, it is evident that his role must be less aggressive than
hers: tyranny may be imposed; grace and love may be only
received. In *The Son of Man,* discussing the "scandal" of
Christ's failure to win more than a handful of followers,
Mauriac points out that no man's love may be claimed by fiat:

> We know . . . that love does_not force itself upon us: the love of
> the Son of Man no more than any other. Love demands hearts which
> either hold back or give themselves. God is love; it is for this reason
> that He can be rejected. If He forced Himself upon creatures He
> would not be God; and man would not be the proud individual
> alone in creation who can turn his head from left to right in a sign
> of refusal. All Christian life is contained in this consent, once given
> and never withdrawn; love does not take by force the being it loves.
> It invites; it solicits; and this is primarily the role of grace.

The statement defines well Monsieur Calou's relationship
to other people, particularly to Jean, the principal object of
his love. Convinced that "the ways of human beings do not
cross by chance," the curé sees Jean as a charge sent by God
and works for the happiness of his soul with no thought of the
sometimes agonized cost of his own unselfish labor. No other
pupil has ever won the completeness of love he feels for this
boy, who, at times, can hardly abide his presence. Neither the
curé's kindly words of persuasion, however, nor even the example of his saintly life serves to win the love of one whose
spirit has for so long been torn by his uncle, his mother, and
Brigitte's cutting him off from his adored Michèle. Yet even
when Jean proves so utterly unfaithful to him, repaying his
kindness by running off with his savings and with Hortense
Voyod, whose satisfaction seems complete only when she brings
the curé to deepest misery—even then Monsieur Calou assumes blame for the disastrous unfolding of events. Entering

in his journal the sentiment that his affection for Jean has clouded his judgment, he condemns himself for overlooking the duty that God lays upon us *"of seeing that our affection for other human beings shall not be an end in itself, shall not usurp the place of that utterly complete love* [of God] *which no one can begin to understand who has not felt it."* Only the saintly character which the abbé is could find in his love for Jean the sin of idolatry. The journal continues: *"How could I hope to overcome in him and conquer those natural instincts of the young animal, if I found them so attractive? It is easier to hate the evil in ourselves than in those we love."* Whatever Monsieur Calou's judgment on himself, the reader knows with Mauriac that his wholly disinterested love cannot conquer, but only invite, only solicit, for such indeed "is primarily the role of grace."

III

It is Madame Brigitte Pian who makes the longest journey and, providentially, experiences the greatest change in the novel whose title is her epithet. And it is precisely at the narrative's midpoint that Louis begins to detect certain budding ameliorative tendencies in his stepmother's character. To that point the quality of her person is accurately intimated in Michèle's remark that she would rather be in hell without her stepmother than in heaven with her! It is, perhaps paradoxically, out of the intricacies of her relationships with those whom she most oppresses that her salvation is effected. In particular her heartless attempt to destroy the tender bond of Jean and Michèle, along with the ensuing intercessory efforts of Monsieur Calou, initiates her persecution of the priest who will finally bring her the peace of grace.

Madame Pian's crucial problem is her difficulty in distinguishing between herself and God, her assumption that she reflects in her every earthly act his will, or, even more arrogantly, her persuasion that God's nature is a mirror of her own. In no situation does she play God more assuredly than with the pathetic Monsieur Puybaraud and his equally pathetic Octavia. She is as pathologically upset by the prospect and then the reality of their marriage as she is by the adolescent tenderness of Michèle and Jean. She seeks confidently to bend them to her will, "tasting the pleasure," as Louis puts it, "that belongs, of right, to God alone: the pleasure . . . of feeling that it was in her power to mold . . . [their] destiny as she willed." As she attempts, in arbitrary selfishness, to prevent their marriage, she attributes "to our Father in Heaven the complexities and perversities of her own nature." In this case as in others the combination of her sense of vocation—"to make clear to others what God had planned for them from the beginning of time"—and her genius for knowing every letter of the law and little of its spirit makes of her a pharisee of stainless perfection.

It is, moreover, ironic though not surprising that Brigitte never characterizes herself more unwittingly and accurately than when she inveighs against the "tricks and subterfuges" of Satan himself. It is not the Evil One, as she affirms, but a far more generous impulse that brings Monsieur Puybaraud and Octavia to a desire for marriage. Brigitte's manner of trying to prevent it—by telling Octavia that her fiancé through such a renunciation of "his apostolic mission" would only be sacrificing himself to her inferior being—is demonic in its cruelty and sophistry. Brigitte's later manipulation to have revealed to her husband the scandalous letters of his first wife, a discovery hastening his death, bears too the mark of a satanic cleverness.

The mammoth, festering sore of Madame Pian's illness is her spiritual pride. She sees herself as hovering over the mountaintops, dispensing tirelessly to creatures of less saintly capacities her self-defined and self-approved gifts of the spirit. There she strikes her pose, blind to the insidiousness and the deleterious effects of her actions. There are, it is true, brief moments of self-doubt, as when she laments her loss of temper in the presence of the Puybarauds, but even then she is more concerned lest her behavior has veiled her true perfection from the eyes of others than that she has offended both them and God. She keeps careful account of her supererogatory dispensations of kindness—and finds her list of debits remarkably inconsequential. That she brings little but misery to her stepchildren and bears partial responsibility for events leading Jean to Madame Voyod, hastens the death of Octavia as well as that of her own husband, breaks the spirit of Monsieur Puybaraud and leads him to temporary despair, causes the most painful of unmerited scandals to break over the head of the Abbé Calou—to all these evidences of her malign influence she long remains oblivious. The mirror in which she admiringly regards herself bears to her the obverse reflection of her real nature: "In the matter of humility," as Louis tells us, "she feared competition with none." And so she pursues her pharisaical way toward an imagined sainthood, unaware that no one is more persuaded of his own unworthiness or more cognizant of that infinity between the best of human deeds and God's righteousness than the true saint. The more she imagines an upward movement of spirit, the more she is under dominion of the very Satan whom she conceives as her polar opposite. She finds, Louis writes, "each day ever stronger reasons for thanking her creator that he had made her so admirable a person." And he continues:

It did not occur to her that never for a single moment, even in the earliest stages of her search for perfection, had she felt any emotion which could be said to have borne the faintest resemblance to love: that she had never approached her Master save with the object of calling His attention to her own remarkably rapid progress along the Way, and suggesting that He give special heed to her singular merits.

In his *Mémoires Intérieurs* Mauriac writes enthusiastically of Nathaniel Hawthorne's *The Scarlet Letter,* a novel

which, like *Woman of the Pharisees,* portrays the malignancy
of pharisaism. To him one great value of Hawthorne's narrative is its illumination of evil:

This book furnishes us with a key to what seems the most impenetrable of all mysteries, especially to the believer: the mystery of
evil. Evil is in the world, and in ourselves. Yet, "all is Grace." Those
are the last words of Bernanos's country priest. The very principle
of our regeneration is to be found in what is worst in us.

Certainly one of Mauriac's own most compelling fictional
achievements is his ability to delineate with such precision
"what is worst in us," to understand the least admirable inclinations of the human heart and mind, and in this respect
his characterization of Madame Pian is superb. But if the first
part of *Woman of the Pharisees* is the intensive anatomy of
the sometimes subtle, and by no means universally recognized,
workings of pharisaism, the last part shows the motions of
grace, the persuasion that the worst in man, once acknowledged and repented, gives way to regeneration.

Woman of the Pharisees is a study, of course, not only of
the mystery of evil, but of the mystery of grace as well. The
former is illuminated by the latter: it is the gift of grace alone
which enables Madame Pian, finally, to know the depth and
scope of her earlier evil. There are intimations too that her
evil was born of ignorance, not of malicious and deliberate intent. In a letter to Louis, written shortly after Brigitte first
acknowledged the imperfect equation between God's will and
her own, Monsieur Calou accounts for her awakening:

*Up to now she has seen only the edifying aspect of her activities.
Suddenly, and without any warning, her eyes have been opened on
to a new and horrible view of herself. When Christ makes us see
clearly, and we become aware of our actions pressing in upon and
surrounding us, we are as much astonished as was the man born
blind who, in the Gospel story, saw "men as trees walking."*

Though the flow of grace does not purge every trace of
her pharisaism, Brigitte shows unmistakably the fruits of her
regeneration. For the first time she faces with humility her

approach to the Communion, recognizing within herself a state of mind, an unshriven impurity, which would make her participation in the Eucharist a sin. And she feels the impossibility of conveying the full nature of her iniquity to a priest-confessor, who simply could not, as she says, "grasp the fact that evil can sometimes poison a whole life, that evil may have many shapes, may be invisible, incomprehensible, and, consequently, incommunicable—impossible to put into words." It is Louis who suggests that the one priest to whom her sins are already known is the Abbé Calou. And Brigitte, following her stepson's counsel, confesses to the curé and returns home with the assurance of pardon, for the first time knowing "the impulse of gratitude that set her in the presence of God . . . [with] something of a tenderness that was at once humble and very human." Little of the cloak of pharisaism falls upon her remaining years. She receives Jean into her home and, later, his marriage to Michèle with a graciousness previously unknown. She enters a tender betrothal with Dr. Gellis, undaunted by the ridiculing laughter with which their engagement is greeted, and responds to his death with admirable courage and loving memories. To Louis she brings a fond and appreciated maternal care. Most significantly, she forms a deep friendship with Monsieur Calou, long regarded as an enemy. And to the pharisaism which dominated her soul until she was fifty, he *was* an enemy. To fight it, he crossed her will, losing his parish as a consequence and finding his "road to Calvary," like every such road, a suffering approach to God's Kingdom. To the sad gratification of both, he dies in her arms. Madame Brigitte Pian, most of whose life voyage was spent in ignorance of her true nature, comes at last to know the meaning of both evil and grace, as the novel's closing words make eloquently clear:

In the evening of her life, Brigitte Pian had come to the knowledge that it is useless to play the part of a proud servitor eager to impress his master by a show of readiness to repay his debts to the last farthing. It had been revealed to her that our Father does not ask us to give a scrupulous account of what merits we can claim. She understood at last that it is not our deserts that matter but our love.

I V

In his Nobel Prize acceptance speech, "An Author and His Work," delivered in Stockholm in 1952, Mauriac acknowledges his reputation as a writer who presents a museum of horrors and specializes in monsters—a familiar and frequent charge made against his novels. It is important to note the kind of monsters his characters are. They are *not* accomplished villains, not Iagos or Edmunds or protagonists of the kind found in the plays of Christopher Marlowe or John Webster. There is about them a morbidity, an unwholesomeness, rather than a greatness; they are objects of loathing or despisement rather than hate or grudging admiration. At worst their reduction to sickly caricature evokes a reader's impatience and distaste. I think, for example, of those relatively early companion pieces, *A Kiss for the Leper* and *Genetrix,* in which the characters of Jean Péloueyre or of Félicité and Fernand Cazenave are of caricatural proportions to strain our credulity. And *The Lamb,* a much later novel, does indeed resemble a chamber of horrors where we meet again with Jean, Michèle, and Brigitte, older than they were in *Woman of the Pharisees.* Both *The Desert of Love* and *The Knot of Vipers* come off considerably better, especially the former. From a Christian writer one would expect, of course, full recognition and portrayal of man's ingenuity in sinfulness, but in much of Mauriac we find attention not only to depravity of spirit but to sheer sordidness and physical repulsiveness. Mauriac's eye is fascinated, not unlike Graham Greene's, by outward loathsomeness of the human body, with the result that a Jean Péloueyre, the Cazenaves, even the Puybarauds are repulsive to the reader's physical senses. *Woman of the Pharisees* is relatively free of this quality, though in the Puybarauds and in the brief sketch of the schoolmaster, Monsieur Rausch, near the novel's beginning, we find traces of it.

However Mauriac might define the chamber of horrors of which he is accused, he asks in his Nobel speech that we look beyond its blackness to "the light that penetrates it and burns there secretly." He asserts that in one essential respect his characters are almost unique in contemporary fiction: "They are aware that they have a soul." Even though some of them, responsive to the hypothesis of God's death, "do not believe in the living God," they are nonetheless "all aware of that part of their being which knows evil and which is capable of not committing it. They know what evil is. They all feel somehow that they are responsible for their actions, and that their actions in turn affect the destiny of others." Of the major characters in *Woman of the Pharisees,* such a description is eminently true. Louis recognizes even in early adolescence his disposition to scandal and deceit. Jean feels a sense of shame at his ungrateful treatment of Monsieur Calou. Most importantly, of course, Brigitte Pian moves (and is moved) from a tardy recognition of the depths of her evil to the remorse and contrition indispensable to her salvation. Beginning with a biblical parable, Mauriac argues the possibility that the sin springing from ignorance may well give way to the flow of grace, and that however depraved the world as a whole may be, there are individual hearts which respond to God's love.

The Lonely Journey

"Hospitality is not our custom here; we have no use for visitors." *

In the meantime she had come to know the malice of the world, compared with which all one's own malice fails and becomes senseless.

"Winter has been with us long, a very long winter, and monotonous. But we don't complain about that down there, we are safe from the winter. Well, yes, some day spring comes too, and summer, and there's a time for that too, I suppose; but in memory, now, spring and summer seem as short as though they didn't last much longer than two days, and even on those days, even during the most beautiful day, even then sometimes snow falls."

I

"I have nothing to say about Kafka except that he is one of the rarest and greatest writers of our time." These words of Jean-Paul Sartre (in the essay "Aminadab," found in *Situations,* I) are a model of self-restraint, particularly for a critic who wrote three hundred thousand words on Jean Genet even before Genet had written his major plays. The comment, a lit-

---

* *The Castle* by Franz Kafka, translated by Willa and Edwin Muir (New York: Alfred A. Knopf). Copyright 1930, 1941, 1954 by Alfred A. Knopf, Inc. Reprinted by permission of the publisher. The novel was first published in 1926.

tle extreme for those of us who would like to understand
Kafka more fully, is at the same time a healthy counterbalance
to critics who have said far too much about him—not in terms
of sheer volume, but of attributing to his works overly detailed, specific, and limiting interpretations. R. M. Albérès and
Pierre de Boisdeffre, toward the end of their *Kafka: The
Torment of Man,* argue wisely that to study Kafka's texts
"with a view to finding *one* interpretation will always be
childish. They [the texts] are designed to provoke successively
every possible interpretation even as each of these interpretations—and their sum as well—remains inadequate. As for a
privileged, definitive interpretation [of the human condi-
tion], this does not exist for the simple reason that Kafka was
not familiar with it and wrote these very texts only to show
that it was not to be found." Every great writer, of course, is
too richly complex to be interpreted in a simple declarative.
But I am acquainted with no writer, I think not even Shakespeare, whose works seem to me so elusive as Kafka's of anything approaching definitive interpretation. His fiction is the
happiest of hunting grounds for the critic who finds, to be
sure, a partial truth, but then takes off on the wings of ingenious imagination, claiming along the way too much for his
partiality. Camus's remark about Kakfa's work—"that its nature, and perhaps its greatness, is to offer us all interpretations
and to confirm none"—may serve as cautionary warning to the
Kafka critic that he resist, in his eagerness to make sense of
his subject, the temptation of making overly extensive claims
for *any* single interpretation. There are many possible interpretations, but, as Albérès and de Boisdeffre affirm, not even
all of them together suffice to provide Kafka's meaning. Mod-
esty and moderation are most highly desirable.

The first problem in reading Kafka is simply to try to
make sense of him. Generally, we feel that we are "making
sense" of literature when the text's situations and actions, as
well as the characters' responses to them, conform in some
way to our own experience of life. Persons, places, and things

of the text; actions, passions, and reactions of the characters; sequential and causal relationships of the events—all will then be familiar to us or, at least, not beyond what we can imaginatively conceive as possible, even if unusual. And we do, in reading Kafka, find a remarkable exactness of realistic detail, a precision of description, which may initially persuade us that we are looking at our own world. In the opening paragraphs of "The Metamorphosis," for example, Gregor Samsa awakes in a familiar bedroom containing the commonplace cloth samples of his sales trade, a picture of a regally dressed woman on the wall, and a window looking on an overcast day. He contemplates the ordinary routine of his business—his office work, his travel with its inconveniences and lonelinesses, the unattractiveness of his employer. Ordinary as his setting and reflections are, however, we find nothing of the familiar or even imaginatively conceivable in Gregor's waking up to find himself transformed into a gigantic insect. The narrative thus presents a world which is ours and not ours, a juxtaposition of striking and eerie effect. *The Trial* and *The Castle* too offer their wealth of realistic everyday detail. But the courtroom and garret and cathedral scenes of *The Trial* are in most ways frighteningly removed from our common experience of life, and the labyrinthine journey of *The Castle*'s K. crosses terrains quite foreign to us.

When a literary text does not reflect our own immediate sense of common experience, we usually ask if it is allegorical, calling for its own appropriate reading technique. Do the persons and episodes point beyond themselves to some more universal meaning? As we read the first sentence of John Bunyan's *The Pilgrim's Progress*, for example, we find something not quite "real" about the man clothed in rags, his back to his house, a book in his hand, a burden on his back. The tale becomes less real as it progresses, the traveler encountering bizarre adventures and making hairbreadth escapes. Whatever its lack of correspondence with ordinary life, however, it bears allegorically the most precise correspondence with a familiar

Christian theology concerned with the journey of a man of growing faith from this world to the next. The rags denote unrighteousness; the burden, original sin; the book, the Bible, the pilgrim's guide from his earthly home, to which his back is turned, to the Celestial City. *The Pilgrim's Progress* "makes sense" by means of its step-by-step accommodation to a carefully worked out, readily familiar theological system. But Kafka's fiction, so foreign to our day-to-day experience, does not open itself to allegorical interpretation either, for as Wilhelm Emrich has remarked, it points beyond its events *not* to the known, but to the *unknown*. Thus we have little to fall back on, no norm through which certain allegorical events may be interpreted.

Frustrated in an attempt to understand a narrative either in realistic or allegorical terms, we may then look for help from an omniscient narrator. Joseph K. of *The Trial* and K. of *The Castle* may be unable to penetrate certain of life's mysteries, but perhaps we can look to Kafka for an illumination of what to his characters is obscure. But we find scant help here either, for in however many ways Kafka's novels may be ironic, there is a minimum of the dramatic irony in which author reveals to reader something unknown to the literary characters themselves. For Kafka *is* Joseph K. and K. and Gregor Samsa too; his fiction is spiritual or psychical autobiography. K. of *The Castle* guides our understanding of the nature of human life as far as Kafka himself can. And if Albérès and de Boisdeffre are correct, Kafka writes in part to show, in novels resistant to dogmatic interpretation, that the human condition is equally obdurate to precise elucidation. Kafka's understanding exceeds that of his characters in few respects, perhaps mainly in his keener recognition of the limits of human understanding.

In our attempt to comprehend Kafka's understanding of life we may find some illumination in his diaries and notebooks, where we observe his persistent attempt at self-definition. We may begin with a few of his reflections on himself as writer and as person. As early as December 16, 1911, he writes: "The moment I were set free from the office I would yield at once to my desire to write an autobiography." * On August 6, 1914, he speaks of his "talent for portraying . . . [his] dream-like inner life." And the bulk of his fiction is, as I have already noted, in the form of spiritual autobiography, projecting his "dreamlike inner life." To present a "dreamlike inner life" is to write in a surrealistic mode—something beyond the "real," or more real than the real, or of more significance than what is generally taken for real. Surrealist writers—the absurd play-wrights are good examples—seek to make known man's soul-scape, not the world's outer landscape so readily perceivable to the senses. *The Castle* is in this tradition.

Kafka's autobiographical fiction is an attempt at self-definition and, by extension, human definition. His diaries, as well as his fiction, convey to us his extravagant sense of his own imperfections. He notes on July 19, 1910, for example, that, "if I lacked an upper lip here, there an ear, here a rib, there a finger, if I had hairless spots on my head and pock-marks on my face, there would still be no adequate counter-part of my inner imperfection." Of similar tenor, though applicable to all men and not just to Kafka, is an entry for February 7, 1915:

At a certain point in self-knowledge, when other circumstances favoring self-scrutiny are present, it will invariably follow that you find yourself execrable. Every moral standard—however opinions may differ on it—will seem too high. You will see that you are nothing but a rat's nest of miserable dissimulations. The most trifling of your acts will not be untainted by those dissimulations. These dissimulated intentions are so squalid that in the course of your self-scrutiny you will not want to ponder them closely but will instead be content to gaze at them from afar. These intentions aren't all compounded merely of selfishness, selfishness seems in comparison an ideal of the good and beautiful. The filth you will find exists for its own sake; you will recognize that you came dripping into the world with this burden and will depart unrecognizable again—or only too recogniz-

* *The Diaries of Franz Kafka, 1910–1913*, ed. Max Brod, translated by Joseph Kresh (New York: Schocken Books, 1948).

able—because of it. This filth is the nethermost depth you will find; at the nethermost depth there will be not lava, no, but filth. It is the nethermost and the uppermost, and even the doubts self-scrutiny begets will soon grow weak and self-complacent as the wallowing of a pig in muck.*

Kafka writes often of his sense not only of imperfection but of frustration and alienation as well. He speaks of himself as a well gone dry, as more lonely than Robinson Crusoe, as imprisoned within "an impenetrable bramble thicket" in a public park. He is in every way cut off from what or where or with whom he would like to be—trapped by his inner imperfection, his aridity, his loneliness, his thicket. It is no wonder that he expresses with some frequency what he describes (April 8, 1912) as "the metaphysical urge . . . toward death."

Meanwhile he writes, thereby finding a cathartic exorcising of the world's real wretchedness through the outpouring of words which express it. The therapeutic, life-giving effect of such composition is made clear in the diary entry of October 19, 1921:

Anyone who cannot come to terms with life while he is alive needs one hand to ward off a little his despair over his fate—he has little success in this—but with his other hand he can note down what he sees among the ruins, for he sees different (and more) things than do the others; after all, dead as he is in his own lifetime, he is the real survivor.

The writing—of the diaries and notebooks, of *The Trial* and *The Castle* and other works of fiction—frequently anatomizes the search for some splinter of light which may challenge the world's at least highly apparent darkness. At times Kafka speaks with a degree of confidence, as on October 18, 1921, when he asserts the conceivability "that life's splendor forever lies in wait about each one of us in all its fulness, but veiled from view, deep down, invisible, far off. It *is* there, though,

* *The Diaries of Franz Kafka, 1914–1923*, ed. Max Brod, translated by Martin Greenberg, with the cooperation of Hannah Arendt (New York: Schocken Books, 1949).

not hostile, not reluctant, not deaf. If you summon it by the right word, by its right name, it will come. This is the essence of magic, which does not create but summons." There is thus some intimation of hope—if one only possessed the magic wand which summons! Kafka is persuaded of a real and living goal, but equally persuaded that it seems beyond human attainment. Perhaps most frustratingly, he finds himself ignorant not only of *how* to reach this goal, but even of *what* the goal is. His own goal he does not see as a Kierkegaardian Christianity or a Zionistic Judaism. Whatever it may be, he senses that the suffering he endures may be the goal's necessary mode of approach. "Occasionally," he writes on March 13, 1915, "I feel an unhappiness which almost dismembers me, and at the same time am convinced of its necessity and of the existence of a goal to which one makes one's way by undergoing every kind of unhappiness." In a masterful aphorism of March 9, 1922, he plays a variation on the same theme: "Somewhere help is waiting and the beaters are driving me there." Kafka's diaries and notebooks convey a nightmarish sense of that "dreamlike inner life" which will form the basis of his spiritually-psychically autobiographical fiction. In them we find the self-portrait of an introspective questioner, a man oppressed by the weight of his real or imagined unworthiness and by a world offering little solace or encouragement, and yet a man—not unlike some of Samuel Beckett's protagonists —who continues his quest with rugged perseverance.

In his fiction Kafka would convey to us his inner response to the life which proves so thwarting. He does so through finding for his response what T. S. Eliot defines in his essay "Hamlet and His Problems" as an "objective correlative": "The only way of expressing emotion in the form of art is by finding an 'objective correlative'; in other words, a set of objects, a situation, a chain of events which shall be the formula of that *particular* emotion; such that when the external facts, which must terminate in sensory experience, are given, the emotion is immediately evoked." Kafka's fiction is the chain of events which, when read, conveys to and induces in the reader Kafka's own emotional response to life. Thus we find in "The Metamorphosis" Gregor Samsa's (or the narrator's) innermost sense of his relationship to his family, not through a camera-eye report of hostilities and humiliations encountered in realistic, daily experience, but through the objective correlative of Gregor's nightmarish transformation into a large insect. His family role, this literary method suggests, is in all but a literal sense that of an insect. Gregor's father treats him with scornful brutality; his more sympathetic mother is nevertheless frightened by her son's loathsomeness; and his sister, despite a tender compassion, views him as noisome, finding his room offensive to her smell and the dishes from which he has eaten offensive to her touch. Gregor's metamorphosis merely confirms that his person is an insect in all but physical appearance. He knows that his death, like that of the beetle within the narrative, will be a welcome relief to his family; that upon that death, as upon the insect's death, fog will turn to sunshine, a father long sickly will become robust, a mother long fretful will become calm, and a sister long repressed will welcome a new and happy day. Gregor's death, in short, will be a relief to everyone, including himself. "The Metamorphosis," enigmatic when attempted realistically or allegorically, assumes meaning and clarity only when we become absorbed in the fabric of Gregor's situation, finding evoked within ourselves his own, and presumably Kafka's, response to his at least imagined grievous imperfection and insignificance.

The Trial and The Castle may be read in much the same way as "The Metamorphosis": as Kafka's attempt to convey surrealistically the inner response of his total being to life's phenomena. Thus a sensitive reading of the novels enables us to experience the totality and, frequently, the bewilderment of that response. To follow The Trial's Joseph K. through the crucial year of his arrest and death is to feel the anguished struggle of a man who is suddenly awakened to a knowledge of, and then persistently denies, his human guilt. To accompany *The Castle*'s K. on his lonely journey is to feel the agonizing frustration of a man whose most passionate yearnings fall short of their goal.

I I

The whole of *The Castle* has both the frustrating indecisiveness and the sharp intensity of a dream. At the novel's beginning K. arrives in a village strange to him and overlooked by a castle. Whether his arrival is the product of his own purposeful decision, pure chance, or some unfathomable magnetic power of the village and Castle is uncertain. That the villagers at the Bridge Inn where K. immediately goes for the night neither expect him nor graciously welcome him is clear. Whether he is, in the role of land-surveyor, expected by the Castle hierarchy which rules the village is not clear, as two contradictory phone calls reveal. Whatever motivates K.'s arrival, however, he gains in the less than one-week time span of the novel's action an implacable determination to stay, and whether or not the Castle hierarchy expected him, it resists successfully K.'s every effort to survey its terrain. The narrative is the struggle of a lonely man to gain some degree of recognition and acceptance by the this-worldly community of the village and the other-worldly community of the Castle. It also etches the resistance of individual persons and a bureaucratic hierarchy to his presence.

The village which is the novel's exclusive setting and through which K. seeks access to the Castle is lacking in every manner of vitality except its intensive interest in and, with few exceptions, hostility toward K. The short days of winter bring much cold and little light. The climatic oppressiveness seems to have blighted the health and vigor of the inhabitants, many of whom suffer physical defect or disease. The peasants seem in perpetual stupor "with their open mouths, coarse lips, and literally tortured faces," their heads appearing to have been "beaten flat on top," and their twisted features seeming to bear witness to "the pain of the beating." The coachman Gerstäcker is afflicted with a limp and severe coughing fits; the parents of Barnabas, Olga, and Amalia are invalids, their father suffering from gout, their mother from obesity and rheumatism; the mayor of the village is confined to his bed with a throbbing foot. The winter which casts its pall over the whole landscape and its creatures follows, moreover, no ordinary calendar: when K., toward the novel's end, asks the barmaid Pepi how long it will be until spring, her reply makes clear winter's truly remarkable endurance:

Till spring? . . . Winter has been with us long, a very long winter, and monotonous. But we don't complain about that . . . we are safe from the winter. Well, yes, some day spring comes too, and summer, and there's a time for that too, I suppose; but in memory, now, spring and summer seem as short as though they didn't last much longer than two days, and even on those days, even during the most beautiful day, even then sometimes snow falls.

Bleak and unenticing as the village is, K. bends his full energy and employs his every stratagem to make within it a place for himself—apparently out of conviction that it is the only gateway to the Castle, the destined object of his ultimate hope. If his determination is undaunted by the village's physical unattractiveness and sickly pallor, it is equally undaunted by the suspicion, unfriendliness, and disdain of many of its citizens. He is treated rudely in the Bridge Inn where he seeks his first night's rest. When, the next day, he essays his first visit to a home in the community, he is brusquely informed that "hospitality is not our custom here; we have no use for visitors" and shoved out of the house to the ridiculing laughter of its inhabitants. He is later told by the village mayor that he has come in vain, there being no need whatsoever for a land-surveyor. And when, perhaps as a kind of sop, he is given the position of school janitor, he is told that there is no more need for a janitor than for a land-surveyor, and is treated most humiliatingly when he and Frieda, his betrothed, take up their scant quarters at the school.

K.'s village life bears close correspondence to Kafka's as-

sessment of his own life as reflected in the diaries and notebooks. For neither K. nor Kafka, it seems, is there a place in
the normal life of their human communities. But as the diarist
Kafka senses the possibility "that life's splendor forever lies in
wait about each one of us in all its fulness, but veiled from
view, deep down, invisible, far off," so K. looks toward the
Castle for the fulfillment of this possibility. The Castle, however, is terribly unavailable. It is shrouded in mist and darkness when K. arrives in the village. And how disappointing its
appearance is when K. does get his first clear glimpse of it
the next day: it is a crumbling clump of most unimpressive
stone buildings circled by swarms of crows, harbingers of
death. The village road, reasonably supposed to lead to the
Castle, does not in fact do so. K. is told at one time that a
road which may lead to the Castle bears no traffic and at
another that there are various such roads, fashion (whose
whims are incomprehensible) decreeing which of them is at
any given moment the broad way to the shattered heap. Yet
the Castle, shoddy and wretched as the village itself and so
difficult or impossible of access, remains K.'s goal. If the Castle
is some vague surrogate for Heaven, then one of Kafka's notebook aphorisms is appropriate to K.'s dismal situation:
"[h]eaven is dumb, echoing only to the dumb."

Few aspects of *The Castle* are so remarkable as K.'s perseverance in the face of every conceivable frustration and
rejection. He bends much of his effort toward meeting a man
named Klamm, the Castle's chief representative, whose visits to
the Herrenhof Inn suggest his availability to the village. To
reach Klamm, to see him and be seen by him, to present a
land-surveyor's petition to him K. views as his own main hope
of reaching the Castle. It is to Frieda, barmaid of the Herrenhof and former mistress of Klamm, that K. turns for help. It
is she who gives K. his first and only glimpse of Klamm,
through the peephole of the door behind which the mysterious Castle official ruminates on his visits to the village. And it
is she who seeks more than anyone else to ease K.'s way into

acceptance by the village community so hostile to him. On the very evening of their first meeting and the peephole episode she hides him in the inn from the landlord who would have ejected him, and enjoys with him their first tryst (and right by Klamm's door), "where they lay among the small puddles of beer and other refuse scattered on the floor." She seeks to solace, comfort, and protect him in every way, accompanying him to the miserable janitorial quarters at the schoolhouse and awaiting with patient devotion the time of their marriage. When she later breaks their engagement, she does so only through her conviction of K.'s unfaithfulness.

To what extent K. is attracted to Frieda by her intrinsic virtues, to what extent by her being a presumed avenue to Klamm is difficult to say. Perfectly clear, however, is K.'s grasping at every source which seems a promising mode of approach to or knowledge of Klamm. Since he observes Klamm only through a peephole, he must gain knowledge of him through the words of those who have known him. No one gives a more awed account than Gardena, landlady of the Bridge Inn. Over two decades earlier Gardena had been Klamm's mistress, and the intervening years have in no way diminished her original ardor. Her most precious possessions remain three keepsakes, relics of that now distant relationship: a thoroughly ordinary woolen wrap; a faded, cracked, crumpled photograph of the messenger who had first summoned her to her erstwhile lover; and a nightcap. She ecstatically recalls that Klamm sent for her three times, and sadly that there was, inexplicably, no fourth. She sees her continuing passion as in no way inconsistent with her expressed fidelity to her husband, now of many years. It is her comparison of Klamm to an eagle, however, which gives K. perhaps his most lasting and accurate impression of Klamm's nature. At a later time, we are told, K.

thought of Klamm's remoteness, of his impregnable dwelling, of his silence, broken perhaps only by cries such as K. had never yet heard, of his downward-pressing gaze, which could never be proved or disproved, of his wheelings, which could never be disturbed by anything that K. did down below, which far above he followed at the behest of incomprehensible laws and which only for instants were visible—all these things Klamm and the eagle had in common.

It is no wonder that Gardena views as the height of impertinence and frivolity the attempts of K., in her view an unwanted troublemaker, to break into Klamm's majestic privacy. That Klamm has distributed his favors rather widely and seemingly arbitrarily among a number of women disturbs her not at all.

K. thus learns something of Castle officialdom through his limited, hearsay knowledge of Klamm. He learns more, again indirectly, through the family of Barnabas, a lowly Castle messenger and deliverer to K. of the Castle's infrequent and confusing communications. Barnabas's sister Amalia is the only villager ever openly to scorn a Castle official. She had, a few years before K.'s arrival, been seen at a village celebration by a little-known but powerful official named Sortini, who, apparently smitten, had on the same evening sent her an obscene note demanding that she come to him immediately. Amalia's enraged tearing of the note into pieces and flinging them into the face of Sortini's messenger inflamed all the perverse forces of the mysterious Castle. Her father was deprived of his highly cherished avocation in the fire brigade, and of his vocation of cobbler also, for the villagers, horrified by Amalia's intrepid independence, wished only a complete severance from her entire family. The father became a broken man, apathetically and vainly making every attempt to placate the angry, distant rulers so offended by his daughter's rare conduct. Most frustrating, and thoroughly in accord with the Castle's spineless tyranny, was the fact that no charge was made against Amalia, who could consequently offer no defense. When her family petitioned for forgiveness, the Castle's petty officials, the only ones to whom the villagers had access, feigned ignorance of the case. Olga, Amalia's sister, who relates the whole sordid, frightening episode to K., conveys a sense of her family's desperation:

Nothing more could be done through the servants. Sortini's messenger was not to be found and would never be found, Sortini and his messenger with him seemed to be receding farther and farther, by many people their appearance and names were already forgotten, and often I had to describe them at length and in spite of that learnt nothing more than that the servant I was speaking to could remember them with an effort, but except for that could tell nothing about them.

It is difficult to conceive a more cruel and capricious abuse of power than that exemplified through the Castle's reaction to Amalia's rebuff of Sortini. The villagers are utterly helpless against the arbitrariness, evasiveness, and tyranny of Castle officials who stand well beyond anything that might normally be designated as responsibility or accountability. Yet it is the Castle which K. would storm.

Some of the humiliations and frustrations visited upon K. have already been enumerated, among them his rude reception by the villagers and his inability to find a geographical route to the Castle, to which can be added the ineffectiveness of his presumed and clownish assistants, Arthur and Jeremiah. He finds himself in the absurd dilemma defined best by Camus in *The Myth of Sisyphus* as the "divorce between the mind that desires and the world that disappoints." There is a reluctance, both of individual persons and of what might be called the world's bureaucratic machinery, to accommodate K.'s yearnings. The reluctance of individuals stems in large part from their assumption of an immense gap between the quality of K.'s person with its manifold imperfections and the splendor attributed to life within the Castle. No one is more impressed by this disparity than Gardena, who expresses her sentiments to K. angrily and eloquently:

Herr Klamm is a gentleman from the Castle, and that in itself, without considering Klamm's position there at all, means that he is of very high rank. But what are you, for whose marriage [to Frieda] we are humbly considering here ways and means of getting permission? You are not from the Castle, you are not from the village, you aren't anything. Or rather, unfortunately, you are something, a stranger, a man who isn't wanted and is in everybody's way, a man who's always causing trouble, a man who takes up the maids' room, a man whose intentions are obscure, a man who has ruined our dear little Frieda and whom we must unfortunately accept as her husband. I don't hold all that against you. You are what you are, and I have seen enough in my lifetime to be able to face facts. But now consider what it is you ask. A man like Klamm is to talk with you.

But K. must sustain more than verbal assaults on the degree of his personal insignificance. He finds too that the world's machinery, the confusion of its bureaucratic system, works against him. We may consider, for example, his visit to the village mayor, from whom he hopes to gain information and authority for the carrying out of his land-surveying activities. The mayor's easy availability affords K. initial hope that he may be taken seriously, though he reflects immediately that such access may be only a delaying, mollifying tactic, one designed to induce a false confidence which may later prove damaging. One of the mayor's functions, he quickly concludes, is to "guard the distant and invisible interests of distant and invisible masters," something quite different from seeking to promote K.'s own concerns. K. finds to his dismay that the official papers which might have defined his authority and duties have been misplaced among a welter of other papers, or perhaps lost altogether. He is repeatedly informed by the mayor, not so much of his personal insignificance, but of the insignificance of his "case" or his "affair." K.'s petition for clarity, his effort to give substance to his avowed vocation of land-surveyor, the mayor classifies, among all the cases which have come before him, as "one of the least important among the least important." Thus there is an effort to impress upon K. not now his serious imperfections of person, but his lack of any vocation: not only *is* K. nothing; he can *do* nothing. We find, therefore, persistent attempts, by Gardena and the mayor among others, to undermine K.'s confidence in both his personal and vocational attributes: what he is and what he would do are seen as extravagantly insignificant.

The fact is, however, that K. is by no means insignificant. It takes him but a few days to become the most famous (or infamous) inhabitant of the entire village, his presence causing a stir unfelt since Amalia's rugged assertion of independence. He is, first, the very center of expectant attention of the peasants within the Bridge Inn on the evening of his arrival. Those persons whom he meets thereafter, most of them total strangers to him, know immediately who he is. Late in the novel, during his night of interrogations by and with Bürgel and Erlanger, he upsets completely the hitherto relatively placid nature of such occasions, scandalizing the landlady and landlord of the Herrenhof Inn, persons most familiar with what normally transpires on similar nights. He gains his immediate reputation and large significance through refusing to be intimidated by forces that have reduced most of the villagers to spiritless automatons. Showing every evidence of tenacity and independence he also refuses to leave the village until he penetrates the Castle or dies in the attempt. He remains firm against both those who wish to be rid of him and the urgent plea of his beloved Frieda that they search for their happiness together elsewhere. "Here in this world," Frieda tells him, "there's no undisturbed place for our love, neither in the village nor anywhere else; and I dream of a grave, deep and narrow, where we could clasp each other in our arms as with clamps, and I would hide my face in you and you would hide your face in me, and nobody would ever see us any more." K. sees no escape, in life or in death, and we must assume that, if he could turn the calendar back a week, knowing all that he knows in the novel's closing pages, he would still choose to enter the village. He would change only his mode of attack, for he has learned much from the mature composure of Frieda, even if he rejects her entreaty to flight. As he tells Pepi late in the novel, he remains mystified but has learned much:

My own guilt is by no means clear to me; only, when I compare myself with you something of this kind dawns on me: it is as if we had both striven too intensely, too noisily, too childishly, with too little experience, to get something that for instance with Frieda's calm and Frieda's matter-of-factness can be got easily and without much ado. We have tried to get it by crying, by scratching, by tugging—just as a child tugs at the tablecloth, gaining nothing, but only bringing all the splendid things down on the floor and putting them out of its reach forever.

The Castle never ends, or at least does not conclude, so that a reader can only surmise what might have been K.'s future course. It is inconceivable that he would have relaxed his efforts, and I think equally inconceivable that the Castle authorities would have become more receptive to him. Since an enduring stalemate seems most likely, an extension of the novel would serve little purpose. Kafka has guided us to the very limits of his own experience and refuses to speculate beyond it. Life on this earth is a tenacious human struggle to achieve a goal whose attainment is blocked by seemingly arbitrary, malign, sadistic forces, and whose precise nature is not known in any case. Man does not know exactly where he would wish to go, and he is restrained from going he knows not where. From every point of view, I think, it is fortunate that Kafka did not affix to his novel an ending which, according to Max Brod, he disclosed in answer to Brod's inquiry. Brod is quoted in the Publisher's Note to the English definitive edition:

The ostensible Land-Surveyor was to find partial satisfaction at least. He was not to relax in his struggle, but was to die worn out by it. Round his deathbed the villagers were to assemble, and from the Castle itself the word was to come that though K.'s legal claim to live in the village was not valid, yet, taking certain auxiliary circumstances into account, he was to be permitted to live and work there.

Far better, I believe, for a writer of Kafka's uncertainties, that the novel end as it does.

III

"This inescapable duty," reads Kafka's diary entry for November 7, 1921, the year of *The Castle*'s probable beginning, "to observe oneself: if someone else is observing me, naturally I have to observe myself too; if none observes me, I have to observe myself all the closer." *The Castle,* like most of Kafka's writing, is the product of self-observation and the successful effort of a writer to convey to his readers a profound sense of his "dreamlike inner life." The novel is what Aristotle might have called the imitation of a soul in action. To come to know this, Kafka's, soul at its deepest level is to empathize with K., to endure with him every moment of his eerie and uncertain journey. The self-condemnation and self-deprecation of the diaries give way in fiction to the castigation of the usually autobiographical protagonist—in *The Castle* by Gardena, the mayor, and a host of others. K.'s basic problem is Kafka's: that of an outsider exerting every means toward becoming acceptable in a secular and a religious order and enjoying only the barest modicum of success. Enumerating some of the projects in which he had failed, Kafka once listed "piano, violin, languages, Germanics, anti-Zionism, Zionism, Hebrew, gardening, carpentering, writing, marriage attempts, an apartment of my own." It is the plaint of a man searching persistently and vainly for his vocation. K., land-surveyor and janitor in name only, faces much the same frustration. And a vocation is generally prerequisite to community membership.

Without membership in a community of this world, it is difficult to envisage one's place in the community of the next: the way to the Castle, K. believes, lies through the village. What a dismal prospect, trying to gain approving recognition in the hostile village of this world, with its "ludicrous bungling that in certain circumstances may decide the life of a human being," in order to gain entrance to what seems to be the coldly heartless and irresponsibly capricious Castle of the next. Even the relatively insensitive Pepi is said to have "come to know the malice of the world, compared with which all one's own malice fails and becomes senseless." We may surmise that Kafka, despite all his self-directed criticism, must at times have felt that he was no match, in wickedness or imperfection, for this world or the next. His long, detailed "Letter to His Fa-

ther" evidences not only the indignities and oppressions Kafka
suffered in his life, but also the feeling of mingled repulsion
and attraction with which he faced his God-figure. His father,
indeed, may have served as prototype for the Castle officials:
to read the "Letter" and *The Castle* is to receive much the
same sense of awed response to the figure of authority.

We may recall Kafka's diary notation asserting his occasional persuasion that a man makes his way toward an exis-
tent goal "by undergoing every kind of unhappiness." Perhaps
most depressing about *The Castle* is not that K. suffers but
that his dimly perceived goal seems so unworthy. Ionesco
writes of Kafka's "theme of man astray in the labyrinth,
without a guiding thread," and we can only wonder, should
K. have found that thread, whether it would have guided him
to an end justifying the journey's wretchedness. Ionesco is
correct in attributing to Kafka's works a religious character.
Though too sweeping in his generalization that contemporary
man can reach out "only unconsciously and gropingly for a
lost dimension that has completely vanished from sight," he is
pointing toward a truth. In Kafka's case it is the biblical dimension that is lost and there is nothing to suggest that there
is anything resembling the Kingdom of God lying beyond the
village. Neither Kafka nor K. possesses the Pauline or Kierkegaardian fear and trembling which stems from a deep sense of
personal inadequacy in the presence of a God who, though
fearful, is also loving: the Castle officials are most notable for
an exclusiveness nurtured by hardness of heart. We may
wonder why K. continues to pursue his quest, concluding as
we may, after living with him for twenty chapters, that he is
far too good for either the village or the Castle. Perhaps we
are also to conclude that anything is better than loneliness
and exclusion—even if other men and the gods now available
are hardly to our taste. On one matter we are clear: K.'s
tenacious endurance gains our sympathy and respect.

Waiting for the Logos

Things fall apart; the centre cannot hold;
*Mere anarchy is loosed upon the world . . .**

Surely some revelation is at hand;
Surely the Second Coming is at hand. .
　　　　W. B. Yeats, "The Second Coming'

"Many must die, many must be sacrificed, so that a
path may be prepared for the loving redeemer and
judge. And only through his sacrificial death can the
world be redeemed to a new innocence. But first
the Antichrist must come—the mad and dreamless
Antichrist. First the world must become quite empty,
must be emptied of everything in it as by a vacuum
cleaner—nothingness."

I

In the year 1888 a perceptive observer of the seventy-year-old
Herr von Pasenow could discern his character and personality
through his style of walking: undignified, overweening, vulgar,
rakish, swaggering. His walk bore the marks of the Devil himself, or—taking into consideration the walkingstick and passing
more charitable judgment—it resembled a dog hobbling
briskly and zigzaggedly about on three legs. His son Joachim

* *The Sleepwalkers* by Hermann Broch, translated by Willa and Edwin
Muir (New York: Pantheon, 1947). Copyright 1947 by Pantheon Books,
Inc. Reprinted by permission of the publisher. The novel was first pub-
lished in 1931–32.

(main protagonist of "The Romantic," Part One of Hermann Broch's trilogy *The Sleepwalkers*) once noted the resemblance between his father's walk and his handwriting, whose sloping, running quality also seemed of a three-legged nature. Joachim liked neither his father's walk, nor his handwriting, nor the man himself.

If Herr von Pasenow's walk is the key to his whole style of living, Joachim's military uniform is the key to his own. About military uniforms Joachim's friend Eduard von Bertrand, a onetime soldier turned businessman, has a theory. There had, he believes, been a time when the priest, set off from the rest of mankind by his ecclesiastical garments, prescribed the judgment of good and evil, thus holding off the forces of anarchy. But the Church, fallen in luster and authority, has given way to the secular, particularly the army, and the new absolutism is clothed in military, not priestly garb. Such a secular exaltation of itself as the absolute Bertrand defines as "romanticism." The romanticism of his time is "the cult of the uniform," whose function, like that of priestly robes of a time past, is "to manifest and ordain order in the world, to arrest the confusion and flux of life." Though Joachim sees in Bertrand's theory, as in various of his other pronouncements, an underlying cynicism, he knows that his beloved uniform does bear witness to his style of life. To him the uniform symbolizes a noble code of living and a secure hierarchy of values. In mufti he feels naked and indecent, for civilian life, unrestrained by priest or soldier, spells for him the anarchy consequent upon an absence of discipline.

Joachim's uniform, outward and visible sign of an inward and spiritual sense of honor, signifies his nostalgia for past values, his eagerness to hold on to what of them remains, and his fear of "new values" which seem to him disconcertingly like "no" values. Among the old values is chivalry, particularly as it embraces the relationship between man and woman. He is disquieted by the small liberties his father takes with the charming, if unfastidious, Ruzena. And when Joachim becomes her lover (chivalry allows such liaisons), he is as chivalrous toward her as a man who is simultaneously moving toward marriage with another can be. While his code demands that he protect his mistress from the ravages of sensual men, it also demands that he enshrine his intended, Elisabeth von Baddensen, in the cult of the virgin. Upset that his father should caress Ruzena's hand, he is upset too that his father should encourage his marriage to Elisabeth, leading as it certainly would to the violation of a saint. He is keenly mortified when Baron and Baroness von Baddensen, inviting him to a tour of their house, actually suffer him a view of their bedroom, where stand side by side and in embarrassing proximity the two beds sullied by concupiscence and crying loud of the baroness's degradation. That Elisabeth should be destined for the same fate, "that indeed he himself should be the man chosen to perform that act of desecration, filled him with such compassion that he longed to steal her away, simply that he might watch before her door, so that undisturbed and unviolated she might dream for ever in a dream of white lace." The wedding night, which (with Joachim distinctly loath to divest himself of his uniform) slowly and awkwardly leads to awakening from that virginal dream, is presented with tender ridicule. Had Eduard von Bertrand—who has long since shed his uniform, who looks forward rather than backward, and who loves and is loved by Elisabeth—married the young beauty, the consummation would have been more precipitate, for Bertrand is free of Joachim's cult.

Joachim and Bertrand, destined to constant interaction in the year 1888, are polar opposites, a fact attributed in part by Joachim to their disparate breeding grounds: the country, whose pastoral security was thought by him to nourish faith and stability; and the city, whose labyrinthine ways connoted to him a diabolical underworld and helped account for Bertrand's peculiar blindness to the claims of honor. "It seems to me," Bertrand tells Joachim to the latter's disapproval, "that honour is a very living feeling, but none the less all obsolete forms are full of inertia, and one has to be very tired oneself to give oneself over to a dead and romantic convention of feeling. One has to be in despair and see no way out before one can do that." From this moment on Joachim's feelings toward Bertrand oscillate between repulsion and attraction. At times he views his more sophisticated, less sentimental acquaintance as an emissary of the Devil, as a Mephistopheles sent to tempt him away from his most precious values. But with equal frequency he feels close dependence upon a man clearly more knowledgeable than himself in the practical affairs of the world.

As a late nineteenth-century romantic, Joachim feels allegiance to the cult of the uniform his surest stay against chaos. Had he lived in an earlier age, he might well have found his security in the priesthood. Indeed, his adult nostalgia for the Church of his childhood is strong. Shortly after his brother's death—by "honourable" duel—he enters his church and tries "to recapture the feelings which as a child had been his when every Sunday he had stood . . . [there] as before the face of God." As Bertrand seems to him more and more to take on a demonic coloration he seeks increasingly the consolation of religion; and to contemplate the religious is, to Joachim, to contemplate Elisabeth. Once as he attempts to pray, he recalls from childhood a picture of the Virgin, whose hair seems now to blend with "the maiden tresses of Elisabeth." Later, proposing to Elisabeth, he sees in her "the vision of Mary wandering on earth before her assumption into heaven," and he even entertains the wish that he and Elisabeth, like Mary before them, might already have passed into the heavenly kingdom! His marriage to Elisabeth he views as her sacrifice and his redemption. Even on his marriage bed, thoughts of a Christian household as a way of grace take precedence over the more secular aspects of his present situation.

If Bertrand counters Joachim's romanticism with a modest cynicism, he is at the same time the only really hopeful—in an ultimate sense, even optimistic—character in Part One of

The Sleepwalkers. The other characters are gripped by fear
and loneliness. Herr von Pasenow is "tormented by some secret
fear that abated only when he was in his bedroom." Elisabeth's
fear of the unfamiliar and unconventional is a strong factor
in precluding marriage to Bertrand, and Joachim too dreads
change. Doubtless one cause of their fear is a sense of terrible
isolation. We learn, for example, that a visit of Joachim to
his parents serves only to intensify their loneliness, and that
between husband and wife is "an impenetrable wall of deaf-
ening silence . . . a wall through which the human voice cannot penetrate." Only Bertrand seems free of such miseries.
Aware of the destructiveness brought by fear and loneliness
to the relations between man and man, he nonetheless believes in "a kind of human solidarity and an understanding
that bridged the years." Joachim, with all his romantic no-
tions, seems more despairing than hopeful, perhaps because,
his eyes on the past, he cannot see ahead to a time when the
world, having plunged to its deepest abyss, may once again
move to a love long lost. It is, perhaps oddly, the "cynical"
Bertrand who foresees a renewal of love, however distant:

I believe, and this is my deepest belief, that only by a dreadful
intensification of itself, only when in a sense it becomes infinite,
can the strangeness parting two human beings be transformed into
its opposite, into absolute recognition, and let that thing come to
life which hovers in front of love as its unattainable goal, and yet
is its condition: the mystery of oneness. The gradual accustoming of
oneself to another, the gradual deepening of intimacy, evokes no
mystery whatever.

II

On March 2, 1903, August Esch lost his job in Cologne for an
alleged error in bookkeeping. The charge, fabricated as a protective shield for the misconduct of others, is ironic: Esch is as
wedded to and expert in the cult of bookkeeping as Joachim
was to the cult of the uniform. His art he views not simply as
a practical mode of keeping commercial ledgers but as a right-

eous means of rendering the world its moral due; reference to "the upright book-keeping of his soul" affords some sense of the avowed scope of his intention. He seeks stability with a passion rivaling Joachim's, though the seeking is implemented not through a romantic sense of honorable behavior but through a mathematical sense of balancing credits and debits. Kneeling at the altar of what he calls "law and order," Esch hardly conforms to the title—"The Anarchist"—of Part Two of *The Sleepwalkers*. If Part Two has an anarchist it is Martin Geyring, whose "anarchy" is of the gentlest of sorts. Esch himself is opposed to anarchists, largely because, in their world, "no one seemed to know whether he was on the right or on the left, in the van or in the rear," a situation hardly pleasing to a bookkeeper who worships precision.

Esch sees himself as a man with a conscience; as a courageous knight whose strictest duty is to uphold certain absolute principles of law, order, and justice; as a person called to preside over the books of both a commercial firm and the world's morality. He is distressed to note, behind the apparent orderliness of a business enterprise, "all manner of infamies," and to find in the world itself a chaos sprung from confusion between "[t]hings as they were and things as they ought to be." His task, he believes, is to set the world right. So Esch sees himself, at least in the late winter and spring of 1903.

But there is in Esch's self-analysis a flaw, one that issues from his very devotedness to bookkeeping. For a bookkeeper *as* bookkeeper must be more intent upon the balancing of accounts than upon the accounts to be balanced: his first interest is mathematical, not moral; his eye is on form, not content; he is a computer rather than a judge. And in Esch's hallucinatory meeting with Bertrand, whose judgment we learned to respect earlier in the novel, Bertrand accurately defines the speciousness of Esch's claim to moral uprightness: "Your order, Esch, is only murder and counter-murder—the order of the machine." An efficient machine serves its master well, and Esch's mechanical bookkeeping logic performs for him some remarkable services, particularly through its ability to justify any actions or judgments in which Esch wishes to indulge himself. To cite an example: Esch, betrothed to Mother Hentjen, can sleep with Erna Korn and, for a time at least and through the most complex machinations of illogical logic, persuade himself that he is remaining faithful to his affianced. To cite a more desperate example: Esch is gratified by the pathetic suicides of Bertrand and young Harry Köhler, for in these deaths, he reflects, "murder and counter-murder, debit and credit cancelled each other, here was for once an account that balanced itself perfectly."

It is evident that the cult of bookkeeping, like the cult of the uniform, may lead into strange ways, but the order of "murder and counter-murder" is a more serious threat to the world's weal than the order of romance and chivalry. The rules of bookkeeping, moreover, can not only make of infidelity a virtue and see in murder a happy balancing of accounts; they can also, with their attention to form and neglect of substance, lead a man to believe himself free of personal responsibility and to attribute whatever might ordinarily be deemed human guilt to an abstract system, not a living being. Thus the world of behavior can in the end be neither moral nor immoral, but only amoral: men are not individual beings, but ciphers, reduced to their nothingness by a mechanical system. "Somewhere it was not a matter merely involving human beings," Esch once meditates, "for human beings were all the same and nothing was changed if one of them melted into another, or one of them sat in another's place—no, the world was not ordered according to good and evil men, but according to good and evil forces of some kind."

Esch has intimations, despite the confidence with which he sometimes speaks, that not all is well. His zealous dedication to the cult of bookkeeping does not bring him the sense of solace and security he so desperately wishes. He is as fearful as Joachim, and even more lonely. And like Joachim he seeks consolation in both religious faith and human love. His religious leanings are frequently seen in his theological imagery. When he first witnesses the knife-throwing act of Herr Teltscher and Ilona, he envisages her as a "crucified girl," hears "the fanfare of the Last Judgment," feels a desire to replace her as the crucified one, and essays tireless efforts to rescue her from oppression. He is obsessed with the idea of sacrifice (though he sees this too as in part a balancing of accounts), and he sees himself as the sacrificial victim called to redeem Ilona from her misery. Even his early (unsuccessful) attempt to seduce Erna he approaches with religious overtones, as he is led to her room by "the yearning of the captive soul for redemption from its loneliness, for a salvation which should embrace himself and her, yes, perhaps all mankind, and most certainly Ilona"! He sometimes views human love as the supreme earthly religious journey. When he first evokes from the habitually rigid, emotionless Mother Hentjen an ecstatic response, he discerns in the act of physical love (as do the homosexual Harry Köhler and the musician Alfons) the very annihilation of time, and thus a condition of eternity associated with the redemptive state and its attendant goodness and righteousness. He believes that love is thus a good which reaches beyond its earthly manifestation:

For the man who wills Goodness and Righteousness wills thereby the Absolute, and it was revealed to Esch for the first time that the goal is not the appeasement of lust but an absolute oneness exalted far above its immediate, sordid and even trivial occasion, a conjoint trance, itself timeless and so annihilating time; and that the rebirth of man is as still and serene as the universal spirit that yet contracts and closes round man when once his ecstatic will has compelled it, until he attains his sole birthright: deliverance and redemption.

We are reminded of Bertrand's earlier words to Joachim, stressing the wonderful "mystery of oneness" wrought by love's transformation of persons formerly isolated.

Parts One and Two of *The Sleepwalkers* introduce us to the young adulthood of Joachim von Pasenow in 1888 and that of August Esch fifteen years later, both men rather inflexibly bound to their respective cults. In Eduard von Bertrand and Martin Geyring the protagonists find persons of more mature and composed demeanor. When we encounter Pasenow and Esch again, in 1918, the time of Part Three of the trilogy, we discover that they in large degree throw off the rigid patterns of their younger years. That Bertrand, to the young Pasenow half-angel and half-devil, was a wise mentor to the young soldier has already become evident. Though Esch only imagines a meeting with Bertrand, of whom he has heard much, the Bertrand who addresses him in a dream sequence speaks, as is his custom, wise words, quoted verbatim by Esch fifteen years later: "No one stands so high that he dare judge his fellows, and no one is so depraved that his eternal soul can lose its claim to reverence." Esch himself has presumptuously arrogated the role of judge, yet his depravity is by no means complete. As we will discover, it is Broch's view that the world's spiritual health is with the passage of years spiraling downward toward an abyss whose coming will bring with it a purgation clearing the way for a rising motion and a regaining of health. Again Bertrand is the prophetic spokesman:

Many must die, many must be sacrificed, so that a path may be prepared for the loving redeemer and judge. And only through his sacrificial death can the world be redeemed to a new innocence. But first the Antichrist must come—the mad and dreamless Antichrist. First the world must become quite empty, must be emptied of everything in it as by a vacuum cleaner—nothingness.

III

In the year 1918 the soldier Wilhelm Huguenau, who already before his military service enjoyed the reputation of "an energetic, prudent and reliable man of business," deserts the German Army, sheds his uniform, and takes up quarters in the town of Kur-Trier. For him *The Sleepwalkers'* third part— "The Realist"—is named. As Joachim worshiped his uniform and Esch his bookkeeping, Huguenau worships himself. By a coincidence which is the novelist's prerogative, the trilogy's three protagonists are met together in Kur-Trier and largely guide the town's activities: Joachim as Herr Major von Pasenow, town commandant; Esch as owner and editor of the town newspaper, the *Kur-Trier Herald;* Huguenau as the town realist, which is to say its sower of discord and suspicion, its traitor, rapist, and murderer. Yet it must be admitted that Huguenau's boundless ingenuity as a "realist" does evoke a certain grudging and horrified admiration. In the brief span of six months, which he views as a holiday from his more normal round of activities, he works quickly and confidently. He deserts, takes up residence in Kur-Trier, ingratiates himself into Major von Pasenow's trusting confidence, engineers the "sale" of the town newspaper to no one's advantage but his own, moves into Esch's house, vilifies Esch and challenges the major's judgment and competence, rapes Frau Esch (formerly Mother Hentjen), murders Esch with a bayonet in the back, gains a military escort from the town in charge of the wounded Pasenow, and by the middle 1920s is a flourishing merchant and father of a family.

Tempting as it is to pass moral judgment on Huguenau, we should remember that this realist is simply the epitome and microcosm of the style and spirit of his time, and that, in the earlier judgment of Esch himself, the world is "not ordered according to good and evil men, but according to good and evil forces of some kind." Realism is that style of life which leads a man to base his every choice and decision on self-interest, without regard to the consequences upon other persons. Huguenau's style could be described through the following syllogism: *Major Premise:* All that is to my self-interest is good; *Minor Premise:* Murder is to my self-interest; *Conclusion:* Murder is good. The world that the time's style has produced is described in various ways by different characters: "the whole world goes on crutches . . . a hobbling monstrosity"; "the whole world is a prison"; it is "full of devils"; "[c]haos was invading the world on every side . . .

darkness was spreading"; the world is "in the midst of fear
and tribulation." And as we recall Bertrand's designation of
Esch's bookkeeping kind of order as "murder and counter-
murder—the order of the machine," a triumph of technical
form over substantive moral content, we are not surprised at
Huguenau's fondness for machines. His interest in gaining
control of Esch's newspaper is further kindled by sight of the
printing press. He is a man whose "sympathies were with the
machine," who bears an "affectionate attitude to machines,"
and who, during the town's looting, is clutched by fear that
the looters "would smash his machine to pieces." His constant suit for the young Marguerite's affection is doubtless
partly due to his feeling that "there was some vague kinship between the child and the machine." There is, moreover, implication that both Marguerite and the machine were
born of the Devil. As she dances and chants in apparently
sympathetic rhythm to the town's frenzied looting, we are
told that Pasenow "gazed at the dancing child whose laughter
seemed to him strangely mechanical, strangely evil, and horror overwhelmed him." And Esch, his ears assailed by the
pounding of the printing press, once remarks:

Sometimes it seems as if the world were only one huge dreadful
machine that never stops . . . the war and everything . . . it runs
by laws that we don't understand . . . impudent self-assured laws,
engineers' laws . . . every man must do what is prescribed for him,
without turning his head to right or left . . . every man is a machine
that one can only see from outside, a hostile machine . . . oh, the
machine is the root of evil and the Evil One is the machine. Their
order is the void that must come . . . before Time can begin again.

If man is a machine who can be seen only from outside,
it is no wonder that he feels isolated. And the loneliness
which oppressed the worlds of 1888 and 1903 is no stranger
to the inhabitants of Kur-Trier. To Lieutenant Jaretski,
whose gas-poisoned arm has been amputated, "everyone is
pledged to his own loneliness." Hanna Wendling suffers intensively the anguish of isolation, and both Pasenow and

Esch carry into the year 1918 the loneliness which has long been theirs. But that terrible year is not without signs of joyous metamorphosis in the lives of them both as they free themselves from the cults that once dominated their actions and frustrated their lives.

Esch's remarkable transformation from concern for the mechanical form of bookkeeping to concern for the content of the accounts grows out of a newspaper editorship leading him to a panoramic view of man's suffering. He learns, finally, that the balance between murder and counter-murder brings only a mathematical, not an ethical gratification, and that the commercial rules of bookkeeping are simply not applicable to a scaling of good and evil. He now turns not only in theory but in practice to a righting of the world's wrongs, struggling, as editor of the *Kur-Trier Herald*, "for precise evidence of the world's doings, and against the false or falsified book-keeping entries which people tried to fob off on him." He exposes the abuses of his time and fights its evil with a fervor quite outdistancing the rebellious anarchy of his earlier friend Martin Geyring. "Small wonder," we are told, "that Herr Esch, himself at odds with the world, should begin to feel a brotherly sympathy for his oppressed and downtrodden fellow-creatures, and should become an obstructionist and a rebel."

It took Esch fifteen years to free himself from the mechanical cult of bookkeeping, and Pasenow thirty years to free himself from the romantic cult of the uniform. In the June 1, 1918, issue of the *Kur-Trier Herald* appears an essay by Pasenow entitled "The Turning-point in the Destiny of the German People," its religious basis foreshadowed by its epigraph: "The devil leaveth him, and, behold, angels came and ministered unto him." The verse is Matthew 4:11 and concludes the passage narrating Jesus' successful resistance in the wilderness to the temptations of Satan. Pasenow urges that his fatherland also cast off its unclean spirit and turn to a renewal of Christian faith through which alone his nation may find its salvation. The article is an accurate measure of the major's change from the young man whose uniform seemed the symbol of good. It is the war, the abysmal evil of the new age, that at the same time sparks the redemptive awakening not only of Esch, but of Pasenow as well, for whom the devastating conflict

> had suddenly become no longer a matter of uniform, no longer a matter of red regimentals or blue regimentals, no longer an affair between gallant enemies who chivalrously crossed swords; no, war had proved neither the crown nor the fulfilment of a life in uniform, but had invisibly and yet more and more palpably shaken the foundations of that life, had worn threadbare the ties of morality holding it together, and through the meshes of the fabric grinned the Evil One.

Pasenow's article in Esch's paper leads to a remarkably tender relationship between the two, Esch finding in the essay "a restatement of his own task and his own aims." Their long-time mutual loneliness dissipates in the bond of their friendship. As the major's words lead Esch to renewed hope for the world's redemption, Esch in turn comes to impress the major as one who could "set everything right." Through Esch's laughter Pasenow beholds "the glimmer of a soul leaning out of a neighbouring window with a smile, the soul of a brother, yet not an individual soul, nor yet in actual proximity, but a soul that was like an infinitely remote homeland." In mutuality of trust and love the two men gain together what neither could gain alone, as each moves from anguished isolation within a society knowing only loneliness to membership, partly through their Bible classes, in a Christian Body whose Head brings joy even in the travail of suffering. Fifteen years earlier Esch's dream of becoming a sacrificial intercessor for Ilona bore little fruit, primarily because his rigidly formal mode of keeping accounts blinded him to the larger moral issues involved. But now he has been made ready for his long envisioned sacrifice. Once a sleepwalker whose dreams were misleading and whose actions were of little avail, he can now be accurately described as one who stretches "his arms out like a man waking from sleep or nailed on a cross." It is Esch who rescues his beloved major from imminent death, shelters him in the tomblike cellar of his home, leaves the small light of a paraffin lamp by the unconscious man's side, and returns to the town in the hope of restoring order. As he makes his way into the street, his thoughts, we learn, are "with the man who lay in the cellar, the paraffin lamp at his head. When the light expires the Redeemer is near. The light must expire so that the debt of time might be paid." As Esch goes to his death, victim of Huguenau's back-piercing bayonet, certainly we are to assume that he has met his crucifixion, sacrificing his life that one payment may be made on the very extensive "debt of time." The novel's action ends with Esch's sacrificial death; with the wounded Pasenow carried to safety, not to be heard from again; and with Huguenau, still very much the realist, moving in his kind of triumph to a successful business career and a family life, yet never to dispel a loneliness which he feels most acutely when in the presence of others.

IV

Hermann Broch's *The Sleepwalkers* is a complex and manifold accomplishment, mostly prose fiction, but with its third part containing a symposium in dramatic form, a sixteen-part "Story of the Salvation Army Girl in Berlin" (partly in verse), and ten essays entitled "Disintegration of Values." Each of the trilogy's three parts—"The Romantic (1888)," "The Anarchist (1903)," "The Realist (1918)"—portrays the style or spirit of its particular time in Germany. The young, uniformed, country-bred Joachim von Pasenow possesses the romantic temperament which seizes upon honor as the primary value and looks back to an age presided over by knights and priests. The young August Esch puts his faith in the mathematical precision of bookkeeping, more interested in an account's formal balancing than in the nature of its credits and debits. Wilhelm Huguenau is the prototypical realist, a person whose devotion to self-interest is pursued with the singleness of purpose of a machine.

The Sleepwalkers is a tripartite microcosm of the German people from 1888 to 1918, a portrait of the dissolution of values and disintegration into chaos attending the absolute pursuit of any cult, most particularly that of the realist. But if the novel is a microcosmic portrait of three decades of German history, it is also the microcosmic portrait of a Western civilization which had its roots in Athens and Jerusalem, has become a "lost generation," and may look forward to a glorious rebirth only when the Logos (Greek and Christian) once again becomes the informing Value of all values. So we learn through one "Bertrand Müller, doctor of philosophy," first-person narrator of the "Story of the Salvation Army Girl in Berlin," and, more important, author of the philosophico-theological essays entitled "Disintegration of Values." Through him, Broch's spokesman, the trilogy is taken well beyond its narrative time span and presents a theocentric philosophy of history whose thesis is that the spirit of every age is determined by that period's degree of fidelity or infidelity to the Logos or Christ as interpreted by Plato and the Catholic Church. Broch-Müller sees as civilization's basic conflict a continuing struggle between Christian and antichristian forces and argues that the Western world, since the great Thomistic synthesis of the late Middle Ages, has been moving antithetically toward the Antichrist. The movement, not yet complete, must run its full downward cycle before the reign of Christ may return. As we were earlier apprised by Eduard von Bertrand, the redemption to a new birth must await and be preceded by the coming of the Antichrist, when the world's downward spiral will reach the absolute nothingness toward which it has been moving since the Protestant Reformation initiated the gradual, catastrophic fall from a theocentric world. Broch's lost generation is nearing, but has not yet reached, the nadir. The fortunes and misfortunes, the actions and passions of Pasenow, Bertrand, Esch, and Huguenau provide the narrative counterpart, foreshortened to three decades, of the trilogy's philosophy of history.

Turning specifically to the ten Broch-Müller essays, we may begin with their recognition of "our mass movement towards death," and of the slaughter, insanity, and hatred shaping the style of our age. Nowhere do we find more precise witness to our time's spirit than in the "machine-and-cannon-and-concrete style" of its architecture, whose most marked characteristic is an absence of ornament which, far from being the mere excrescence of architectural form, is in fact the outward manifestation of its whole "inner logic of structure." Our architectural mode is "a writing on the wall proclaiming a state of the soul which must be the non-soul of our non-age." Thus, as we could infer from Herr von Pasenow's manner of walking his whole style of life, we can infer from a period's architecture the spirit of its age ". . . style is something which uniformly permeates all the living expressions of an epoch." To know a man's or an epoch's style, moreover, is to know what is held by him or it to be the "truth," which in turn is the determining and presumably logical motivation of all the actions of the man or the epoch. Huguenau, for example, sees as the true and the good any action that works to his advantage. Once this major premise is accepted, the logic of his thought has a precise rationality. But the actual propositions providing the substance of his syllogisms are profoundly irrational, with the result that the rational logic of thought is used to justify the irrational logic of his actions. As Broch-Müller points out, Huguenau is a fitting complement to the nonornamental architecture of his age:

Huguenau is a man who acts with singleness of purpose. He organizes his day with singleness of purpose, he carries on his business affairs with his eye singly on his purpose, he evolves and concludes his contracts with his eye singly on his purpose. Behind all his purposefulness there lies a logic that is completely stripped of ornament, and the fact that this logic should demand the elimination of all ornament does not seem a too daring conclusion to draw; indeed it actually appears as good and just as every other necessary conclusion. And yet this elimination of all ornament involves nothingness, involves death, and a monstrous dissolution is concealed behind it in which our age is crumbling away.

The ten essays trace the historical process which has brought us to our present "monstrous dissolution," just this side of the abyss which awaits us and which, in turn, will give way to a newness of life once again informed by the Logos. The essays distinguish, as do the trilogy's narrative sections, between the unchanging, purely formal quality of logic and its substantive propositions, constantly varying throughout history. An epoch's propositions, those intuitions or facts that it deems true, spring from that epoch's interpretation of the world. Biblical writers, for example, eschewing a pagan pluralism, interpreted the world as a monotheistic structure with the whole creation emanating from and reaching toward a First Cause, God himself, the beginning and end of all that is. Medieval thought viewed God anthropomorphically, as one whose infinity is nevertheless "finite" in the sense that he is conceived as the very real source and goal of all that is. More recent centuries have come to interpret God as "an infinity of abstraction," with the result that the modern inquiry for ultimate truth does not culminate in a single agreed upon and universally recognized "finite" First Cause. The inquiry has become a series of infinitely extended, never-ending, disparate inquiries, with the consequence "that every solution is merely a temporary solution, and that nothing remains but the act of questioning in itself: cosmogony has become radically scientific, and its language and its syntax have discarded their 'style' and turned into mathematical expressions."

There remains therefore no single common goal or ultimate truth which may serve as a canon for mankind's striving or for its system of values. There are many value systems and many partial truths, each with its own proponents, who respect only their own particular goals and are indifferent or hostile to the goals of others. Each group has its own logic, its own syllogism which would seem to justify its goal, however

irrational that goal may be or however wide it is of what the
biblical God would decree. "The logic of the soldier," for
example, "demands that he shall throw a hand-grenade between the legs of his enemy." And there is the logic of the
army, of the businessman, of the artist—the list could go on
and on. It follows that a romantic like Joachim, yearning for a
"bounded world, a closed system of values," must finally look
backward to the Middle Ages, which "possessed the ideal
centre of values . . . a supreme value to which all other
values were subordinate: the belief in the Christian God."
There remains no predominant style of life catholic in in-
clusiveness; there remain only innumerable and mutually in-
compatible styles, never touching, each moving autonomously
and in parallel order, and never reaching an infinitely regress-
ing, quite abstract First Cause. Every man is consequently
isolated in his own system or style, unable to communicate
with other men:

. . . [man] is helplessly caught in the mechanism of the autonomous
value-systems, and can do nothing but submit himself to the particular value that has become his profession, he can do nothing but
become a function of that value—a specialist, eaten up by the radical
logic of the value into whose jaws he has fallen.

Broch-Müller assigns the primary cause of the world's disintegration to "[t]hat criminal and rebellious age known as
the Renaissance, that age in which the Christian scheme of
values was broken in two halves, one Catholic and the other
Protestant." The Protestant Reformation, a movement from
deduction to induction and from Platonism to Positivism, rejected the medieval value system with the result that, in our
time, "values are no longer determined by a central authority,
but take their colouring from the object: what matters is no
longer the conservation of Biblical cosmogony, but the 'scientific' observation of natural objects and the experiments that
can be carried out on them." To the Protestant mind God
loses his transcendence and becomes "the divine spark in the
soul . . . the object of immediate mystical apprehension,"

for "Protestantism is a phenomenon of immediacy." When all values were informed by a central authority, then every activity—that of the soldier, the businessman, the artist—was judged not as an end in itself but in terms of its redounding to the glory of God. But, according to Broch-Müller, it is Protestantism's emphasis on the immediacy of individual objects which has led to individual value systems, each "raised to an absolute of its own," with a series of "absolute values side by side in isolation without reference to each other." For these reasons Protestantism is seen as a lapsing from the medieval synthesis and as "the first great sect-formation in the decay of Christianity." The essayist's description of the twentieth-century Protestant is the diagnosis of all that he finds lamentable in the style or spirit of our age—its multiple autonomousness, abstraction, unornamented barrenness:

[The Protestant,] in excluding all other values, in casting himself in the last resort on an autonomous religious experience . . . has assumed a final abstraction of a logical rigour that urges him unambiguously to strip all sensory trappings from his faith, to empty it of all content but the naked Absolute, retaining nothing but the pure form, the pure, empty and neutral form of a "religion in itself," a "mysticism in itself."

The last two "Disintegration of Values" essays look forward, not backward, prophesying at a time indeterminable the coming in fullness of the Antichrist and the consequent beginning of a reverse movement marked by rebirth of the human spirit. Out of the nothingness of utter dissolution, the unchanging though now neglected Logos will once more be seen as the First Cause, from which and toward which all moves. The world's sleepwalking, which dreads the present night but dimly intuits the distant coming day, will then be at an end; lonely, speechless fright will give way to the spirit of the Logos, the Christ and the Word, to the "condition of possible experience" which makes for communication and thus unity among men. The new age will be free of both an irrationality of action embracing even murder, and a super-rationality venerating formal precision without regard to the propositions treated formally. Actions will be tempered by a reason not lost in worship of its intrinsic self but giving direction to the world's behavior. There will, finally, be a return to the one Truth which informs every truth, though not before the spirit of Protestantism, "the most outstanding expression of the disintegration of values," makes the slow way to its reduction to absurdity: the coming of the Antichrist, end product of immediacy, positivism, and abstraction, and the "zero-point of atomic dissolution."

Broch, like Camus after him, sees the twentieth century as an absurd and a suicide-pondering era. Contemporary man yearns, in Broch's view, "for a Leader to take him tenderly and lightly by the hand, to set things in order and show him the way." The Broch of the early 1930s, unlike Camus a decade later, believes that the Leader *is* and that his spirit will reach again into the world. The Leader is he "who will build the house anew that the dead may come to life again, and who himself has risen again from the multitude of the dead; the Healer who by his own actions will give a meaning to the incomprehensible events of the age, so that Time can begin anew." The world's travail will not cease; sacrifice and expiation will be called for; yet the world will once again be illumined by the presence of grace in the hearts of men and the promise of an imperishable heritage. To the contemporary man whose fragmented world, terrible loneliness, and seeming lostness have brought him to the thought of suicide, Broch's closing lines bring the promise of a human solidarity born of hearts touched by grace:

In the icy hurricane, in the tempest of collapse all the doors spring open, the foundations of our prison are troubled, and from the profoundest darkness of the world, from our bitterest and profoundest darkness the cry of succour comes to the helpless, there sounds the voice that binds all that has been to all that is to come, that binds our loneliness to all other lonelinesses, and it is not the voice of dread and doom; it falters in the silence of the Logos and yet is borne on by it, raised high over the clamour of the nonexistent; it is the voice of man and of the tribes of men, the voice of comfort and hope and immediate love: "Do thyself no harm! for we are all here!"

Hermann Broch's *The Sleepwalkers* is a remarkable achievement and is among the most neglected, certainly in the United States, of our century's great novels. With all its philosophical depth, it is yet a novel whose prominent thesis never dominates or renders puppetlike its characters. Pasenow, Esch, and Huguenau, representative as they are of "styles" of life, are first of all, like the characters of Proust, Joyce, and Mann, protagonists whose actions are never imposed upon them but spring from their fully drawn inner beings. The trilogy is of both epic scope and notable unity. The person and influence of Eduard von Bertrand are among the unifying factors of the entire work, as is the coming together of the three major protagonists in the novel's third part. Providing an overarching unity is the counterpoint between the narrative of relatively brief duration and the philosophy of history encompassing a span from Greek and biblical times to a future viewed apocalyptically. As the narrative has its integrity, so does the philosophy or theology have its own. It is difficult in the twentieth century to express messianic hopes without cloying sentimentality or without a leap of faith, as Camus defines it, seemingly made in partial blindness to the world's ways or as a last resort of despair. Though we may feel inclined to dispute Broch's reading of history, particularly his diagnosis of Protestantism and his prophecy of a new age, we—at least I—find his position consistent and not beyond credibility. *The Sleepwalkers* argues most convincingly of the twentieth-century novels known to me that the biblical God, withdrawn as he may now be, is the force and being in the light of whom history has made most sense. A belief in the triune God, Broch's "Leader," has been history's primal motivating force. No serious philosophical novelist can ignore the idea of God, much as he may rigorously dispute his being. Broch, accepting God's being, has in my judgment "placed" him in the world's history with rare and exciting brilliance.

One of Broch's stunning metaphors may serve fittingly to conclude this chapter. He writes of a dancer's relationship to music, described by Plato, we may recall, as the harmony of the celestial spheres. Broch's sense of the relationship between dancer and music is the metaphor of God's relationship to man:

The dancer is removed beyond the reach of this world. Wrapped in the music, he has renounced his freedom of action, and yet acts in accordance with a higher and more lucid freedom. In the rigorous security of the rhythm that guides him he is safely sheltered, and a great relief comes to him from that security. Thus music brings unity and order into the confusion and chaos of life. Cancelling Time it cancels death, and yet resurrects it anew in every beat of the rhythm.

Afterword

The several years spanning the making of this book have fulfilled one of their goals: they've added at least a cubit to my self-understanding. I've searched my beliefs, brought them into sharper focus, and seen them change. My creditors are twentieth-century fiction; the Bible, particularly the New Testament, read again with renewed delight and attentiveness; my many young college and seminary students who have taught me that in vital academic communities there are as many teachers as there are learners; my three children—Martha, Bill, and Mary—from whom I have learned, sometimes maddeningly, that the child is indeed father (and mother!) of the man; and the quiet wisdom of my wife, Frances.

Jean-Paul Sartre has been my most influential mentor in the mysteries of vocation. From him among others I've learned that vocation, more than a summoning to life's work, more than becoming a butcher, baker, or candlestick maker, is a response to every moment of time's unfolding, an honest deliberation of how best to invest every molecule of human action and passion. By D. H. Lawrence I've been persuaded that vocation is a call more to being than to doing. To concentrate first on doing is often to be more resolute than thoughtful; and since doing is more comfortably measurable than being, a doer may fall to the temptation of exalting the quantitative over the qualitative. Lawrence, in one of his essays in *Phoenix*, speaks for the later Sartre as well as for himself:

The glory of mankind has been to produce lives, to produce vivid, independent, individual men, not buildings or engineering works

or even art, not even the public good. The glory of mankind is not
in a host of secure, comfortable, law-abiding citizens, but in the
few more fine, clear lives, beings, individuals, distinct, detached,
single as may be from the public ("Study of Thomas Hardy,"
chapter 5).

The ideal man of whom Lawrence here speaks is motivated from within and knows, with Sartre, that if the good
society is ever to come, it will be the product of individual
men each attentive to his own drummer, not to the demands
of an existing society all too assured of the sacredness of its
ways. The immaculate model of unthinking conformity is
Sartre's Jean Pâcome, so enamored by the ease of following
the leader that he never looks within himself: he *does* a great
deal; he *is* nothing; and if one *is* not, he cannot *become,* cannot transcend himself. St. Paul, who would hardly agree with
Sartre in all matters, entertains a like abhorrence of a this-
worldly conformity: "Do not be conformed to this world but
be transformed by the renewal of your mind, that you may
prove what is the will of God, what is good and acceptable
and perfect" (Romans 12:2).

Since many twentieth-century novelists either proclaim
or tacitly assume God's death, they hardly turn to his will for
guidance. But if God has for them disappeared, the biblical
ethic has not. They and their characters call me to forgiveness,
to humility, to examination of motives as well as deeds, to
keeping my brother, and to loving my neighbor and respect-
ing myself. No earlier literature has been richer or more
varied in its reflections on vocation. Stephen Dedalus is called
to rouse the conscience of his race, Roquentin to provoke his
people to a Sartrean good faith, the invisible man to bring to
the disregarded a visibility, Rieux to minister to the suffering
and help forge human solidarity, Mrs. Dalloway to be grateful for the world's abundant gifts. I am called by all of them
to that Sartrean transcendence which is a thoughtful, courageous commitment to each of this life's admittedly few moments.

My reflections on vocation, stimulated as they were during the composition of this book, enjoyed nevertheless a long prior history. But it was a reading of Conrad's *Nostromo*, perhaps five or six years ago, that first encouraged systematic thinking about my relationship to the physical universe. With that reading I realized that the "feeling of fellowship with all creation" which Conrad commends in his Preface to *The Nigger of the "Narcissus"* was lacking in me, and that the natural world had been to me almost as invisible as Ralph Ellison's protagonist was to other men. That the world might exist for more than my personal indulgence, and for that of other men, had apparently never seriously occurred to me. Conrad's San Tomé silver mine then came to symbolize the Aggrieved, its pillagers the Aggrievers, and I suddenly recognized that the large world of nature, if capable of harboring the feelings of an avenging justice, must surely wish all men dead. If the universe is as indifferent and hostile as Camus's rebel deems it to be, is it really but a capricious victimizer of men—or is it first man's aggrieved victim? Or is there perhaps a cruelly arbitrary god who delights in cosmic conflict? But whether man may have struck first against nature, or nature against man, or whether there is a sadistic and greater force ruling both, I found in my reading helpful instruction for my own meeting with nature. Conrad's call for solidarity not only among men but between the human and the natural orders is eminently salutary. And Camus, whatever his ontological persuasions about nature may be, has few peers in his celebration of nature's splendor: his essays "Summer in Algiers" and "Return to Tipasa" are among the most eloquent and moving evidences of man's joy in nature's beauty that I know.

If Conrad and Camus stress the pathological in the man-nature confrontation, Lawrence, working from different premises, stresses the curative. The tragedy of our age he attributes in part to our alienation from what he calls the living universe, whose harmony would beckon us back to its graceful rhythms. Like Wordsworth, Emerson, and Thoreau he sees in the world's diurnal motions a habit of perfection for those with eyes to see and ears to hear. Like Conrad he calls us to a communion not only with other men but with all that is. Of the "discoveries" that have come to me with the forming of this book, none has emerged more freshly and forcefully than a new sense of nature's sanctity.

Twentieth-century fiction also speaks fluently of man's relationship to other men. The main impact of Orwell's *1984* is the terrifying portrayal of man's vulnerability to betraying other men. The theme of betrayal is both ancient and commonplace, but Orwell's placing of it in modern political context brings it so close to our lives that we respond with sickened and horrified immediacy. As we sense the approach of those sharp-toothed rats to our pain-sensitive eyes, and as we hear Winston Smith's hysterical "Do it to Julia!" we know on how thin a thread our love for those most dear to us may hang: to protect ourselves, we are led to suspect, the sacrifice of parent, child, or spouse may not be too great a price.

Far more encouragingly, from Lawrence we have the promise, though not the fulfillment, of the height and intensity that may be found in the closest of human relationships, that between a woman and a man. Even if we believe ourselves too frail to experience that full mutual tenderness which is Lawrence's ideal, we nevertheless come to know some of those barriers which hulk between ourselves and another. We learn to distinguish between that self-love battened by our sense of power over another, and a love nourished by mutually generous and grateful giving and taking. We are once again impressed by St. Paul's truth that "love does not insist on its own way." Lawrence *is* guilty of occasional male chauvinism, but at his best he has few equals in the defining of a loving human relationship.

Mrs. Dalloway's kind of love is in lower key than the Lawrencian ideal, but it well shows that man's ingratitude to man (and to dogs and canaries as well!) is not universal. Clarissa Dalloway's gratitude embraces both everyone (except

Miss Kilman and brutal psychiatrists) and everything that falls within her scope. Virginia Woolf persuades me above all that man is called not only to love his neighbors but to give thanks for all the world's rich diversity. Mrs. Dalloway's presence is a fitting conclusion to the first three sections of this book: her vocation is to be grateful; her sensitivity to the living universe is most keen; her love reaches out to those she knows and to those of whom she but hears.

The fiction of recent decades has persuaded me that I am called at every moment of my life to make an honest choice among a myriad of alternatives, that conformity for its own sake invites a coward's death-in-life, and that Pauline transformation and Sartrean transcendence are not the polar opposites I once may have imagined. The novels read, in their rendering sharp visibility to air, earth, fire, and water, to beasts and birds, to trees and grass, and to subterranean minerals, have brought to me a hallowed sense of the universe which neither the Greek philosophers nor the biblical writers succeeded in doing. And the novels have, in their reflections on man's relationships to other men, added to parables of the Bible parables of their own. Only one thing is lacking: a celebration of the God of whom Scripture speaks. Few twentieth-century novels, as I remarked earlier, are grounded in "the acceptance, by the writer and at least some of his characters, of the presence of God's grace in and beyond history."

I have come to realize, perhaps subconsciously at first but now quite consciously, that the ultimate object of my search through these past half-dozen years has been the biblical God. Fiction, including that of Mauriac and Broch, has been of little help. And so I have, hardly surprisingly, turned again to the New Testament, particularly to the synoptic Gospels, to try to see if the God who is affirmed is dead for me —or, perhaps more accurately, if I am dead for him. And in the Gospels I seek first a knowledge of him who said, "no one knows the Father except the Son and anyone to whom the Son chooses to reveal him" (Matthew 11:27).

The witness which the Jesus of the Gospels bears to a way of life and a way of death is for me an inestimable gift. Through his life and teachings he has revealed the multidimensionality of human life and the meaning of righteousness, humility, givingness and forgivingness, and love. Through his death he bore ultimate witness to all he believed and taught. I am far less certain that he has chosen to reveal to me the Father, whose personal being seems not quite within my comprehension and focus. And so I am led to an anxious question. Can a person of doubtful faith follow the will of the biblically affirmed Father, be endowed with the kind of love celebrated in the thirteenth chapter of I Corinthians, be a disciple of Jesus under the terms of the "new" commandment that he love others as Jesus loved him (John 13:34-35)? The prevailing New Testament assumption seems to be that a person in that condition cannot. Yet there does seem to be one strong minority report: the parable of the sheep and the goats in the twenty-fifth chapter of Matthew. When the Son of Man invites to inheritance of the kingdom those "sheep" who, he tells them, have ministered to him when he was hungry, thirsty, lonely, naked, sick, and imprisoned, they are nonplussed. It must, they infer, be a case of mistaken identity. Not only have they not ministered to this gracious judge; they do not even recall ever having known him or seen him. That they cannot be identified with the faithful, with those who have acknowledged and knowingly served the Son of Man, seems to me evident; that they have been eminently Christlike in their loving ministry to the least of the brethren is beyond dispute. Would not *The Plague*'s Jean Tarrou, who aspired to be "a saint without God," and the unbelieving Bernard Rieux, who ministered indefatigably to the brethren, be first among peers in the gathering of the sheep?

How, finally, would I sum up the personal fruits of my recent studies? The title of this book is a clue. Though the phrase "celebration of life" is not meant to imply that all doubts have been resolved, it does point to a direction of

spirit. Even the novels least inclined to celebrate—*Nostromo,
1984, The Castle*—even they share the most striking common
denominator of all the other novels: insistence upon the wondrous, nearly incredible degree of human endurance. That the
world is a vale of tears and thus absurd I find indisputable;
but that the best of men respect what they are given and,
with or without a sense of God's grace, tenaciously pursue
their thoughtfully chosen ideals, is equally indisputable. Thus
the phrase "celebration of life" issues, I hope, not from self-
deceptive whistling in the dark, but from honest response to
a world which, even at its darkest, has its shafts of light.

My recent secular readings have led me to an increased
skepticism of biblical doctrine and proclamation (as em-
bodied, for example, in the Apostles' Creed), and to an increased devotion to the person and teachings of Jesus. This
result has led me to seek anew the relationship between belief
and works. I believe, with Scripture, that a tree is known by
its fruit, but I am not as convinced as Paul that a tree can
bear good fruit only if nourished by a Pauline conception of
faith. I know men of profound and orthodox faith who are
moved to most righteous deeds, and I know skeptics who
minister in love to the brethren. It is possible that such skeptics may possess a faith beyond their knowledge, that faith
and works may be in fact inseparable: "But some one will say,
'You have faith and I have works.' Show me your faith apart
from your works, and I by my works will show you my faith"
(James 2:18).

Twentieth-century fiction has the parabolic power of pre-
senting vividly and concretely men and women devoted to
various biblical imperatives and responding to the call to
love their neighbors and to comport themselves with courage,
endurance, gratitude, sympathetic understanding, and love. I
find in no other literary period authors and characters of more
intensive and thoughtful commitment to those Greco-Judeo-
Christian qualities long held to be the ideals of our civilization.

I find myself convinced that every man is called—whether

by divine will, by his society's needs, by his own intrinsic being, or by all of these—to a transcendence or transformation of his present being. I find myself convinced of the sacramental quality of the natural world. I find myself convinced that love is the source of every righteous action, particularly as it embraces one's neighbor. But I also find myself absurdity's disappointed victim: that satisfying vision or grasp of the Godhead for which I yearn is at this time beyond my reach. In one of his sonnets, John Donne urgently petitions God to be a little less sparing of his grace; the opening lines express a hope and an impatience with which I am in earnest sympathy:

> Batter my heart, three-personed God; for you
> As yet but knock, breathe, shine, and seek to mend;
> That I may rise and stand, o'erthrow me, and bend
> Your force to break, blow, burn, and make me new.

I too await such renewal. Rejoicing in the gifts of the life, teachings, and death of Jesus, I continue to long for the faith not only to believe in his righteousness as I do, but to believe that there exists the Father whom Jesus claims to be uniquely his Father *and* to believe that Jesus is the Son of that Father. As I search my beliefs, I am reminded of that distraught father in the ninth chapter of Mark who brings his possessed son to Jesus. The disciples having failed to exorcise the demonic spirit, the father asks Jesus to help him if he can. When Jesus answers, "If . . . [I] can! All things are possible to him who believes," the father cries out, "I believe; help my unbelief!" That father's petition I understand.

Bibliography

This bibliographical section I present apologetically: its sins of omission will be patent to experienced students of modern fiction. There are more good critical works appropriate to this study than those that appear below; the problem is an embarrassment of riches. For those that do appear I need make no apology. Readers will, of course, find additional bibliographical notices in most of the secondary works listed.

JAMES JOYCE

Burgess, Anthony. *Re Joyce*. New York: Ballantine Books, 1966; first published in 1965 by W. W. Norton.
Connolly, Thomas E., ed. *Joyce's "Portrait": Criticisms & Critiques*. New York: Appleton-Century-Crofts, Goldentree Books, 1962.

Nineteen essays on *A Portrait*.

Ellmann, Richard. *James Joyce*. New York: Oxford University Press, Galaxy Books, 1965; first published in 1959.

An absolutely superb biography.

JEAN-PAUL SARTRE

Cranston, Maurice. *Jean-Paul Sartre*. New York: Grove Press, Evergreen Pilot Books, 1962.
Murdoch, Iris. *Sartre: Romantic Rationalist*. New Haven: Yale University Press, 1953.
Thody, Philip, *Jean-Paul Sartre: A Literary and Political Study*. New York: Macmillan, 1960.

RALPH ELLISON

Klein, Marcus. *After Alienation: American Novels in Mid-Century.* Cleveland: World Publishing, Meridian Books, 1965; first published in 1964.

See chapter entitled "Ralph Ellison," pp. 71–146.

JOSEPH CONRAD

Guerard, Albert J. *Conrad the Novelist.* New York: Atheneum, 1967; first published in 1958 by Harvard University Press.

The most helpful of the book-length studies I have read.

Kimpel, Ben, and T. C. Duncan Eaves. "The Geography and History in *Nostromo*." *Modern Philology* LVI (August, 1958): 45–54.

A great help in unraveling chronological complexities.

Tillyard, E. M. W. *The Epic Strain in the English Novel.* London: Chatto & Windus, 1958.

See chapter entitled "Conrad: *Nostromo*," pp. 126–67.

ALBERT CAMUS

Brée, Germaine. *Camus.* rev. ed. New York: Harcourt, Brace & World, Harbinger Books, 1964; first published in 1959 by Rutgers University Press.

Cruickshank, John. *Albert Camus and the Literature of Revolt.* New York: Oxford University Press, Galaxy Books, 1960; first published in 1959.

Merton, Thomas. *Albert Camus' "The Plague."* New York: Seabury Press, 1968.

Scott, Nathan A. *Albert Camus.* 2nd rev. ed. London: Bowes, 1969; first published in 1962.

Thody, Philip. *Albert Camus, 1913–1960.* New York: Macmillan, 1961.

THOMAS MANN

Heller, Erich. *Thomas Mann: The Ironic German.* Cleveland: World Publishing, Meridian Books, 1961; first published in 1958 by Little, Brown under the title *Ironic German: A Study of Thomas Mann.*

An exceptionally fine study.

D. H. LAWRENCE

Ford, George H. *Double Measure: A Study of the Novels and Stories of D. H. Lawrence.* New York: W. W. Norton, Norton Library Paperbacks, 1969; first published in 1965 by Holt, Rinehart and Winston.

Hough, Graham. *The Dark Sun: A Study of D. H. Lawrence.* New York: Macmillan, 1957; first published in 1956 by Duckworth, London.

Leavis, F. R. *D. H. Lawrence: Novelist.* New York: Simon & Schuster, Clarion Books, 1969; first published in 1956 by Alfred A. Knopf.

Polemical and cantankerous, this fascinating book should be read as one *among* other studies of Lawrence.

Mudrick, Marvin. "The Originality of *The Rainbow.*" In *A D. H. Lawrence Miscellany,* edited by Harry T. Moore, pp. 56–82. Carbondale, Illinois: Southern Illinois University Press, 1959; first published in *Spectrum,* Winter 1959.

GEORGE ORWELL

Thomas, Edward M. *Orwell.* New York: Barnes & Noble, 1967; first published in 1965 by Oliver and Boyd Ltd., Edinburgh.

VIRGINIA WOOLF

Blackstone, Bernard. *Virginia Woolf: A Commentary.* New York: Harcourt, Brace, 1949.

Daiches, David. *Virginia Woolf.* rev. ed. Norfolk, Connecticut: New Directions, 1963; first published in 1942.

FRANCOIS MAURIAC

Jarrett-Kerr, Martin. C. R. *François Mauriac.* New Haven: Yale University Press, 1954.

Jenkins, Cecil. *Mauriac.* New York: Barnes & Noble, 1965.

FRANZ KAFKA

Albérès, R. M., and Pierre de Boisdeffre. *Kafka: The Torment of Man.* Translated by Wade Baskin with an introduction by Margaret C. O'Riley. New York: Philosophical Library, 1968.

Emrich, Wilhelm. *Franz Kafka: A Critical Study of His Writings.* Translated by Sheema Zeben Buehne. New York: Frederick Ungar, 1968; first published in Germany in 1958.

Politzer, Heinz. *Franz Kafka: Parable and Paradox.* rev. and expanded ed. Ithaca, New York: Cornell University Press, Cornell Paperbacks, 1966; first published in 1962.

HERMANN BROCH

Arendt, Hannah. *Men in Dark Times.* Translated by Richard Winston. New York: Harcourt Brace Jovanovich, Harvest Books, 1970; first published in 1968.

See chapter entitled "Hermann Broch: 1886–1951," pp. 111–51.

Ziolkowski, Theodore. *Dimensions of the Modern Novel: German Texts and European Contexts.* Princeton, New Jersey: Princeton University Press, 1969.

See chapter entitled "Hermann Broch: *The Sleepwalkers,*" pp. 138–80.

Index

Literary works are not listed as headings, but as subheads under their authors. The twelve major novels discussed are not indexed; their authors are indexed only to head a listing of their works other than the twelve novels.

"The Russian Point of View,"
190, 191, 206

Yeats, W. B., "The Second Coming," 251

Zamiatin, Eugene, *We*, 6, 170,
171, 172, 173, 176
Zionistic Judaism, 238